THE DIVINE
BETTE MIDLER

In *Divine Madness*, 1980.

THE DIVINE

BETTE MIDLER

JAMES SPADA

Collier Books
Macmillan Publishing Company
New York

Collier Macmillan Publishers
London

BOTH PAGES:
In her first film, *The Rose*, 1979.

Macmillan Publishing Company
866 Third Avenue, New York, N.Y. 10022
Collier Macmillan Canada, Inc.

Library of Congress Cataloging in Publication Data

Spada, James.
  The divine Bette Midler.

  1. Midler, Bette.   2. Singers–United States–Biography.
I. Title.
ML420.M43S6 1984   784.5'0092'4 [B]   84-12189
ISBN 0-02-612590-0
ISBN 0-02-007070-5 (pbk.)

Macmillan books are available at special discounts for bulk purchase for sales promotions, premiums, fund-raising, or educational use. Special editions or book excerpts can also be created to specification. For details, contact:

Special Sales Director
Macmillan Publishing Company
866 Third Avenue
New York, New York 10022

10 9 8 7 6 5 4 3 2 1

First Collier Books Edition 1984

Printed in the United States of America

The Divine Bette Midler is also available in a hardcover edition published by Macmillan Publishing Company.

In *Salvation*, 1970.

Books By James Spada

The Divine Bette Midler
Hepburn: Her Life in Pictures
Judy and Liza
Monroe: Her Life in Pictures
Streisand: The Woman and the Legend
The Spada Report
The Films of Robert Redford
Barbra: The First Decade

Designed by Ken de Bie

FOR
TONI NICKENS,
WITH FOND REMEMBRANCE

At the premiere of *The Rose*, 1979.

ACKNOWLEDGEMENTS

Special thanks to Bob Scott, Larry Paulette, J.B. Annegan, the Hansons, and Greg Rice, whose extensive collections of Midler memorabilia made researching this book much less arduous. Thanks also to Michel Parenteau, Richard Brezner, Frank Teti, Bob Deutsch, Greg Gorman, Bruce Mandes, Jeff Schaffer, Ben Carbonetto, Michele Rosen, Vito Russo, Gary Herb, Ramon Hervey, Andy Powell, Teresia Fox, Paul Grein, Keith Lyle, the staff of the Lincoln Center Library of the Performing Arts, the Seattle *Times*, the *Tonight Show*, Fairchild Syndicate, Los Angeles *Times*, Joe Goodwin.

For their reminiscences, thanks to Charlotte Crossley, Linda Hart, Bruce Vilanch, Ula Hedwig, Marta Heflin, Peter Dallas, Paul Aaron, John Graham, Norman Kean, Kenny (Claude) Sasha.

For their friendship and moral support, love as always to Dan Conlon, Chris Nickens, Paul O'Driscoll, Karen Swenson, Kathy Robbins, Loretta Fidel, Larry Alexander, Ken deBie, John Cusimano, Nora Ehm, Ken and Martie Weiss, George Schulman.

Special appreciation to Barry Lippman for his encouragement and belief in this project.

Contents

PART ONE

BEGINNINGS

(1945–1970)

One

Bette Midler is a woman of astonishing contrasts. Performing, she can be touchingly vulnerable one minute, outrageously vulgar the next. On stage, she can completely dominate the most cavernous theater with a larger-than-life glamour that leaves her audiences wildly cheering; off stage, she often goes unrecognized even at intimate functions until introduced.

Her public persona, The Divine Miss M, is a dazzling creation who positively glows with self-confidence; Bette Midler admits to sometimes crippling bouts of insecurity.

There are other, equally intriguing dichotomies in Bette Midler today. But perhaps the starkest contrasts in her life—the ones which set the stage for all the others—were those of her childhood, those she had no control over: between how the little Bette Midler perceived herself and the way she was preceived by those around her; between the loveliness of Hawaii and the sometimes grim situation of her family; between the restlessness of her spirit and the restraints of her environment.

She would later call that environment, in her inimitably self-mocking style, "kind of weird." The Midlers were a Jewish family who moved to Hawaii from Passaic, New Jersey not long before Bette was born on December 1, 1945. Fred Midler, nicknamed "Chesty" because as a young man he worked out with weights until he had a notable physique, was a part of the "dry-cleaning Midlers" of Paterson, New Jersey when he met Ruth Schindel, from Passaic. They married, had two daughters, then decided to move to Hawaii, which Fred had seen for the first time during his tenure in the Navy and which he thought of as "paradise." Another reason Fred wanted to leave New Jersey, according to Bette, was "to put some distance between him and his mother."

Ruth Midler was a starstruck movie buff who had named her first two daughters after Judy Garland and Susan Hayward. Her third daughter she named after Bette Davis. But like many others, Mrs. Midler thought the star pronounced her name "Bet," and that's what the new baby was called.

Both Fred and his wife became so homesick for New Jersey after several years in Hawaii that they moved back to Passaic. But the lure of the tropics proved too great, and after six months they returned there permanently. "They always talked about how beautiful New Jersey was," Bette recalled, "and how they missed their family there. So I always wanted to go to New Jersey. When I got there I almost died. It's the dirtiest, tackiest place in the world."

Fred Midler was a housepainter, and he did a great deal of work for the Navy. For a time, the family lived in inexpensive but pleasant military housing. When that became scarce, however, all non-military personnel were relocated by the government without much concern for keeping people in equally good quarters. The Midlers were sent to "Halauua housing—poor people's housing," says Bette. "It was tough on the family, you know. It was like a step downward. People like to think their lives are going to improve, and ours was getting worse."

The family's lack of money, coupled with the fact that they were the only white people in a community made up almost exclusively of Fillipinos,

Samoans, Japanese, and Chinese, made life difficult for them. As she grew up, Bette let the other children think she was Portuguese, a group which made up another large segment of her neighborhood. "It was easier than anything else. Portuguese people were accepted. Jews were not. I was an alien, a foreigner—even though I was born there."

There certainly were enough outside forces to make Bette Midler feel like a pariah, but there were also a great many inside her as well. Almost from her earliest memories, she recalls having a rich fantasy life. "I believed in the things in fairy tales," she says. "I lived in a cloud. I was afraid of people. . .I always worried what they thought of me. I was very shy, lived very much in my head, in my daydreams."

Bette's mother encouraged her little one in those daydreams. "My mom was a fabulous woman. I adored her. She was the fastest thing on two feet. I can remember trying to hang on to her skirt, her purse—anything—so I wouldn't be left behind." Ruth Midler's preoccupation with Hollywood was something her daughter gravitated to immediately. Fascinated by her mother's collection of movie magazines, Bette developed a "passion" for Debra Paget (a publicized starlet of the day) and imagined herself as Sadie Thompson, the sultry heroine of Somerset Maugham's *Rain*, played so memorably by Rita Hayworth.

Baby Bette in 1946.

But reality was too often a rude intruder into Bette Midler's fantasy world. "I was an ugly, fat little Jewish girl with problems," she has said. "I kept trying to be like everybody else, but nothing worked." Chief among Bette's problems was her home life. Fred Midler, it seems, was a very difficult man to get along with. "My father was a bellower. To get a word in you had to bellow back. (The) family household was fairly violent. I'm not talking about whipping each other or anything but. . .we expressed ourselves in very strong terms. Yet there was a lot of thwarted emotions. My father was always right, never wrong. It was simple: he was the loudest and the oldest and the heaviest. It was usually us against him. My mother tried to be a soothing influence, but she wasn't very successful at it."

The friction between Fred Midler and his family increased as his children grew up. Bette has referred to him as a "minor tyrant. He would scream and carry on. He thrived on it. My sister Susan and Pa, they'd have terrible riles. She used to call the cops on him!"

Aside from his apparently formidable nature, Fred was also something of an eccentric. He fancied himself a "Mr. Fixit," as Bette put it, and she remembers up to 35 lawnmowers sitting around their yard, along with twelve refrigerators, and various other gadgets, none of them in working order or likely to regain it. He wasn't very good at it, Bette recalled. "One day the roof was leaking, so rather than hire a roofer, Mr. Midler gets up there with his tar paper. He didn't have a roller for it, so what does he haul up there? One of his lawn mowers! There he was on the roof, mowing the shingles flat!"

When Bette was six, the Midlers had another child, their first boy, Danny. After an illness in his infancy, the child was diagnosed as mentally retarded. "My father always wanted a boy," Bette says, "and instead he got three daughters and a retarded son. So it sorta freaked him out."

Fred wasn't the kind of man to abandon his son, though. Neither parent would agree to put the child away, as the public health authorities advised. They did follow the advice of a doctor who told them he would have to cut away some of Danny's tongue, which he said was too long. In doing so, the doctor severed a nerve, and Danny could no longer move his tongue; he was unable to chew or speak correctly. His abilities improved over the years, but the situation left the family bitter.

Fred Midler decided to teach his son at home. "Pa would start kind of quietly," Bette said, "but by the time 4:30 rolled around, he was *screaming* at the top of his lungs, and Daniel would be crying. He's not so retarded that he doesn't know it. But eventually Danny did learn. It took a lot of love for my father to do that. Or some heavy guilt."

By the time Bette approached adolescence, she felt more apart from everyone else than ever. "I was miserable—I guess it was because I looked like I do." She was poor, she was white, she was Jewish, she was homely, and the older she got the worse the treatment she received from the kids around her. Her neighborhood was a "tough" one, she says, "equivalent to any of the tough neighborhoods in Harlem or Brooklyn, except from a different perspective because the racial balance was different. You rarely saw blacks—it was mostly Filipinos—and the Filipinos were always the toughest."

Her schoolmates would mock and taunt Bette, threaten to beat her up, and chase her home in tears. But she found out, in high school, that there was a way to gain the acceptance of her peers. She had a small taste of it in grammar school. "I first realized I was funny in fifth grade. Me and this girl, Barbara Nagy—I remember *everybody*—we decided to put on a skit for the class. She was the man, I was the woman—Herman and Oysterbee (I don't know where the hell *that* name came from). But when we got up to give the sketch, we couldn't remember any of the stuff we rehearsed, so we wound up improvising the whole thing. She was wearing her father's shoes and one of them had a hole in it and I put my finger in the hole—and it brought down the classroom! It was so strange! People were laughing at something I did. . .it was a real nice feeling, though."

The following year, Bette entered the school talent show and sang "Lullaby of Broadway." "All the class voted," she says, "and I got the $2 first prize! I will never forget that flush of happiness." She began to sing the song at every opportunity, but once, planning it for a Class Day, she overheard one of the girls say, "Oh no, she's gonna sing that song *again*." She was crushed, and years later, when she recorded it on her second album, she remembers thinking, "This one's for you, Mary Jane!"

Bette became more and more enamored of glamour, of the colorful life that seemed to exist somewhere just beyond the boundaries of her life. Even the mundane occasion of her mother teaching her how to sew—a craft Mrs. Midler taught all her daughters in order to save money—was turned from what Bette calls "an ordeal" into something bordering on escapism. As she wrote in her 1980 book *A View from A Broad*, "Now I could make the clothes of my dreams, ensembles inspired by the revolutionary Mr. Frederick of Frederick's of Hollywood. It wasn't long before I was the first eighth-grader in Honolulu to come to class wearing a flawless copy of Freddie's Satin Surrender. Of course, Freddie's version was black. Mine was crimson and lilac."

Bette's innate theatricality found its focal point on a fateful day when she was twelve. A local librarian who had taken a shine to this strange little girl ("Mrs. Seto. I'll never forget her. She believed in fairies") gave her a ticket to her first live theater performance. It was a revelation to her. "I looked up at the stage and there were all those shining people. They were dancing and singing, looking so happy. It was the most wonderful thing I'd ever seen, and I just thought—I want to do that. I want to *be* one of those rosy, rosy people."

Bette's fantasy world became more and more important to her as the realities of her life became harsher. She was not a popular girl. "I never had any parties when I was a kid—I never went to any and I never gave any." By the time she entered high school, her *differentness* had become even more distinct, and in a somewhat strange way: Bette developed a prematurely ample bosom. It gave her tormentors one more reason to single her out for ridicule. The boys made rude remarks, the girls catty ones, and once more Bette was made to feel badly about herself. "I'll never forget eighth grade. My mother wouldn't buy me a bra. I used to get teased, and I remember coming home weeping, so she broke down and got me one for my birthday. Oh, I was *so* relieved. Oh my dear, *so* relieved."

With the taste of peer approval she had gotten with her singing in grammar school, Bette figured there was only one way to get along with her classmates. "The position I found myself in as a girl was having to entertain the enemy...I always felt the only way to get any love at all was through performing. I never said it out loud to myself, but by the end of high school I had entrenched myself into performing very heavily...I was always working on a show or some kind of presentation."

She filled her partyless and dateless Saturday nights by heading up a Lennon Sisters-like trio called the Pieridine Three ("It means 'Like a butterfly'") and rehearsing songs they could perform in school. "I came into glory in high school. I *bullossomed*. I blossomed into a D-cup and there were finally white kids in my school. I was even popular. It was a real surprise...in high school I became a person. That was when I began to realize I wasn't as bad as I thought."

The big change in Bette Midler occurred in her junior year. She transformed herself from a shy, basically quiet girl, intimidated by those around her, into the class wit, a good-time girl whom her peers liked and gravitated toward. Penny Sellers, a classmate, recalls, "When I first met Bette—she spelled her name Betti and we pronounced it "Betty"—she was a quiet and serious student. She wore harlequin-shaped glasses, thin shirt-waist dresses, and had sandy blond hair that frizzed in the Honolulu humidity. In our junior year, although she made the requirement of the National Honor Society, she seemed less studious. Her raucous laugh made us all giggle, and her witty remarks were—well—*bawdy*."

Bette was accepted into the Regents, an exclusive Academic girl's club, and was voted its president in the middle of her junior year. So complete was the transformation of Bette Midler from object of ridicule to object of affection that at the end of that year, she was voted "most talkative" and was elected Senior Class President. Penny Sellers wasn't sure she liked this new Bette as much as she had the old one. "Somehow I couldn't quite trust this new, noisy Bette who insisted we now pronounce her name 'Bet.' What happened to the girl I knew? Somehow her behavior was too calculatedly wacky." The change had not been easy for Bette. She wrote in Penny's junior yearbook: "I'll admit that this year has taken its toll—as far as changing me is concerned. Perhaps the change is not for the better...I do so want to make you proud of me—your admiration and respect mean so much to me."

Probably the most influential person in this transformation Bette went through in high school was a girl she met in her junior year and who became her best friend—Beth Ellen Childers. "She was the funniest person I ever

Bette seems to be doing an impression of Lisa Lupner as she poses with some high school classmates. "Those glasses murdered my love life," Bette said. "Thank God they weren't on a chain. It was bad, but it wasn't *that* bad."

5

For her graduation
portrait, Bette seems to have
done quite a bit to
glamorize her image. (1963)

met," Bette has said. "We laughed all through two years of high school. She made me believe in myself. She was hysterically loud and loved noise and a good time. She was the most adorable thing. She made me feel okay to be who I was...My family never made me feel this way. She drew me out of myself."

Beth and Bette became involved in a great many escapades, not the least of which were minor careers as shoplifters. "Oh God," Bette says, "I never after have had the kind of thrill I got when I was shoplifting. It was always cosmetics; lipstick, powder, hairdye—I started dying my hair when I was twelve—and it drove my father wild. He didn't want any of his children turning out to be *whores*. Once my friend and I were shoplifting at a Woolworth's or Piggly-Wiggly's; we were carrying those great big purses women were using then and we were loaded with stuff we'd taken. As we were leaving the store it was pouring rain, approaching a hurricane. My girlfriend had a cold, and she got down on her knees in the middle of this deserted road and repented. She cried, 'Oh God, if I don't catch pneumonia, I swear I'd never shoplift again!' And she didn't, so after that I had to shoplift by myself—I didn't get down on my knees, see. *Never.*"

Bette's close bond with Beth Ellen came to a tragic end when she was killed in a car accident a year after high school graduation. "She was the only real friend I ever had," Bette says. "My mom and I were close, but...when Beth Ellen died, I carried on so much my mom thought we must have been lesbians."

In her senior year, Bette immersed herself more and more in the theatrical life. She joined the Speech Club and won the state-wide championship for dramatic interpretation at a speech contest. Penny Sellers remembers, "In our school variety show, an enormous gala replica of a Broadway production, Bette held the acts together, staggering knock-kneed and cross-eyed. To our intense delight, she hammed and overhammed. Stomps, whistles, and mad applause ushered in her first time on stage as a comedian."

Apparently, few in high school knew Bette could sing; her performances were exclusively "dramatic." But the high school newspaper's graduation edition hinted at it: "Bette Midler, who is considered to be one of Radford's greatest dramatists, is the president. Unknown to many is her scrawny, soprano warble, which can be heard while taking her Saturday night bath...Her ambition is to join the Peace Corps and, perhaps, someday become another Bette Davis."

Bette and Penny Sellers appeared in the senior class play, Cornelia Otis Skinner's *When Our Hearts Were Young and Gay*; Bette played the lead, and Penny had a small part: "She was on stage every minute and I appeared in the third act for about five minutes."

To promote the play, the Radford High faculty arranged for a local television station to provide a live spot. "I remember picking Bette up in front of her inelegant civil servant housing," Penny says, "and driving to the station. I was there for moral support, but Bette managed her first TV appearance with aplomb."

The night of the performance, Penny recalls sitting in the dressing room with Bette, who told her that she was going to become a professional performer and go to New York. "I thought she was talking from excitement. I remembered the tenth grade, when she dreamed aloud about getting contact lenses, a nose job, her hair straightened. Those days were long gone. Now she seemed so ambitious, so sure of herself."

There were four performances of the play, and the first three went off without a hitch. But during the final performance, one of the students forgot his lines, and there was a long, awkward silence. To save the day, Penny recalls, Bette began "laughing and singing, doing the Charleston in crazy circles until we all giggled hysterically and had to drop the curtain. The bell rang, the students thought we were through and filed out. I never got on stage!"

If Bette's life improved at school, things only got worse at home. Life within the Midler household was sterile, stifling. Ruth Midler's own dreams and fantasies didn't have the outlets that her daughter's did. Her frustrations, Bette has said, turned her into "the most negative woman. Hypertense. I saw this misery, this incredible misery that she could not force her way out of, this loneliness and bitterness. But I adored her because I saw in her this somebody who was trying to get out, who had a dream that unfortunately never came true." Mrs. Midler, in turn, delighted in her flamboyant daughter. "She just thought I was *it*," Bette says. "She thought I was so funny and adorable; she just loved all the excitement. She used to say I was the only thing that brought her joy."

Fred Midler continued to rule his family with an iron hand. Susan Midler recalled in *Rolling Stone* that "he didn't like us wearing makeup and we had a curfew, some ridiculous hour like ten o'clock. And if you weren't in the house, you usually got locked out. Us sisters were always sticking up for each other, and sneaking each other in the window at night."

Even her mother allowed Bette to see only movie musicals because she "didn't want me to see '*those* things.' I never swore until I was seventeen. If you said 'darn' in the house, you got beaten within an inch of your life."

The teenage Bette soon rebelled against the puritanism of her home life. "My mother was always trying to make sure I wasn't exposed to the seamier aspects of life. Consequently I was always fascinated by the seamier aspects of life. That was the biggest influence on me. I used to look out the window and watch the girls—you know, the cheap girls, the *bad* girls in the night. I thought those girls were the *best*. I thought they were *great*. I never got over them, I never did. . . they all wore real tight skirts with flounces on the bottom, pointy shoes and pointed bras and sweaters buttoned down the back. And they all had filthy, *filthy* mouths. Sometimes I would follow them and listen to their conversations. They would talk about their boyfriends and who was doing what to whom—and it always made me laugh. Because I was a very *good* girl, you know. I *was!*"

Bette graduated from high school in 1963, and was the valedictorian of her class. Her yearbook "prophecy" column was indeed prescient: "This is the year 1973. . .Bette Midler has made her big comeback on Broadway."

The summer after her graduation, Bette worked in a pineapple factory, on the "assembly line": "You see, only the middle part of the pineapple is used for slices," she explains. "So I would sit there and all those sliced pineapples would come by and I would pick out the good slices to put in the cans. All day long I'd sit there and pick out the pineapple slices. I wore these rubber gloves. . .it was really sickening, but I needed the money."

It was about this time that Bette became involved with a young man and because "I didn't want my ma to know," she moved out of the house.

The following fall, she entered the University of Hawaii to study drama. But she was far too anxious to actually *do* something to remain a student much longer. In 1965, an opportunity arose for her to be an extra in George Roy Hill's film of James Michener's *Hawaii*. She jumped at the chance. "I played a missionary's wife and spent my two minutes on screen heaving over the side of a ship." But an additional assignment as an extra in the film brought her to Hollywood—her first trip outside Hawaii—and gave her enough money to make reality the dream which had become an all-encompassing passion: she would go to New York and become an actress.

At this point in her life, Bette hadn't given much thought to film: she wanted to be a *Broadway* star. "I was sitting in Honolulu with stars in my eyes thinking that I could become Ethel Barrymore or someone of that stature." And she realized that she would have a better chance of succeeding on Broadway—with her unusual looks—than in Hollywood, where, it seemed, you needed to look like Debra Paget or Sandra Dee just to break in.

She left Hawaii in November, 1965. "The day I did you should have seen us all in that car! Everybody cried—even my father cried, which was unusual. I told my family I was gonna be a star...I was wearing a plaid dress and I had on my first pair of nylons and a girdle with a garter belt—for a *ten-hour* flight! But I was too excited to get comfortable, to move. I just sat there in my cramped seat, trying to imagine New York City and what a giant star I was gonna be. I sat there like a big dope and do you know I was so excited I never even took off—my God!—my *red* high-heeled shoes!"

Two

When Bette got to New York she experienced firsthand the "seamier" side of life she had been so attracted to as a teenager. Her first lodgings were unquestionably in one of the seediest places of human habitation in a city with its share of them—The Broadway Central Hotel, which collapsed just a few years later. She rented a tiny room for $15 a week. "There was a hole in my bed," Bette says, "and I was always falling through it at night. And the bathroom was down the hall. And I mean *really* down the hall. You had to get dressed, go out the door, turn right, turn left, turn right again. It was your basic freak scene, that hotel. Winos in the hall, whores in the next room, junkies outside. The dyke bar was downstairs (I had to beat them off with a club!) and the gay bar was down the street.

"I *loved* it! My dear, it was my great adventure. So exciting. No seriously, I got used to it. It became just another trip down life's merry road."

Bette's joy at finally being in New York made all the difficulties of living there no problem at all for her. A few weeks after she arrived, the famous blackout occurred, and soon thereafter the subway workers went on strike. "I had to go up to 119th Street," Bette said, "to get to work every day. I was working at Columbia University—typing. So it was like this incredible hassle. But I just thought it was a lark.

"I just blossomed out when I came here. I never felt I was home until I came here. I became all the things I wanted to be. It was like I was finally free."

Although Bette had stashed away $1000 of her *Hawaii* earnings in case of emergency, she needed to work to make ends meet. The jobs she got were the typically varied and colorful kinds aspiring actresses always seem to find.

In addition to her typing stint at Columbia, she toiled as a hatcheck girl ("I was the worst—I was always giving people the wrong hats"), as a go-go dancer in Union City, New Jersey, and as a sales clerk in Stern's department store. That job lasted four months, until Bette quit. "This old lady came in and, honey, was *she* a killer. She had 'dementia' written all over her face. In an hour and a half the old bitch tried on about a hundred pairs of gloves. Then she started screaming that I didn't show her everything so I threw the gloves down and just walked out."

The jobs paid her bills, but Bette's real work in New York was her pursuit of a showbusiness career. She took acting lessons from Herbert Berghof and Lee Strasberg, singing lessons, dancing lessons. Every spare moment was spent in a single-minded quest for her goal. Trying to explain her drive, she later said, "What I have in me. . .well, it's not hard, and it's not cold, and it's not *fierce ambition*. . .it's a drive, but it's not a drive—it's being driven. It's something I have no control over. It's something pushing me, I'm not pushing myself."

While taking acting lessons at the Herbert Berghof Studio, Bette "made the rounds" of theatrical auditions, the often dehumanizing process all aspiring actors must go through. She attempted to win serious roles, but with no success. "I didn't realize what the theatre had come to—that I would be competing with other girls on a *physical* level. I thought they'd hear my brilliant line readings and say—'Give the girl a gig.' I wanted to be a great dramatic actress back then," she said later. "I had always sung, but I never really thought of becoming a singer at first. The *thea-ter* was my great love, dahling—I was calling people

As Cinderella in
Tom Eyen's musical *Cinderella
Revisited*, 1966.

'dahhhhling' even back then. I got into singing eventually because I had the idea that if I started out in musical comedy, it would open the doors to those great juicy dramatic roles..."

The juiciest dramatic roles Bette was getting at this point were as witches in children's theater productions ("I was a great witch"). Then she heard that playwright/director Tom Eyen was holding auditions for a new show he was putting on at the Cafe La Mama, *Miss Nefertiti Regrets*—"a very strange little musical comedy," as Bette puts it, "but very musical and very funny." She sensed that her looks wouldn't work against her in an off-Broadway production.

For her audition, Bette sang Kurt Weill's "Pirate Jenny," a bitter, rough-edged song. The result was somewhat incongruous. "Tom Eyen thought it was hysterical that this girl from Hawaii was singing 'Pirate Jenny.' He thought it was the silliest thing he'd ever seen." But Eyen was impressed with Bette, and although he didn't have any openings in any of the major roles, he hired her as one of two non-speaking chorus girls.

The show had a short run at La Mama, but was revived a few months later. This time Eyen, who found Bette's wit and comic sense delightful, cast her in the lead as the Egyptian queen—complete with blond wig, bikini and stilleto heels. Bette's performance was sexy and tongue-in cheek. "I was Miss Nefer-*tits*," she says with relish.

Again the run was short, though, and Bette spent the summer of 1966 on the "borscht belt," the primarily Jewish resort area in the Catskill Mountains in New York. She appeared in "An Evening of Tradition" (a presentation of Sholom Aleichem and Paddy Chayevsky stories), and also did some singing at several showcases—"I got a standing ovation at Brickman's, but only one gig came out of it."

Back in New York, she was cast in another Tom Eyen show, *Cinderella Revisited*, at the 13th Street Theater. The cast did a show for children during the day, then for the evening shows changed the spelling to "*Sin*derella" and presented their adult version of the fairy tale.

Bette's arrival in New York coincided perfectly with the trend toward irreverence and experimentation in theater—if only Off-Off Broadway. Her own idiosyncracies—her looks, her clothes, her sexy *chutzpah*—all served her well in these off-the-wall productions, which increased her confidence in being different, outrageous. She tried to see as many shows as possible, and one theater troupe in particular made a lasting impression on her—Charles Ludlam's Ridiculous Theatrical Company.

"I got a great deal of my early inspiration from Charles Ludlam," Bette said. "The first thing I ever saw him do was *Turds in Hell*, which blew me away. It was incredible, the most incredible piece of theater I'd ever seen. And there was this chick in the show called Black Eyed Susan—she was terrific, she really inspired me. She was kind of a running-gag character. In one part she was a hooker on the docks, and she came out and recited this endless Robert Service poem that made no sense at all. Then in this 1930's number she came out all wrapped in toilet paper with dollar bills taped to her. She was the Statue of Liberty and sang 'Wheel of Fortune.' Actually, 'Wheel of Fortune' was instrumental in setting me in my path. I didn't think I could stand up and sing. But after that..."

Still, Bette's dream was the *legitimate* stage, the *thea-ter*. "I figured that the best way to get into the theater was in a musical comedy, because it was the easiest nut to crack. I mean if you don't have a lot of credit in serious or classical acting, they won't even look at you. And I didn't have training when I came to the city. It was all instinct and guts."

The hottest musical comedy on Broadway at this time, of course, was *Fiddler on the Roof*, which had opened in 1965, won ten Tony Awards and charmed audiences of all ethnic and religious backgrounds with its heart-warming look at 19th century Jewish family life. Bette figured she was a natural for the chorus at least—she certainly *looked* the part—but audition after audition proved fruitless. "The chaaaaanges they put me through to get that part," Bette says. "First they said I was too Jewish, then they said I'm not Jewish enough. This went on for *eight months*." Finally, she was hired for the chorus, and understudied the role of Tzeitel, Tevye's eldest daughter.

She appeared in the chorus for several months, then was let go. When she heard that auditions were being held to replace the actress playing Tzeitel, she made an appointment. "But the lady who was casting didn't want me to have the job. She called me up two hours before the audition and said I didn't have a prayer. But if I didn't go in, she said, I could have the chorus job back. But I at least wanted to get a look at [director]Jerome Robbins—I worship the ground he dances upon—so I said, 'I'm sorry, I'm taking the audition.'"

Bette won the role, and "never forgave" the casting director for almost tripping her up. Although she sang "all of 32 bars" in the role, she was ecstatic—*"I was actually on the Broadway stage!"* She was also in better living quarters, having moved to a West 75th Street apartment with a friend.

Marta Heflin, who later went on to play the rock magazine reporter who sleeps with Kris Kristofferson in *A Star Is Born*, became Bette's understudy and remembers being very impressed with her. "Her characterization of Tzeitel was very strong. I had to watch the show when I first came into it, and I was sitting in the audience, and I was incredibly impressed. She had such intensity. I knew the minute I saw her that she was going to go on to be a very big star."

Bette and Marta became friendly. "Everyone really liked her a lot. She was very open, very friendly and bright. She was very encouraging and sweet to me." Bette's friendship with Marta was soon to bring about a tremendous change in her life.

But first, there was this part to be played, and Bette played it for three years. "Tzeitel is a good role. I loved it for two years—which is a long time for anybody to love it." After that, Bette suffered, in her words "a *very* heavy bout of disenchantment. I felt that I was stagnating. What I thought it was going to be like—legitimate theater—was nothing of the sort. . .it was cheap, dirty, full of politicking.

"I was really good for about two years, because I had this little thing in my head that wouldn't let me *not* be on. And I would go out there and for two years—every night—I would be ON. The *third* year, however, I came to a *screeching* halt! There I was in the third year, working for the same money I had during the first year, breaking my ass. . .I said, this is not the way to do it. *This is living?* You call *this* living? I didn't call it living."

She began making the rounds again, looking for a new job, but without success. "I was miserable because I couldn't get into agents' offices. And when they would send me out to auditions the people wouldn't like the way I looked, or the way I sounded—I couldn't make them understand that there was anything there."

She remained with the show another year, and it was during this period that tragedy struck the Midler family. Bette's oldest sister, Judith, while visiting

As Tzeitel
the bride in *Fiddler on the
Roof*. Bette was in the
long-running show for three years.

OPPOSITE: In *Fiddler
on the Roof*, 1968 (with Adrienne
Barbeau and Tanya Everett).

New York to see Bette in *Fiddler*, was killed when a car sped out of a garage in the theater district and pinned her against a wall. Bette's sister Susan recalled to an interviewer that Bette called the family with the news. "I gave the phone to my father, Bette spoke to him first, and then it was passed around to all of us. It was a nightmare. I don't think my mother ever got over it."

Bette adored Judy—she told *People* in 1975 that "she was studying to become a movie-maker. She was the most brilliant, perceptive, sensitive..." The family flew in to New York for the funeral, because most of the rest of the Midlers were still in New Jersey. Marta Heflin sat *shiva* with Bette and her family, and remembers it vividly. "I was sitting in her bedroom with her and she was so strong, so philosophical about it, the tragedy of it. It was very interesting how she dealt with it. She didn't fall apart. *She* was the one keeping her family together, emotionally. And she loved her sister *so* much. It seemed to make her a little tougher all around, you know?"

Marta played Tzeitel for a week, then Bette returned to the show. Before long, Marta's own ambitions would present Bette with the opportunity both to leave *Fiddler* and to begin her progression from Bette Midler to The Divine Miss M.

Three

Disenchanted with the "legitimate stage," and excited by the music scene in New York, Bette had begun going to various clubs and showcases after her night's work in *Fiddler*. "I'm a very timid person, very shy, really," she said later. "And I'm terrified to go anywhere by myself. There were so many places I wanted to go to that I couldn't. . . like I would go to The Scene and I would always hide. . . way in the background. I was always frightened. I didn't want to know them, and I didn't want them to know me. I just wanted to walk in and listen to the music."

Bette and Marta had become more friendly. ("We just hit it off," Marta says. "I'm not sure why. Kindred insanity, I guess.") Marta went to the local clubs too, but she—an aspiring singer—performed in several of the showcase spots, places where hopeful amateurs could get up and sing a few songs or tell jokes. Bette found out about this, and accompanied Marta one night to a club called Hilly's. She was going to take the plunge.

On these "new talent" nights, most of the acts were barely passable, some were awful, others were obviously performers with great promise. Bette watched several acts, including Marta's, then it was her turn. "She was very hesitant, kind of embarrassed," Marta remembers. "She wasn't sure what she was going to do, or even if she *should* do it, you know—the kinds of things people feel when they've never done anything like that before." Bette conquered her fear, got up in front of a noisy, disinterested audience, and began to sing.

"As I was watching her sing," Marta recalls, "I thought, Oh, my God. Something is happening here. This is really hot. Because the audience just was freaked. It was *very* heavy. I had no idea she could do that."

"The first two songs I sang, nothing happened," Bette said later. "But in the third song, something happened to me in the middle. I suddenly knew what the song was about. I had an experience, some kind of break-through —something happened to my head and my body and it was just the most wonderful sensation I'd been through. The song was 'God Bless the Child,' which I never sing. I sang it that once and that was all because it frightened me so— it really freaked me out. I was screaming at the end of it, the song had a life of its own and the song imposed itself on me and I didn't even know what was going on. I was just this instrument for what was going on. Bizaaaaaaaaare! But it was just what I needed to help me decide to become a singer."

Bette went back to Hilly's again and again, constantly trying out different songs. She also accompanied Marta to another club, Bud Friedman's popular Improvisation on West 44th Street, which was known primarily as a showcase for young comics but which often featured aspiring singers. The first time Bette sang there, Friedman remembers being unimpressed. "She sang a lot of heavy stuff and the audience just didn't dig it—or her, for that matter." But Friedman caught her act again at another club called The African Room and was moved by her performance of "Am I Blue?" He invited her back to The Improv.

Friedman recalls that audience reaction to Bette was usually good, but sometimes it took awhile for them to come around. "I remember one crowd started laughing at her, just because of the way she looked as she walked up the aisle. But by the time she finished her first song, they were no longer laughing. It was perhaps the bizarreness of it that they didn't understand. She was bizarre even then."

The house pianist at the Improv once a week was Barry Manilow. He played for Bette when she sang, and before long would begin to play a very important role in her career.

At first, Bette performed in normal street clothes. "But *then*, I saw this picture of Helen Morgan on the cover of one of her albums. She looked so...so lost. She wore a long velvet gown and held a glass in one hand. The image was terrifically romantic. It appealed to me. So I went out and bought a black velvet gown with beaded sleeves from a junk store around the corner. Ten dollars. I really got into the costume thing—the whole image. It was like being bitten by a fever. After *Fiddler* every night, I'd put on my face, do my hair, put on my costumes and take the subway—people stared and called me names, but at least they didn't *attack* me, so I was grateful."

Bette had been introduced to Helen Morgan—and most of the other great female singers—by her boyfriend Ben Gillespie, whom she had met doing *Fiddler*, in which he was a dancer. "He was my mentor," Bette says. "He opened up the world for me. I was crazy for him. He taught me about music and dance and drama and poetry and light and color and sound and movement. He taught me grandeur. He inspired me not to be afraid and to understand what the past had to offer me.

"He used to play things for me, things I had never heard before. He turned me on to *Unforgettable*, one of Aretha Franklin's earliest albums—a sort of tribute to Dinah Washington. When I listened to it, she was talking right to me. That's the essence of art, you know—when someone can communicate like that...I was over at Ben's house one night listening to that album and I was ripped-ripped-*ripped*! Really stoned! I started singing at the top of my lungs."

Bette began to sing some of the classic torch songs—"My Forgotten Man," "What a Difference a Day Makes," "Ten Cents A Dance"—and "the more I sang them the better I liked them, and the more I wanted to sing. Suddenly it took on a whole intellectual bent, I was running around to the library and collecting records." She would spend hours in the Lincoln Center Library of the Performing Arts, researching old songs and adding them to her repertoire.

Bette's relationship with Ben Gillespie ended after three years—"With all that wonderfulness, there was the other side. Once the despair and the destruction overwhelm the creative thing, then I always move on, because basically, I'm a loner. And I always will be."

But a new—non-romantic—relationship had begun for Bette: Bud Friedman became her first manager. They signed a one-year contract, and Bette worked nearly every night at the Improv, while still doing *Fiddler*. But again it was Marta Heflin who gave Bette a chance to move on to new ground. Marta had been hired to appear in an Off-Broadway rock musical by Peter Link and C.C. Courtney called *Salvation*, inspired by the success of *Hair*.

"It was a revue in the form of a revival meeting," Marta recalls. "The people in the cast were all called up from the audience—supposedly—to be saved. I played a nymphomaniac. And you know how with some nymphomaniacs, you'd never know it because they wear Peter Pan collars and are very proper ...but *underneath*. Well, that's how I did it."

When Marta left to do the part in a California production of the show, she told Bette she should audition to replace her. Bette did, and the show's director, Paul Aaron (who went on to direct the movie *A Different Story* and the TV

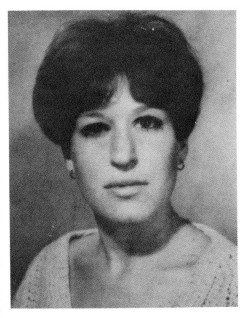

One of the portraits
in Bette's professional portfolio,
circa 1969.

version of *The Miracle Worker*) remembers Bette Midler's audition vividly. "We would bring the girls in one at a time. Barry Manilow was the pianist—he used to do that, play auditions for four or five of the girls and make about 15 or 20 bucks—and he said to me just before Bette came out, 'Wait 'til you get a load of this girl. She's not really what you're looking for to replace Marta—it'd be kind of a strange shot—but give her a chance.'

"So I was prepared for anything—and believe me, she gave a memorable audition. She was almost the last girl I saw, and she came in, walked down the aisle toward me, threw herself in my lap and said, 'Well, you may have seen a lot of girls before me, but you ain't never seen one the same.' And then she proceeded to absolutely blow me away. I thought, This is so special, so terrific, this makes me laugh, this is sexy and raunchy and wonderful. And I wanted to hire her, so I had to tailor the role around her. With Marta, it was always the sex of the virgin. With Bette it was the sex of the vamp—the whole Mae West, Sophie Tucker thing she later became famous for."

Bette's one solo number came early in the show, when she sang of her desire for her boyfriend: "You, I wanted you, in the morning—and over again. You, I wanted you, in the evening—and over again. And in between, and in between, and in between...I wanted *all of your friends*."

"We had these blowup plastic cushions, and she sat on the cushions, and as the number went on, she and the cushions would have an affair, and she's saying all these lines—and with Marta doing it, it was exactly the antithesis of what you would expect. With Bette, the moment she set her hips out, you *knew* she wanted you and all of your friends."

Both Paul and Marta agree that Bette's approach worked just as well as Marta's, despite the fact that the humor of the incongruity was lost. But for Paul Aaron there was another kind of dynamic at work in the way Bette played "Betty Lou." "Bette has gotten prettier as she's gotten older, you know, but when she was a little chorus girl she wasn't the most beautiful girl in the world. The fact that she *made* herself so attractive, so hot—that's what was so amazing about it. It was kind of like, 'I don't give a shit what *you* think I look like, here's what *I* think I look like.' And I *loved* her for it. I loved the guts, I loved the gumption, and I loved the talent."

The only shortcoming Aaron discovered in Bette was her inability to totally immerse herself in the ensemble. "It was very clear to me then that Bette was never going to be an ensemble performer. She had problems with those numbers. But whenever she was 'down in one,' whenever that spotlight was on that lady alone, boy did it light up and she could do it. She radiated. But she couldn't blend herself in with eight people. She was smart enough to realize that and she modelled her career around that. And, of course, the rest is history."

All the while she appeared in *Salvation*, Bette continued to perform in clubs, and once the show closed a few months after Bette joined the cast, Bud Friedman got her some out-of-town gigs. She had been working on her voice, studying with vocal coach David Collier, and her eclectic material set her apart from the usual. She was still singing torch songs—"At that time in my life I was very down," Bette says, "I couldn't get up for love or money, so that's what I sang, nothing but torch songs—'I lost this person, I lost that person.'"

Bette's career was slowly starting to percolate, but one memorable day she received a stunningly fateful telephone call. It was one of her former teachers, Bob Ellston, who told her, "Listen, I know this guy who runs a steam bath and it's a very popular place for homosexuals to go and gather, and he's looking for

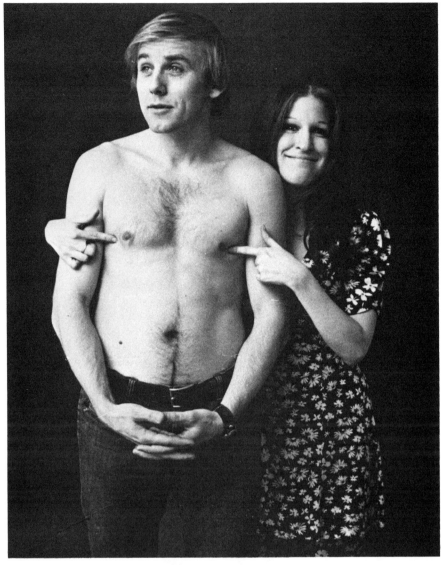

With a fellow cast
member in *Salvation*, 1970.

entertainment. Would you like to work there?"

"I didn't even think twice," Bette said. "I mean, I have been in those circles since I was fourteen years old." It seemed to her like an intriguing opportunity, and something of a challenge – a woman entertaining gay men in their own inner sanctum.

Stephen Ostrow, owner of the Continental Baths, went down to the Improv at Ellston's suggestion and caught Bette's performance. He liked what he saw. The first act he had signed for the baths – a husband-and-wife folk-singing team – wasn't the most appropriate entertainment for such an iniquitous venue; Bette Midler, he thought, would be much better. And since Bette had been working for free at the Improv, Ostrow knew he wouldn't have to stretch his budget too much to get her. He offered her $50 a weekend for one show a night on Fridays and Saturdays at 1 a.m., beginning in July. She quickly accepted.

No one, least of all Bette herself, could have possibly foreseen the impact that her appearances at the baths would have – on her audiences, on her career and, most importantly, on the very person that Bette Midler was.

PART TWO

THE DIVINE MISS M

(1970–1974)

Four

By 1970, tremendous changes were taking place in the sexual mores and attitudes of millions of people in the more liberal areas of the country—New York, San Francisco, Los Angeles. In 1969, an event had taken place which to homosexuals everywhere became the equivalent of the storming of the Bastille—the Stonewall riot, in which the patrons of that gay bar in Greenwich Village fought against policemen who had come to raid the place, rather than meekly allowing themselves to be led away as so many before them had done. It was the symbolic beginning of the Gay Liberation movement which flourished in the 1970s and saw gay people—not without hurdles and setbacks—gain a tremendous amount of acceptance and equality.

Gay bathhouses—places where homosexuals could gather in anonymity for sex and socializing—had existed for years, but they were seedy, dirty, sometimes dangerous places reflecting perfectly the atmosphere in which gay people had been forced to live for decades. The Continental, in this new climate of openness which was developing at the time, changed all that. The facilities were clean, there was a pool, a steam room, a sun deck and a dance floor, in addition to the private areas reserved for sexual activities.

Steve Ostrow was a man who was certainly liberated personally, and he was determined to liberate his bathhouse from the stigma such establishments had carried. With a wife and a male lover, Ostrow was in the vanguard of the entire sexual revolution which swept the country in the '70s. His establishment was a place where gay people could have sex with each other, but he wanted it to be more than that—"a full living cycle, a total environment. . . and after you've been here for twenty-four hours, you want to be entertained. *I* do. Entertainment was a natural thing to make a part of the baths."

The night before Bette was scheduled to make her first appearance at the Continental, her *Fiddler* hairdresser, Bill Hennessy, called her up. He had just visited the baths and thought there was something she ought to know. "You're not going to believe this, but there's some drag queen over at the Continental who's calling himself Bette Midler, and he's gonna appear there tomorrow night." Bette howled—and used the quote as her opening line the next night.

The entertainment accomodations at the baths weren't particularly deluxe; the dance floor was cleared and a small area near the pool was set up with chairs for the performers. A tiny dressing room—off to the right and up a few stairs—was equipped with a barber chair. Billy Cunningham, whom Bette had met at the Improv and who later became musical director of the off-Broadway hit *Let My People Come*, agreed to play piano for her. He gave her a rather grandiose musical introduction and she walked down the stairs on to the floor. There were perhaps twenty or thirty towel-clad men sitting on the dance floor facing her. She was more nervous than she had ever been, and felt more like an alien than ever before—she was the only woman in the entire place. She opened with "Am I Blue?" and several other ballads Ostrow came to call "dirges." It was, as Bette later described it, "a fairly negative, bluesy down trip." And while the audience was appreciative, they weren't delirious.

But it didn't take Bette long to realize that this place was unlike any other she would ever work in—and that she wasn't as different from these people as she might have thought. There was a "camp" sensibility among many gay

OPPOSITE PART TWO:
A 1970 portrait by Richard Brezner. Bette had asked Brezner, an amateur photographer, to take some portfolio pictures of her.

OPPOSITE: Bette sings an emotional "I Shall Be Released" at the Baths, 1971.

Another Midler
appearance at the Continental
Baths, 1971.

men—a daring, a flaunting of convention, a bitchy, dishy humor, a flair for affectation which the girl who called everybody "dahling" in high school warmed to immediately. She knew instinctively that at the Continental Baths she could take chances, experiment, be as outrageous—and as much herself—as she wanted to be. Bette realized early on that here was a chance to be raunchy and sexy and wild without having to appear in a show; at the baths, she could be like Black-Eyed Susan and yet not have to keep to a script. "As an audience, gay men are spectacular," she said. "They're very warm, very responsive. They are the most marvelous audience I've ever had because they're not ashamed to show how they feel about you. They applaud like hell, they scream and carry on, stamp their feet and laugh. I love it." As Bette put it years later, "Ironically, I was freed from fear by people who, at the time, were ruled by fear. And I will always be grateful."

Before this, Bette had never talked with the audience very much; she'd sing one song, briefly introduce the next. But Bill Hennessy reinforced her instincts about this crowd by stressing the necessity of *relating* to them, particularly through humor. "You've got to allow the comedy, the joy in your life to show through. *Be insane*," he told her. She asked him if he would write some funny lines for her, some gay-ish humor. She still wasn't confident enough to rely solely on her own wit—which was considerable—but she knew that she and Hennessy and the audience out there were kindred spirits when it came to laughter. "I have that sense of humor," she said. "I mean, what they think is funny, I think is funny."

She and Bill sat around after the show or during the week and came up with one-liners, or areas in which she could explore her own humor onstage. It was immediately evident that this was the added dimension that was going to make Bette Midler's stint at the baths a success. The men loved her comedy monologues—dishy, self-deprecating, a combination of gay, Jewish, female, show business sensibilities that touched all bases, but which most of all were just plain *funny*.

The incorporation of humor into her act wasn't confined to one-liners; it became all-encompassing. Bette changed her wardrobe from Helen Morgan sophistication to '50s "trash with flash." Out she would come in Spring-o-lator shoes, a black-lace corset and gold lamé pedal pushers, wearing a "Shangri-las Fan Club" button, her hair looking like she had just stuck her finger in an electric socket.

"Oh, my *dears*," she would say to the audience, holding her head in mock dismay. "Do you believe I was allowed to leave the house dressed like this? My hairdresser decided to give me a new look for tonight, so he did my hair with an eggbeater. You might be familiar with him, the divine Mr. Gerard—he works in the salon in the 34th Street subway station. You know, 75 cents a set.

"I went to see him the other day. I go down into the subway, and they had *moved* the thing. Now, I don't mind having my hair done in the subway. I really don't. But in between the tracks? My *dears*! But Mr. Gerard never missed a beat of that finger action as the A-train whizzed by!"

Bette's humor extended as well into her musical material. She had always loved the music she grew up with—the girl groups, the Shirelles, the Shangri-las, the Supremes, the Ronettes. She decided to do some of the campiest '50s numbers—"ShaBoom ShaBoom," "Teenager in Love"—and the audiences loved them. Her entire repertoire changed. She added wild numbers from any era—"In the Mood" and "Chattanooga Choo Choo" from the '40s, "Leader of the Pack," "Da-Do-Run-Run," "Uptown" and "Don't Say Nothing Bad

About My Baby" from the '60s.

Before long, Bette Midler's act became a veritable revue of the best of American pop music from the past four decades, done with a combination of humor, panache—and commitment. She would make fun of the songs and their eras in her patter—but she would sing them in such a way that you knew why they had been so popular, and that Bette Midler loved them.

"Remember the bouffant BMT subway hairdo of the '50s? Remember AM radio? Oh, my dears, *AM*. That's where it was all at. You didn't have to think, just listen. What fabulous *trash*. Remember girl groups? The Shirelles, Gladys Knight and the Pips? Okay, I'll be the leader, you can be the Dixie Cups." Bette breaks into "We're going to the chapel, and we're gonna get ma-a-a-rried . . ." and everyone sings along.

Now, there was more than one dimension to Bette Midler. The rather homely, vulnerable young girl who could break your heart with a ballad now presented a startling contrast to the brassy, vulgar, campy, seemingly self-assured and often bitchy woman on stage just moments before. There was a tremendous dynamic between these two personalities, and both of them were genuinely Bette Midler—a fact never lost on her audiences. The truth of both of these seemingly incongruous personas made each of them all the more effective.

And there was still another side to Midler—a passionate singer who could rip into a rock number with an intensity that left one breathless. Indeed, there had never been anyone quite like her before. Going to a Bette Midler performance was like getting to see three shows for the price of one.

Bette Midler's gay audiences—aside from the fact that they knew they were seeing an incredibly talented new star—sensed, perhaps above anything else, her *honesty*. They knew that she wasn't entertaining them *just* to make some money; that she thought of them genuinely as soulmates, understood them, didn't snicker at them behind their backs. When she sang Bob Dylan's "I Shall Be Released" at the baths, she performed it as though it were a liberation anthem for every oppressed homosexual, stepped-on woman and discriminated-against minority member who ever lived. Her audiences were moved to tears, and they stood and cheered for her when she was finished.

If the rage Bette could express in her songs over the heartache many of these men had to suffer because of their sexuality touched them to their souls, her humor was able to make them feel better about themselves, too. She would dish them good-naturedly about their mating habits, make fun of their idiosyncracies, laugh at some of the very things other people were outraged by. She would mock the penchant of many gay New Yorkers to weekend on Fire Island, where anything went, especially on the beaches at night and in the thick overgrowth which covered the island. "Ah, Fire Island. Health spa for hairdressers. I was going to perform there, yunno, at Cherry Grove." She primps her hair. "But they just *couldn't* find any room for me in the bushes, honeees!"

She was the first non-gay, non-drag queen performer ever to relate to these men in this way. By doing so, she was telling them that it was okay to be themselves, that they weren't wicked sinners who would be struck down by hell fire. It is not difficult to understand why Bette Midler soon became not only a popular entertainer, but a deeply beloved one as well.

Rex Reed put it succinctly and well in a piece he wrote for the New York *Daily News* on what soon became the Midler phenomenon at the Continental: "Magic is in the air. Magic that removes the violence of the cold, dark streets.

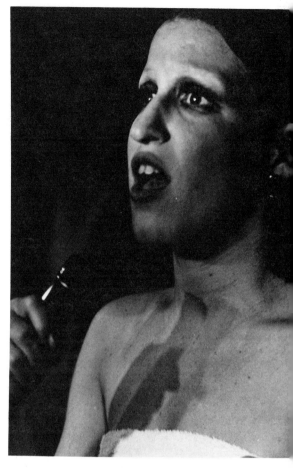

For her encore, Bette returns wearing only a towel.

OVERLEAF: A contact sheet of photographs by Richard Brezner reveals the many facets of the Divine Miss M. (1971)

The Divine One
adopts some attitude.

The insecurities, the hates, the fears, the prejudices outside vanish in a haze of camp. It's Mary Martin asking if we believe in fairies. Yes. We Do. Clap harder. And the Jewish Tinker Bell is right there in front of you. Twinkling, glittering, making soft musical chimes of peace.

"One boy gets so carried away his towel falls off, and he stands there, unshattered in his nudity. The crowd does not faint. They join in the friendly laughter. That's what Bette Midler does to her audience. The boy clutches his towel and says: 'With Bette Midler, the world can overcome anything—*anything*.'"

By the fourth weekend, Bette had improved her show so much that she was now a real attraction, not just something for the guys to do between sexual encounters. The wilder she got, the more her audiences encouraged her. "The audience there wouldn't settle for half-ass," she has said. "If I'd kept my distance, they'd have lost interest because there were too many other things going on in the building that were more fun."

But nothing that was quite so *divine*. The word was used so frequently to describe Bette—"Oh, my dear, she is *so* divine"—that the description turned into a nickname, the nickname into a persona, and the persona into Bette Midler's alter ego. The Divine Miss M was born.

During this time period, Bette was also making an impression on Johnny Carson's *Tonight Show*. Bud Friedman had gotten her booked on the show in the early summer of 1970 on the strength of her appearances at the Improv.

She had to audition first. Getting out of a cab on the way to the audition, she ripped her dress. "Fortunately, I was wearing underwear—one of the few times I was wearing underwear—and it ripped all the way, *right* on the ass. The whole skirt was falling off, so I found a paper clip and I put the dress together. Then I said. . . what *is* this—if they don't like the way you sound they won't buy you anyway, ass hanging out or no ass hanging out. So I got up and I sang."

On the show, Bette sang "Am I Blue" and Mae West's "Come Up and See Me Sometime." The audience was responsive and Bette was pleased: "It was a real good shot." But it was Bette's next *Tonight Show* stint, during which she talked with Johnny for the first time, that established her as one of Carson's zaniest—and most popular—guests. She was to do the show seven times over the next two years.

For her second appearance, just a few weeks after she had begun working at the baths, Bette sang the 1930s song "My Forgotten Man," in a voice of surprisingly pure timbre, sounding remarkably like a vintage '30s recording. Afterwards, she rapped with Johnny and told him, "I'm probably the only female singer in America who sings in a Turkish Bath. It's a health club."

Bette didn't mention it was a *gay* "health club," except to say "it's called the Continental Baths and it's a very *happy* place." Johnny couldn't believe she was telling him the truth. "You're not putting me on, are you? I've never heard of such a thing. They don't have anything like that at my health club. All we have is the guy with the trained duck." Ed McMahon piped in, "We've been going to the wrong place."

"It's true," Bette protested. "They all sit in front of me and when they love me they throw their towels at me." Johnny: "That's better than a big hand, I suppose." Much laughter. "And when they give me standing ovations, all their towels fall to the floor."

She then talked about her days at the pineapple factory. "I worked there for three summers starting when I was sixteen. I was very anxious for money because I never got a cent at home. It was very hard work. I was on my feet for eight hours, with a half hour for lunch and a ten-minute break—at $1.25 an hour. I worked for one of the schlockier outfits. They didn't even pipe in music. Music is important, you know. They've found that when they pipe it in to chickens, they lay better and faster and bigger. . ."

Johnny and the audience went into hysterics, and Johnny managed to blurt out, "Don't we all!" The entire place dissolved into helpless laughter. Bette was a smash on Carson, just the kind of unique, witty guest who can make a particular show memorable.

Her next visit was even better. She told Johnny that her dream was to have a group she would call "Big-Eyed Bette and the Bang Bangs." She then told Johnny, Ed McMahon, Doc Severinsen and Orson Bean that they would be the Bang Bangs and back her up on the next number. "Now all you have to do is sing 'Ooh, ooh, wah-ooh, wah-wah-wah, ooh, ooh, wah-ooh, wah-wah-wah' while I'm singing the lyrics and then when I sing the refrain, you sing along with me—'Why must I be a teenager in love?' You got that? And you also have to pose. Poses are very important." She gave them all their different stances to take, and the song began. It was unquestionably one of the funniest moments in *Tonight Show* history, with the guys screwing up repeatedly, and it guaranteed that Bette was a guest who would be invited back again and again.

For an appearance in April of 1972, Bette sang "Leader of the Pack" and "Delta Dawn." Her rap this time centered around her plants. "Plants have personalities, you know. I have a very aristocratic gardenia, who wasn't doing too well, so my boyfriend gave it a shot of cocaine [the word was blipped, but you could read Bette's lips], and that really perked it up. It was amazing—the plant got *a whole new lease on life.*

"I also have a Venus Fly Trap. I don't have any flies, so I gave it bacon. It *spit it out.* A *Jewish* Venus Fly Trap, I suppose. But they do get hungry. I have a friend who has one of those *big* ones, it's not a Venus Fly Trap but it's like one, yunno, and it grew to *five feet tall.* And my friend's Chihuahua went into the greenhouse and *never came out!* It's true! I *swear* it!"

Charlotte Crossley, who later became one of Bette's backup singers, remembers seeing her for the first time on this show: "I thought to myself, This woman is *very sick.* And I *loved* her!"

In September of 1970 Bette made her "big time" nightclub debut at Mr. Kelly's in Chicago. She opened for Jackie Vernon, whose audience, as Bill Hennessy liked to say, "had passed away many years ago, of course." She toned down her act somewhat, but not as much as one might have expected. She came out wearing a very loud purple dress, no bra, and shook her pendulous breasts to the beat of "ShaBoom, ShaBoom." If it worked at the baths, why couldn't it work in Chicago? She was taking a risk, but Bette sensed that she was on to something bigger than the Continental Baths. "Everybody has the potential for that humor," she said somewhat later. "Most people are never exposed to (it). But as soon as they see it, they see that it's funny."

Rather than talk about hairdressers or Fire Island, Bette got into an unstructured, almost stream-of-conciousness monologue about Frederick's of Hollywood, that Temple of Tackiness which had so captivated her as a young girl. She went on about all the fabulous items you could purchase from Frederick's—like blow-up bras (you blew into a tube to make them whatever size you wanted) and panties with a little heart sewn strategically. It was all tacky, trashy and flashy and just the thing The Divine Miss M loved. Her audiences ached with laughter.

Her musical repertoire was just as popular with these middle-American au-

Another moment
at the Continental Baths.

diences, who felt nostalgia whenever Bette sang a song from their particular era. Bette may have helped create the nostalgia craze during the 1970s, or she may simply have ridden a wave already developing, but in any event she knew it was coming. "In about three years," she said in the beginning of 1971, "the '50s are going to come back so big it's going to be ridiculous. The *best* things about the '50s will be back. That's what's nice about nostalgia. It takes all the good things and forgets the bad things. Living it is really a trip, but *remembering* it is much, much more fun."

Bette's reception at Mr. Kelly's made it clear that she wouldn't be playing the baths forever, but she returned to New York for another eight-week stint there that took her into early 1971. She continued to experiment at the baths, trying out new songs, new jokes. She added some *double entendre* numbers, "Doctor Longjohn" and "Fat Stuff" (much to the delight of the boys), some hard rock ("C.C. Rider," "Great Balls of Fire" and "Down on Me") some additional camp and novelty numbers ("Marijuana" and "Love Potion #9") and Kurt Weill's dramatic and theatrical "Surabaya Johnny," which she turned into a tragedy with a rendition of devastating pathos.

But then again, right away, there would be the jokes. And they were always fresh. The baths forced her to expand, to seek out new material, to avoid relying on the tried and true. Her first few nights there, some of the guys complained that she was doing exactly the same songs and jokes as she'd done the night before. She hadn't realized that many of the men who frequented the baths did so on an almost daily basis.

She took the fact and made it into a joke of its own. "Oh, you're a much better group than last night. (Pause, questioning look at audience.) This *is* the same group as last night! It was just too dark for me to see at first. Isn't it expensive to stay here so long? Oh, that one's been hiding out in the hamper, with the dirty laundry. And that one's been hiding under the bed. Well, I don't blame you. . .this place is *expensive*, you know?"

In the spring of 1971, Bette decided to try her hand at legitimate theater once again. She accepted an assignment from the Seattle Opera Company to star in a limited run of the Who's rock opera *Tommy*, playing both Mrs. Walker and the Acid Queen.

It was the latter character's one number with which Bette made her biggest impression. A frenzied, hallucinogenic nightmare set to music, Bette performed it by jumping out of a carnival box, wearing a G-string with fringe and a ruby-studded bra. "It looked from the audience like I had nothing on. I'd never done anything like that before. I wanted to know what it felt like, and it didn't hurt me. Except that I got bruised a lot jumping out of that box. I had to put makeup all over my legs because I was black and blue for three weeks.

"Anyway, I jumped out and started shrieking, 'I'm the gypsy, I'm the acid queen, pay before you start. The gypsy, I'm guaranteed to tear your soul apart.'

"I really loved that number. As we visualized it, it had nothing to do with drugs but was about the pervasiveness of female sexuality in American life. This acid queen was like all the negative forces of female sexuality, all the things that drive boys to be homosexuals and frighten men and make them run away. Larger than life female sexuality. Suffocating."

Bette's next engagement was opening for Mort Sahl at Mr. Kelly's in Chicago. The stint was a successful one, and Bette received some local press attention. In a story entitled, "Bette comes on strong, and some can't take the heat," a reporter asked her why she didn't perform the Acid Queen number at

OPPOSITE:
Another evocative portrait
of the period.

Mr. Kelly's. She looked at him askance. "I mean, when people go to see a singer at Mr. Kelly's, they don't expect to see some demented lady take off her clothes and expose her body to them and shriek this incredible song at them. They just are not *ready* for it."

Betta also did some local television talk shows, and it was during one such appearance that she met Michael Federal, a handsome, sensitive young man who had played Claude in *Hair* locally. At that first meeting, he asked Bette for a date. She told him to come to the show first. "I went and was knocked out," Michael said. "She was very, very good." Bette stayed with Michael during her remaining two weeks in Chicago, then brought him back to New York with her to play bass in a band she was putting together.

Bette had come to realize that she needed to have her own backup musicians; an unfortunate occurrence in Chicago had made that clear. Bette agreed to do a benefit performance for veterans, and her band was a motley assemblage of musicians who didn't have anything else to do that day. She gave them her arrangements in rehearsal, but they couldn't or wouldn't get them right. Finally, it seemed that they'd be able to muddle through. But during the performance, they played the songs all wrong again. Finally, Bette turned to them and said, "No. This is the one that goes"—and *sang* the song for them. But the band screwed up again.

At the end of the set, Bette thanked the audience for being so patient: "I thought you were all wonderful." Then she turned back to the musicians and said, "And to this band, I'd like to say one thing. Fuck you." And she walked off stage.

The audience, which included some VIPs, was shocked, and the incident created a mini-scandal in Chicago for awhile. But Bette wasn't going to let anything like that happen again. By the time she returned to the Continental for a short gig in early September, she had a band—Michael Federal (who was now her lover) on bass, Kevin Ellman on drums—and Barry Manilow playing the piano.

Bette had met Manilow at the Improv, where he played for the showcase singers for practically nothing, and Bette was able to offer him more than that. She was being paid quite a bit more than $50 a weekend now for her shows at the Continental, and before long she would be making $1500 a night for one-night stands around the country.

Barry, by all accounts, was extremely important in helping to shape Bette's musical genius. He was able to take her raw talent and give it more structure, more traditional boundaries—not, of course, without some resistance.

"Bette and I hated each other in the beginning," Barry says. "It was a case of two strong egos clashing. But we knew we were good for each other, I guess. What she didn't have were arrangements—and pacing. I tried to give her a musical stamp all her own."

He did—and Bette's shows were getting better and better. She had returned to the baths for several brief stints prior to this one in September 1971, but by now her show was top-notch—and the word was *out* that Bette Midler's act was one of the best in town. Stephen Ostrow was now allowing anyone—including women—into the baths just to see Bette. ("Ladies requested to leave after the show" read a posted sign.) Many of the "beautiful people"—Helen Gurley Brown, Mick Jagger, Andy Warhol—started to attend, and each of Bette's appearances was now something of a "happening."

Peter Dallas, Laura Nyro's lighting director who later worked for Bette, remembers seeing her for the first time this September and being astonished

OPPOSITE: Bette as Mrs. Walker in the Seattle Opera Company's 1971 production of *Tommy*. She also played the Acid Queen.

by the reaction. "I had heard of her, but I really didn't know what she did or that she had such a cult following. There were these hoards of fans, and all I can remember is this girl steps out into a seamy basement and people start screaming and cheering and crying. It was the most incredible thing—she hadn't even *done* anything yet. I wondered why they were going on so, and then she proceeded to deliver a show that warranted all that. But even so, the reaction of her audiences was extraordinary. There was something about that time or that place or that combination that was just very magical. Here was a seedy bathhouse, and all these chic people were lined up *around the block* to see this woman!"

By now, Bette had begun to sing some newly-written songs she had discovered, most notably "Friends," which she adopted as her theme song, opening and closing each show with it. The number was especially effective at the baths, as Bette grabbed on to the outstretched hands of the people in the front rows of her audience. It became a symbol of the gregariousness, the warmth and the vulnerability that always shone through any Bette Midler concert.

Bette was constantly on the lookout for new sources of humor, too, of course, and absolutely nothing was sacred. Once, Peter Dallas remembers, she saw a priest in the audience. "During the break, she ran up to her dressing room and snapped her fingers at Bill Hennessy. 'Quick, quick—ya got any gay priest jokes?'"

By now, it had become a running gag that each of Bette's shows at the baths was going to be her last. "This is my 800th farewell appearance," Bette told the audience one night, primping her frizzy, fire-engine red hair. "Stephen, the owner of this dump, has been making a concerted effort to fill my shoes"—she looks down at her bosom—"and my blouses. He got in touch with Josephine the Plumber to replace me. She came down to look the place over and declined—even *she* couldn't get the stains out of these sinks, honey!

"But this really is the last time I'm gonna be here"—she laughs and looks at an imaginary watch—"for at least two days." Then she holds her head in her hands and cries, "Oh, God! Why can't I be like other girls?!"

Bette then told the audience about her next appearance—her nightclub debut in New York. "On the 20th, I'm going to be at the Downstairs . . . and I could use all of you coming down and saying hello to me, because I don't know anyone in that neighborhood."

As it turned out, Bette did need the help of her "friends" with this one. The Downstairs at the Upstairs was an important, "big time" nightclub, and this was a major engagement for Bette, her first in New York City outside the baths—but luck wasn't with her. Peter Dallas remembers what happened vividly. "The opening night, we were having a hurricane, there was deadly weather, it was Rosh Hashana, and there were eight people in the audience. She was heartbroken and kind of muddled through the show. Her opening line was, 'I want to thank all eight of you for braving the wrath of God to come out and see the dirty Jewish girl from Honolulu.'

"The second night was no better; the third night there were five people. So Bette did something which is very revealing, and which makes me believe that although all the elements were right for her success—the time, the place, the attitudes of the day—Bette would have made it no matter what. She went out, scrambled up some money, and bought a big ad in *Screw* magazine saying 'Bette from the Baths—at the Downstairs!' With a picture of her. Well, of course, she was tapping into her people, her lifeline. By the sixth night, the place is packed. Standing ovations. People are screaming. The seventh night, they're sitting on the rafters. The *creme* starts arriving—John Schlesinger, Truman Capote, Karen Black, Johnny Carson. She gets extended, and extended and extended. Her two-week gig becomes a ten-week gig. She's a smash."

Bette's first major review, in the New York *Times*, is very revealing, telegraphing many of the complaints Bette would face in the years to come from people who didn't "get" what she was trying to do. Spelling her name "Milder" in the headline, critic John Wilson commented that "she has presence, she has a fine voice, she has wit and she has total mobility, including an unusually expressive face." But he complained that her "satire achieves no focal point...she catches nothing of the Andrews Sisters, good or bad. She does a Carmen Miranda number that is little more than an approximation of Carmen Miranda."

It was clear from other parts of the review, however, that Wilson's opinions were definitely of the minority variety: "Bette Midler is creating quite a commotion at the Downstairs...Johnny Carson, on whose television show she has appeared several times, came in to lend her support a few nights ago and she is attracting audiences at other times that go into continuing cries of joy and enthusiasm from the moment she is announced."

Bette was getting a great deal of attention in establishment circles by this time, and she and the people around her were starting to think *recording contract*. Through several connections, Clive Davis, then President of Columbia Records, was invited to see Bette at the Downstairs. Peter Dallas remembers that Davis was "completely unimpressed" and left without coming backstage to greet Bette. "Of course, she was wrecked."

But her luck, so bad at the start of the engagement, had turned around completely. The next night, uninvited and unbeknownst to anyone in Bette's party, Ahmet Ertegun, the President of Atlantic Records, caught the show. It was probably the wildest night of the entire ten-week stint. A group of Bette's fans from the baths had packed the place in order to have a party, and they simply worshipped at her shrine—cheering, stomping, throwing confetti. Ertegun saw all this and was astonished—both by Bette's performance and by the reaction she was eliciting from otherwise seemingly sane people.

"She was overwhelming," he later told *Newsweek*. "I couldn't believe that a young person like her could not only understand those old musical styles but capture the flavor of the periods and make them a part of herself. It was the wittiest musical performance I'd ever seen." At another point, he elaborated: "People of all types—grandmothers, couples, drag queens, everyone was screaming and jumping up and down on the tables for this woman. She was doing everything—she was trying to seem raunchy and tasteless *and* exude a certain elegance, and she pulled it off. What she had was *style*."

Not too much later, Ertegun signed Bette to a major recording contract. But already, Bette Midler was on the verge of one of the most astonishing climbs to stardom in entertainment history. There would be, however, another year of fits and starts, highs and lows, pain and problems until everything came together to make 1973 "The Year of Bette Midler."

Five

February 1972, Bette made what was billed as her "farewell appearance" at the Continental Baths. By now, it was a *major* event whenever The Divine Miss M performed there. A full-page article by Rex Reed, accompanied by a photo of Midler performing as Carmen Miranda, appeared at this time in the New York *Daily News* and other papers around the country. It was Bette's first "big time" interview. "Gawd, I don't know how long I've been here," she told Reed. "It seems like forever, but I know it can't be, 'cause I'm still so young. Ver-ry *young*, have you got that? Tonight is my last night, really. I mean it. I'm on my way, and like Thomas Wolfe, I feel I can't go home again. Lissen, you better get out of here. I've gotta dress for my 'farewell performance,' and besides, my rear can't take this seat any longer."

Reed then told his readers that he realized with a start that he had conducted the entire interview while Bette sat on the john—"the only empty seat in the house. In a city where nightclubs are shutting down faster than a row of stand-up dominos can tumble, there are 3,000 people waiting to get into the Continental Baths to see the freaky Miss M."

Reed may have exaggerated the numbers just a bit, but Steve Ostrow *had* enlarged the performing area to accomodate the Midler crowds, and they were as ecstatic and demonstrative as ever. More and more celebrities were attending her shows, and she constantly improved them, making even those people who had come with a "show me" attitude cheer her lustily by the end of the evening. It was clear that Bette Midler was a performing phenomenon, and that she would not be playing a bath house and relatively small clubs for long. But there were still dues to be paid. She told Reed, "Listen, you think the baths are the pits? Next week, I'm playing Raleigh, North Carolina, in a place called The Frog and The Nightgown. Who do you think lives in *there?*"

Bette was now getting enough bookings to necessitate going "on the road." Peter Dallas remembers that Bette felt she had to put together something more than just herself and a small band. "It was like, you don't really have an *act*, you don't have a *show*, but you're getting $1500 a night from the University of whatever to appear. It's not $50 a weekend anymore, and it's—'Oh my God, I better get a show together!'"

Bette Midler's "show" would develop spectacularly over the next two years, but at this point the only addition was a trio of backup singers. The notion appealed to Bette because of her passion for the "girl groups" of the fifties. Now she *had* her "Bang Bangs"—the cheese-bomb version of the Ronettes, appropriately called the Harlettes. They were also variously called Bette's "celestial choir" and MGM—for Melissa Manchester, Gail Kantor and Merle Miller.

"My girls," as Bette called them, were a terrific addition to her act. They were talented, sassy gals who could complement Bette musically by singing backup vocals and comically by helping her dish—and being, sometimes, the butt of her dishes.

So now there was a Bette Midler Traveling Troupe, and Peter Dallas remembers that it was "a low-paying grind." (Bette may have been getting $1500 a night, but she in turn had to pay everyone else.) "But it was a wonderful experience, a lot of fun. We went to Boston, Philly, places like that to play

OPPOSITE: Bette performs in front of a mixed, packed house at the baths, February, 1972. Later, she called herself "pea-hen to the stars—Barry Manilow, Melissa Manchester, platform shoes."

clubs or colleges, and it was before she had a record out, so we'd play to half-filled houses. But it was this incredible growing period. We had Barry Manilow at the piano, Bill Hennessey writing the dialogue, Melissa, Gail and Merle—and there was just the *synergy* of all this talent traveling around in a little baker's van putting on shows. It was wonderful. And it was really like some kind of miracle when you think of all those people who were on the same bus at the same time. *Barry Manilow*. And Melissa Manchester. Who knew that she, very quietly—she always kept to herself—was penning these little *tunes* that were going to become giant hits. Who could have guessed that so many stars would emerge from that little bus? I'll tell you, *everybody* knew that at least one great star was emerging in Bette. That was always so plain, so evident."

But Dallas recalls, too, that the pressures of what Bette was trying to do—and the speed with which she was gaining fame—put a tremendous strain on her. "There were scenes that I'd rather not go into and that are probably best forgotten by everyone," he says. "It was real hard, and you were dealing with a very insecure woman and things were happening much faster than they should have been happening. Sometimes, there was just a lot of blind terror at work."

Undoubtedly, Bette's most terrifying experience at this point in her career was opening for Johnny Carson in the Congo Room (or "the Congoleum Room," as Bette called it) at Las Vegas's Sahara Hotel in April 1972. It was an offer she obviously couldn't refuse, but she was petrified, and with good reason. Vegas audiences are notoriously indifferent to new—especially *different* and new—performers, and Bette's brand of humor and eclectic musical show was a risky proposition at best.

Enormously nervous as she began, Bette put on a terrific show, but, she said, "I had a lot of trouble dealing with the audience. I have to have love from an audience—when I feel warmth, then I'm warm. They just didn't know what to make of me. . . I hated Vegas, but it was fascinating as an experience, to have it behind you, you know?"

Craig Karpel, who wrote a piece called "Notes on Bette" for *Oui* magazine a year later, described the reaction of a typical audience to her show: "The gentlemen in the audience furrowed their brows and clamped down on their cigars: 'For this I left a hot roulette table and let the captain hold me up for a 20?' Bette's patter included lines like, 'In this one, I shake my tits for all they're worth.' The ladies in the room opened their eyes wide and swallowed hard: 'Tits? Did she say. . . *tits*?'

"Vegas audiences like their *entendres* double. Single *entendres* they consider crude. Single *entendres* delivered by femme songstresses they do not consider. Is it worth $100,000 a week to Bette to stop saying 'tits'?"

Clearly, Vegas wasn't The Divine One's kind of town. Still, her reviews were generally good. *Variety* wrote, "The debut of Bette Midler is a startling change from the norm. Her first words, and there are plenty in the thirty minutes, lay it on with candor as she describes herself as 'the last of the truly tacky women.' That could be possible, in costume only. The tie-around blouse and black slacks are certainly bizarre, although not too far from *Harper's*, yet cannot hide a whale of a voice. She uses it cajolingly; and for those who care to make comparisons, odious or otherwise, the texture and thrust are somewhat triangularly electric from Streisand to Joplin to West. . . The '60s flashback is particularly effective. . . Miss Midler's obvious jitters on opening night will probably be dispelled early, leaving only the enor-

Doing her Carmen
Miranda number. To the left of Bette in
the photo are Francesco Scavullo
and actress Monique Van Vooren.

mous chutzpah to come through naturally in her gabbity-gab and the unique quality of the voice and material to take precedence, as it should."

Bette's association with Johnny Carson led to one of her best jokes: "People ask me what Johnny Carson is really like. And I tell them, 'Well, have you ever noticed that his first wife was named *Joan*; then he divorced her and married *Joanne*; then he got another divorce and married a woman named *Joanna*. Well, you see, there's a reason for this. When he was a little boy, he had a sled named Jo Ann!'

"Isn't that brilliant?" Peter Dallas comments when reminded of the story. "Of course, only about four people ever *got* it, but it was brilliant nonetheless."

Less than a month after Vegas, Bette did a six-day engagement at the Bitter End in Manhattan, one of New York's classier clubs. Every show was a sell-out, Bette was more outrageous than ever ("This next number is for the divine dick . . . you know, Nixon," and "At intermission, dahlings, we have slides of Martha Raye giving *downs* to the Viet Cong!") and her performances gained Midler her first exposure in a national magazine—no less a publication than *Newsweek*. "Next to the likes of Lainie Kazan, Lena Horne or Dionne Warwick," the article began, "Bette Midler is an ugly duckling. Her tiny, 5-foot frame seems absurdly inadequate for her ripe, over-size torso and her large oval face with its ski-jump nose, toothy mouth and mop of curly red hair that is vaguely reminiscent of Rita Hayworth as Sadie Thompson. Her movements are a spasmodic series of clutching, wild arm-waving and little–girl vamping. Her songs are a kaleidoscopic grab-bag of everything . . .

"Yet somehow it all comes together to make her one of the freshest, most captivating of the new girl singers . . . Bette Midler is—to use one of her favorite expressions–'hot.'"

Bette was *so* hot, in fact, that her next venue was one usually reserved for the legendary greats of show business—the hallowed Hall of Carnegie. "Can you dig it?" Bette asked Rex Reed. "From the steam baths straight to Carnegie Hall." Bette and Barry had hired the hall themselves in order to put on the show, which they never expected to sell out. It did.

"At Carnegie I was *terrified*," Bette said later. "I have a tape of myself that someone made for me and all I said all night was *Oh my God...Oh, I'm so freaked out...* all night long! I listened to the tape and couldn't believe it. It wasn't the people, it was the *big*. It was just so huge...it just went up and it was pitch black up there...a second show at Carnegie, if we had done one, would have been sensational—because I was just getting warmed up by the end of that show, I was just getting comfortable."

The audience, of course, never knew that Bette was feeling anything but great. Filled to the rafters with Midler's faithful, the show was a smashing success, and Bette's performances were fabulous. The evening was much more musical than a typical Midler concert, with a minimum of comedy. John Graham, who did the lighting, feels that Bette wanted to give a more traditional concert because this was, after all, Carnegie Hall. "And she wanted to be taken seriously as a musical artist. This was her chance to prove herself as a singer of the first rank."

She did so. Despite her nervousness—which she did refer to again and again throughout the evening—Bette was in top form. After some hot scat singing to introduce the song, she did a wonderfully suggestive version of Bessie Smith's "Empty Bed Blues," showing us graphically how her man grinds her coffee, boils her cabbage, slips the bacon in and *overflows the pot*.

She then altered the mood totally by giving a touching, vulnerable rendition of Helen Morgan's "Give Me Something to Remember You By."

After "Boogie Woogie Bugle Boy," Bette did an intense version of "Superstar," with a driving arrangement and a great deal of anger as the song builds to a crescendo. She never did the song quite the same way again, reportedly because she found the power of that arrangement frightening. She asked Barry to change it, and she performed it much more desolately from then on.

Barry opened the second act, backed principally by Melissa Manchester, who sounded quite a bit like Bette ("We used to call her Melissa Mimic," a member of the audience says). Michael Federal did a solo of Barry's rock number "Buried in the Ruins of Love," with a strong, pleasant voice.

After being re-introduced by Barry as "The Pearl of the Pacific," Bette returned to the stage wrapped in a sarong to sing "Moon of Manakoora." For reasons known only to Bette, she dedicated "Fat Stuff" to Annette Funicello. Her performances of favorites like "Delta Dawn" and "Leader of the Pack" were all first-rate.

What humor there was in Bette's Carnegie Hall concert was very funny. She told the story of doing the *Mike Douglas Show* with Lawrence Welk. "I'll never recover from that particular blow to my ego. Lawrence Welk *hated* me. We were supposed to do the polka—well, he wouldn't put his *hands* on me. He said I was gonna give him the *crabs*. I told him he should be so *lucky*. Then I overheard him telling Mike Douglas that years ago he had a band called the Honolulu Fruits. I told him, 'Lawrence, you shoulda stuck with that one.'"

The concert ended with "Chapel of Love," and when Bette returned to a standing ovation there were rousing calls for her to do a wide variety of songs as an encore. "I don't do requests," she said quietly. "I'll do a song I stopped singing. But you've been very kind to me. I don't understand it. But I really appreciate it. When people treat me like this, I feel just like Mick Jagger."

Then Bette said, "This song is from me—" and gestured "to you" widely with her arm. She sang "I Shall Be Released" with more passion and ferocity than ever before, practically sobbing at its end. The audience rose to its feet and

OPPOSITE: "The happiest night of my life": Bette singing in Central Park, August 1972.

gave her a thunderous ovation.

Midler fan J.B. Annegan remembers the night vividly. "It was an incredible experience for everyone there. Imagine, a $6 top to see Bette Midler, Barry Manilow and Melissa Manchester. There was such a feeling of joy and *camaraderie* in that house. Every one of us felt as though we all knew Bette, and that we all knew each other. God, she gave us some good times. She made us all feel so much better about everything–our lives, the world–everything."

As good and as exciting as it was, Bette's Carnegie Hall appearance did not become the milestone in her career that it had with some other performers–it wasn't, after all, a stunning comeback à la Judy Garland or the culmination of a thirty-year career. What it represented more than anything else was a certification that she wasn't just a freaky flash-in-the-pan, that she was well on her way to genuine stardom–and that she could sell out a house the size of Carnegie Hall.

At this point in her career, Bette was worried that the Divine Miss M persona she had created would overtake her own identity, that the public might not accept Bette Midler without all those Divine trappings. She needn't have worried: her next New York appearance proved otherwise.

In August, she performed in New York's Central Park as part of the Schaefer Music Festival. Thousands of fans jammed the open-air Woolman Rink, the overflow sitting on rocks and tree branches to get a glimpse of Bette Midler. "I thought I was in a newsreel," Bette said shortly afterwards. "It was like the Marilyn Monroe newsreel, you know, when she was in Korea, that's exactly how I felt. It was the happiest I've ever been in my whole life. When I started and I was doing Miss M, I was hiding. . .I have found recently that I don't have to hide anymore. That Schaefer Concert was a real knockout for me. I mean I had some makeup on, but I wasn't dressed very peculiarly at all. I was dressed very normally. That was really the happiest night of my life because I found out that they would take me for what I was, that I had succeeded and that I had achieved what I had started out to achieve, which was to come to myself, to come back to Bette Midler."

Ironically, the knowledge that she could do without zany trappings freed Bette to take them to absurd new heights throughout the rest of her career; and it was just this combination of the life-size Bette Midler and the outrageous Miss M that lifted her from talented performer to international superstar. The next eighteen months would be the most exciting, tumultuous, exhausting year-and-a-half in Bette's life. Within that time, she would begin a passionate, stormy romance with a Svengali-like manager; make a Gold album that would win her a Grammy; and conduct two national tours that culminated in a *Newsweek* cover and a record-breaking, Tony-winning show at New York's Palace Theater. She would also, by the end of this period, very nearly suffer a nervous breakdown.

Wearing a "Shangri-La's Fan Club" button, Bette sings "Leader of the Pack" at Manhattan's Bitter End nightclub, May 1972.

Six

uring the fall of 1972, Bette Midler's life was in the midst of major transition. She was, of course, becoming a major star with dizzying speed, but her personal life was going through important changes above and beyond career considerations. She had lived with Michael Federal for more than a year before moving into a Greenwich Village apartment from her Upper West Side digs early in the year. "I'm good when I'm in love," she said at the time. "I'm hot on stage, too. I just enjoy it. I try to be in love all the time...I keep my eyes open."

By the early summer of '72, Bette and Michael were no longer living together, but were still friends and colleagues—Michael continued to play bass in Bette's band. Described by a reporter as "a lean, handsome young man with bright blue eyes and a shy Carolina drawl" who "looks like anything but the lover of a campy, decadent torch singer," Michael was asked by *Rolling Stone* to comment on Bette. "Well," he replied, "I used to be her lover. What would you like me to say? That she was great in bed? Actually Bette and I still love each other, but we can't live together. She's always rushing somewhere but she's never there in time. I'm just the opposite. I'm very mellow and laid back, so I couldn't take it anymore."

It wasn't long before Bette met a man who was anything but mellow and laid back, and who would have a profound influence on her life and career: Aaron Russo. "Baron Bruiso"—as he came to be called—was a New York boy who left his family's ladies' underwear business, went to Chicago and hustled, huffed and bluffed his way into the ownership of a rock club called The Kinetic Playground during 1968 and 1969. That venture collapsed, and he began to operate a strictly minor-league record label called Kinetic, and managed a group called The Flock. When Columbia Records wanted to sign The Flock, Russo got them to agree to distribute Kinetic's records. None of it ever amounted to much.

Late in 1970, Russo was watching *The Tonight Show* when Bette Midler made an appearance. He thought, This girl is hot, and he called Clive Davis, President of Columbia, the next day to say he wanted to sign her. Davis told Russo that he was totally unimpressed by Midler. Russo figured he better get out of this ridiculous business, and moved into commodities trading.

Two years later, at The Bitter End, Russo and his wife Andrea saw Bette's show. Russo, who still had show business ambition coursing through his body, was as thrilled as everyone else with the Midler talent. He knew he was witnessing the start of an extraordinary career, and he began thinking anew about becoming involved in it. He went backstage to meet her, and soon became a prominent member of her entourage. Russo made himself very *available.* Bill Hennessey recalled that Russo "was conspicuous by his presence" and Gail Kantor said, "Aaron's the kind of person who has a very strong image of himself—a very strong, macho image—and he really was seeking to ingratiate himself to the band and the girls. He was almost *too* friendly."

But Bette was ready for Aaron Russo. Described by one writer as "a big, beefy drink o'water," Aaron's strength and his *chutzpah* were exactly what Bette needed at this key juncture in her life. "Aaron was very forceful," she said. "And at that point in time, I just wanted to be looked after."

Bette was afraid of losing control of things—everything was happening so fast. She wanted someone she could rely upon totally and trust completely, someone who could protect her, guide her career, help her make decisions. Aaron seemed to her just the kind of person she was looking for. And she found all the qualities that would make him a good manager appealing on a personal level, too: "We met, and it was instant love and devotion," she said later. "He's a lot like my father. He's a bellower and in that way he intimidates people, but he's a real softie underneath."

When Bette and Aaron first talked about his becoming her manager, he asked her what she expected of him. "Make me a legend," she replied.

"When she told me that," Aaron said later, "I knew I had to do it. It wasn't money, it wasn't stardom—it was more than any of that. It was a chance to do something intelligent. To design a gem of a career."

Bette explained, "I was half joking and half desperate. And what I meant was that I didn't want to be just another chick singer. I don't want to go to Vegas and wind up singing other people's stuff. I want to be what I think I can be, which is certainly not a legend. But you know, Aaron loved that stuff. That was like throwing down the gauntlet, dearie. His eyes just lit up."

And it was exactly that reaction that convinced Bette she had made the right decision to hire him. But the reactions of her associates shocked her. Almost everyone warned her against Russo, told her that he was trouble, a sleazy hustler. Ahmet Ertegun, who was producing Bette's first album for Atlantic, was the most important of the voices raised against Aaron. Bette was wracked with doubt. It got so bad, Russo told *Crawdaddy*'s Timothy White, that "she got a call in the middle of the night from somebody, saying I was part of the Mafia, a hired killer, and it scared the shit out of her. She called me and said, 'Look, I don't think you can manage me. I'm afraid. People have told me all these things about you.'"

Russo told her that if she were that concerned, he wouldn't press the issue of managing her. But after they talked a while longer, Bette blurted out, "Fuck them all! I want you to manage me!"

"When she showed that faith," Russo told White, "There's nothing in the world I wouldn't do for her. How could I not repay that kind of belief in full? I think I would die for her."

Bette was then being managed by Norman Weiss and Michael Liebert of Artists Entertainment Complex (she had let her contract with Bud Friedman lapse after a year.) Aaron had her write a letter informing AEC that she no longer required their services, and they responded by having Bette served with a summons while on stage at Mr. Kelly's. (She thought it was a mash note from a fan and joked about it.)

But Aaron's business acumen can be gauged by the fact that he not only worked a deal out with AEC that allowed him to manage Bette, but got himself an office with AEC as well.

So Bette Midler had a new manager—and a new lover. The romantic aspects of their relationship, of course, didn't do much to enhance the solidity of Russo's marriage. He has intimated that his relationship with Bette broke up the union: "I couldn't say directly how, but in some ways I'm sure it did, yeah."

As late as 1977, Aaron was quoted in *California* magazine as saying, "Sometimes I think that Bette and I are actually in a marriage...sometimes it seems that way. We were lovers for years..."

Bette denies this, maintaining that after the first six months, their relationship was strictly business. Asked about this disparity in *Rolling Stone*, Bette replied, "What do you think he's going to say? That I schtupped him once and threw him out because he wasn't good enough? That wasn't the way it was, of course, but he has his pride."

Whatever the truth of the matter, Aaron Russo at this point in Bette's life

A campy ad for
Bette's last appearance at the
Continental, 1972.

was a welcome guiding influence. His presence freed Bette from worrying about a myriad of details, and his advice was impeccable.

Bette *needed* advice at this point: there were serious problems with her debut album. She had been working on it for eight months, and it was a trial for everyone. "Bette's first album was the most painful experience of my life," Barry Manilow has said. And Bette agreed. "It was so difficult to do! I was so disappointed I cried every single day. Everybody had something to say about what should go where. Everybody! It was the horrors!"

The problems were many and varied. First, there was Bette's strange eclecticism. "She didn't fit into any categories," Ahmet Ertgun has said. "It's very hard to make a record that doesn't fit a category and then find an audience. Also, it was obvious a lot of her appeal was her onstage magic."

Capturing Bette's "onstage magic" was particularly problematic. Atlantic had hired Joel Dorn, a top-notch producer who had just worked with Roberta Flack, to produce Bette. Barry Manilow had hoped to be much more involved in the album than he turned out to be at first. "I was called in at the very beginning, to lay down basic arrangements," Barry told Craig Zadan in *New York* magazine, "and they said, 'Thank you very much. Good-bye.' It was Bette's first time out so she didn't know what to do. I said, 'Bette, how could you let me leave?' But she was scared."

Once Joel Dorn's version of the album was completed, however, it was clear to Atlantic executives that it did not capture Bette's incredible in-person excitement. Barry had the tape of Bette's Carnegie Hall concert, and he played it for Ertegun. "Yes, that's what's missing from the album," Ertegun told Barry.

43

"Can you fix it?" Barry said he'd try, and he re-did nine of the songs.

It was all very tough on Bette. "I just did not know what went down in a studio, so it took me all that time to learn, to hear it in my brain."

The final product, released in November 1972, credits Dorn, Manilow, Ertegun and Geoffrey Haslam; six of the twelve cuts are attributed to Dorn. The production problems were all finally worth it, because *The Divine Miss M* turned out to be a terrific—and very successful—album.

There were still many people who felt it should have been a live album, among them Steve Ostrow. "The biggest mistake Bette made was not recording a live album," he said. "If she had put out a first album called *Bette at the Baths*, now wouldn't that have been beautiful?"

According to Ahmet Ertegun, the notion *was* entertained. "But Bette was resistant to the idea of doing one at the Continental Baths because she didn't want to be known only as 'That girl who sings at the Turkish baths.' Personally, I don't think Bette has to worry about such things."

She needn't have. While it is true that none of the album's performances are as exciting on record as they are live, *The Divine Miss M* stands on its own. It is an amalgam of all the various songs and styles Bette had incorporated into her act, and as such it is a vivid demonstration of Bette's astonishing versatility.

Nowhere is this more evident than on side one. With the exception of "Chapel of Love" (which seems curiously out of place in this context), Bette turns each of the songs, no matter what its original interpretation, into a torch song, a lament about lost or unattainable love. But every number represents a different *kind* of lament, a different woman, a different reaction. In each song Bette plays a unique role, and she does it brilliantly.

"Do You Wanna Dance," a mid-tempo hit for its author Bobby Freeman in the 1960s, she turns into a breathless young girl's sensual fantasy that equates dancing not just with the obvious—sex—but with every joy that can come with first love. In "Superstar" she is a woman whose starstruck fantasies about a rock performer came true—but left her broken. Her voice quavers not only with the pain of lost love but with the fear that she will never be able to escape from the dreariness of her life, made all the more intolerable by the small taste of possibility he had given her. None of this is necessarily in the song itself, but it is there in Bette's performance—and by its end, her voice cracking, she expresses heartbreaking hopelessness. She knows he will never come back.

With "Daytime Hustler" she shifts gears and becomes a street-wise tough cookie who isn't going to fall for the hustler's line—but there is an undercurrent of vulnerability, a sense that this girl is trying to convince *herself* as much as him.

The best interpretive performance on the album, though, is "Am I Blue," which has been sung by practically everybody, but never quite as Bette does it here. Rather than the abject desolation of the girl in "Superstar," this woman tells us her story with a resigned stoicism, a matter-of-factness that suggests that she realizes she has to accept her condition. It is only when she begins to recall how things used to be ("Was I gay? 'Til today") that Bette lets us see the heartbreak as her voice begins to crack. But she recovers, and as the song ends we know that this woman is not going to let her sorrow destroy her.

Side Two, with its dramatic shifts between the playfulness of "Friends," the pathos of "Hello, in There," the campiness of "Leader of the Pack" and "Boogie Woogie Bugle Boy" and the passion of "Delta Dawn," further demonstrates Bette's range.

Bette, at heart an actress, approached her songs as she would a play, experimenting with various interpretations of the "role," and sometimes using

OPPOSITE: Recording her first album, *The Divine Miss M*, 1972.

more than one in the same song. An interview she gave *Club* magazine is revealing in this respect. Discussing "Delta Dawn," about a child-woman whose life revolves around her search for "a mysterious dark-haired man" who had promised to marry her years before, Bette said, "I do identify very strongly with Delta Dawn. I sing that song and a lot of people don't understand what I'm singing. I sing it fast and I sing it gruff. My idea of the song was always that it was a woman's anthem. Alex Harvey didn't mean that when he wrote it, but I changed the lyric around. The end of the lyric is that 'he's going to take you to his mansion,' and it was almost like, 'look at what a fool you are for believing that, for falling for the oldest line in the world.' But at the same time it also had more than that, it had the added dimension of, 'I really understand why you fell.' And then it had the dimension which followed, that of, 'Oh, please don't let it happen to me.' I try to put all that into it."

Bette's revolutionary approach to rock made her first album the subject of much critical analysis. Most of the reviews were quite favorable, and many went to great lengths to explain why Bette Midler could well change the face of pop/rock music. Dave Marsh and Robbie Cruger wrote in *Creem*, "Bette Midler loves old rock and she knows how to divert some of the energy of '60s material into a torchy style that is unique. She can also do it backwards—impart torch songs with some rock and roll spunk—and that is her biggest plus. No matter how much she moves about stylistically, she defines herself so acutely that each song has its own veracity...This is not a perfect record, but like its maker, its strength is that it transcends what flaws there are. And rises above, at its best moments, any of the ideas anyone has about making Bette Midler into a symbol of anything but master of her own talent. True, she operates out of a showbiz tradition that is much older than rock...but she has transmitted to that tradition the joy that it has always managed to resist. The joy is rock and roll's joy, and Bette Midler loves that music to her very core. With Rod Stewart and the Rolling Stones, alone, she can make us laugh and cry, she can make us care whether her records and performances are perfect, and it seems to us that that is the kind of star the '70s needs most."

Because there was such apprehension that Bette's album would suffer in comparison to her live performances, it is somewhat ironic that several critics felt the record couldn't be completely enjoyed without *first* seeing Bette. Robert Hilburn of the Los Angeles *Times* was one of them: "I didn't really care for this album until I saw Bette Midler in person...By fluctuating between so many styles, she undercuts the effectiveness of her vocals by failing to establish a clear identity. To be effective, a singer has to be believable and this album—for those who haven't seen her in performance—suggests in some selections that Miss Midler is rushing through the various styles in hopes of merely coming up with something commercial.

"But most of these reservations are erased once you see Miss Midler in person. She's a wonderfully original, free-spirited performer and vocal interpreter, one who borrows from the various musical styles in an attempt to sample the various emotions that our multi-directional pop music has given us at different times in our lives...her every move on stage is an effort to challenge an audience, an attempt to tell the audience to enjoy itself, to free some deep emotion, to step out from the protective shell that engulfs so many in these troubled, isolated times. When you see the strength and direction of her music on stage, it is easier to understand what she is doing in the album and to accept the vocal arrangements as authentic expressions."

As good an album as *The Divine Miss M* was, there was considerable fear at Atlantic that it might fail to find an audience, that perhaps Bette was too

OPPOSITE: An exuberant publicity photograph released by Atlantic Records, 1972.

"special" to appeal to a broad record-buying public. But by the middle of 1973, the album had sold nearly a million copies and been certified Gold. An even more important indication that Bette was more than a cult figure was the fact that the album produced two hit singles, "Do You Wanna Dance" and "Boogie Woogie Bugle Boy."

Ahmet Ertegun did not want to release "Boogie Woogie Bugle Boy" as the follow-up to "Do You Wanna Dance," because he felt it was too faithful a re-creation of the Andrews Sisters' version and as such was not hit material. But when Bette went to England to tape a Burt Bacharach TV special in 1973, Barry Manilow put together a different version which Ertegun heard and thought would work. "The difference between mine and Joel Dorn's," Barry has said, "is that his is really authentic and mine is bright. I didn't go after the authentic part, maybe because I didn't know how to do it, and it probably wouldn't have come off good on television anyway. I went after a record. I wasn't doing a TV show, I was making a record. It's what I know how to do."

Despite Barry's feeling that the single was less "authentic" than the album cut, Patty Andrews said, "When I heard it on the radio, I was certain it was us until the ending. She copied everything but the ending. But it's great. Makes me feel that the Andrews Sisters' style is coming back again." Within a year, Patty and Maxene were on Broadway with the smash hit swing musical *Over Here!* and they definitely had come back again—thanks to Bette Midler.

Sales of *The Divine Miss M* were helped immeasurably by the three back-breaking coast-to-coast tours that Aaron Russo arranged for Bette throughout late 1972 and all of 1973. Her appearances in cities like Philadelphia, San Francisco and Los Angeles were wildly successful, with throngs of fans waiting for hours to see her and cheering practically everything she did. On the eve of her Los Angeles debut at The Troubador (Peter Allen opened for her), Bette held a press conference and talked about what she hoped to accomplish with her act: "I would really like to wake up people in this country a bit, say to them that they are really alive. They've had a bad time of it for the past ten years. There isn't a lot of humor around today. I'm trying to say, 'Let's have fun. Don't be afraid to show your emotions.'"

A large segment of the American public was ready to embrace that message of Bette's, as evidenced by her sometimes *three* sold-out shows a night. And her greatest triumph to date was just around the corner: her New Year's Eve concert at Lincoln Center's prestigious Philharmonic Hall.

But first, Bette made what turned out to be *truly* her last appearance at the Continental Baths. It was a typical triumph, but there was a great deal of behind-the-scenes acrimony between Bette, Aaron Russo and Steve Ostrow, because Bette felt that Ostrow had dangerously overcrowded the place. The controversy was aired in a *Rolling Stone* magazine piece on Bette in February, 1973. "When I looked out and saw how many people that bastard Ostrow had packed into that place, I was sick . . . it must have been a hundred degrees the way he packed those boys in. At first we couldn't even get through the crowd to get back to the dressing room."

Russo added, "Bette has outgrown the Continental Baths. I mean, she's a star now, she needs the baths like a hole in the head, right? But we agreed to do one last show as a favor. So what does Ostrow do? He decides to make a killing. He throws us to the lions."

Ostrow defended himself. "That's just Bette for you . . . if the place wasn't crowded enough, don't you know she would have accused me of not promoting it well enough? . . . Bette came to me and *asked* me for that date . . . I think she wanted to dispel some of the rumors going around that she was

becoming sort of...well, anti-homosexual. I think she wanted to show that it wasn't true by coming back and doing a show for the boys at the Tubs."

What Ostrow was referring to was an incident in Chicago, where Bette was quoted in a local newspaper as saying, "I have no gay friends. I wouldn't know a homosexual if I saw one." It is inconceivable that Bette meant this in anything but a tongue-in-cheek way, but the interviewer reported it as a matter-of-fact statement. There was a short-lived backlash in the gay community against Bette, but the prevailing wisdom was that the remark had been misreported.

Bette's final stint at the baths was a smash (and removed any lingering doubts about Bette's affection for gay audiences), but for her Philharmonic Show, she decided to really knock 'em dead. On this night, there are more production values than she has ever had before—for what was essentially a one night stand: She is carried on stage in a sedan chair with draped windows, one leg waving seductively through the red velvet. The crowd roars as the curtains part and Bette, her dazzling smile lighting up the entire theater, breaks into "Friends," running frantically back and forth across the enormous stage. Her energy is phenomenal, and it transmits to her audience, who react with delirium.

She does a little dishing. "I loved Tricia Nixon's wedding, didn't you? I was very put out that they did not send The Divine an invitation. But I sent a present anyway—I sent her a man-eating plant. I thought maybe she'd get the message. After all—she did marry a man named Cox," and "It's a good thing Helen Reddy's singing 'I Am Woman.' Who could tell?" But always, after the most outrageous lines, there is the radiant Midler smile that tells everyone it's all in good fun. She even mocks the stature of the hall and herself: "My dears, are you ready for this—Philharmonic Hall. Heavy on the Danish Modern. From 74th Street to 65th Street in a single year."

Someone in the balcony calls out, "We love you, Bette!" She looks up and says quietly, "I hope you won't get mad at me when I change...because I have to, you know? I hope you'll stay with me." The audience isn't quite sure what she means, but they scream their reassurances and the moment is quickly over as she introduces her next song: "Now I'm going to use my tough *shiksa* voice. Are you ready girls? First we assume a posture of extreme hostility"—and she breaks into "Leader of the Pack."

After the intermission, it is a few minutes into 1973. The audience anticipates Bette's return. A platform slowly rises out of the orchestra pit and on it stands Bette Midler, dressed in a baby diaper with a "1973" sash across her bosom. The audience roars with delight and joins her in a rousing rendition of "Auld Lang Syne."

Later, she does a stunning version of "Higher and Higher" and a "Do You Wanna Dance"/"Do You Love Me?" medley.

The evening ends with "Chapel of Love." Brought back by a thundering ovation, she thrills her audience with her impassioned "I Shall Be Released" and finishes up with "Friends." She is given an ecstatic standing ovation and her audience leaves the theater stunned by the intensity, the humor and the excitement of what they have just seen. Bette Midler's Philharmonic Hall show has just entered the history books. No less a newspaper than the New York *Times* headlined its review of the show, "Good, Better, Best, Bette!"

Bette Midler spent the first few hours of 1973 partying, accepting congratulations on her show, eating herself into a stupor (she hadn't had a bite to eat all day) and collapsing exhausted at six in the morning. The Year of Bette Midler had begun in suitably rousing fashion.

After Dark magazine's
1972 Ruby Award as Entertainer of the
Year goes to Bette, 1973.

Seven

Nineteen-seventy-three proved to be the most tumultuous twelve months of Bette Midler's life. She would experience triumph and despair, dizzying acclaim and numbing problems, public adulation and private loneliness.

The year began on a rather poor note. The installation of Aaron Russo into every facet of Bette's life and career created tremendous tensions between her old guard and this abrasive new element. Some of Bette's people knew or had heard of Aaron before he joined up. Charlotte Crossley, who would soon become a Harlette, remembers Bette asking her what she knew about Aaron. "I knew his reputation, being from Chicago," Charlotte relates. "I told Bette, 'I don't know anything good about him.' She said, 'What do you mean?' And I explained that I used to go into the Kinetic Playground a lot, and I'd hear things about him from the people who worked there, the artists. And they all told me, 'He's a bastard.'" Many of Bette's acquaintances came to agree, and over the year several members of her performing "family" would decide not to stick around.

Melissa Manchester was the first to leave. "She called me up *two weeks* before we were supposed to go on tour and said she was leaving," Bette said. "Things like that upset the hell outta me." Bette has since said she bears no resentment toward Melissa, but Melissa's husband-manager Larry Brezner indicates that she would rather forget the entire thing. "Melissa's association with Barry and Bette," he said after Melissa had become a star, "through no fault of theirs, has caused her a lot of pain both personally and professionally. They're all friends, understand, but she's suffered as a result of comparisons to Bette. You put anyone up next to Bette Midler and they're gonna suffer...I think Melissa would prefer that the press just forgot the past. It really has not been easy for her."

Bette says she was "chagrined" to lose Melissa not only because it put her in a panic about finding a replacement, but because "she was *fabulous. I adored* her and I really liked having her work for me."

Charlotte Crossley, who replaced Melissa, felt that she was the best of the three original Harlettes. "I'd see these three white girls up there with Bette being *quiet as mice*. And Bette would scream at them—during the performance—'Look alive girls! What *are* you three yentas up to?' They looked real trashy, but because they were three Jewish girls, they were all kind of afraid to do anything wrong. The only one who was willing to take any liberties was Melissa, and she was always my favorite. She had a lot of sparkle."

Charlotte (who pronounces her name Char-*low* since a trip to France) met Bette Midler during the summer of 1971. "I had seen Bette on *The Tonight Show* late in 1970, and all these people who knew her kept telling me, 'You remind me so much of Bette—you have the same sense of humor.' I'd say 'What?' And I kept running into people who told me, 'You're just like her, your attitude and all.'

"So I got to New York in August of 1971 and was doing *Jesus Christ, Superstar.* I went to this party and the host said, 'I've got a surprise for you'—and in walked Michael Federal with this girl. Now, I knew Michael from when we were in *Hair* together in Chicago, and he said, 'This is my girlfriend, Bette.' And I said, 'Oh, Hi,' and I just didn't even know who she was. An hour goes by and we're talking and I'm going on and on and she says, 'God, you re-mind me so much of me.' And I said 'Oh, yeah? What do you do?' And then I went, 'Oh my God–didn't I see you on the Carson show?'

"So I told her, 'You are very sick–and you're going to be a *smash*.' And we just started screaming and carrying on and it was just like friends for life, you know. We started hanging out together, going shopping, those kind of things."

Bette thought of Charlotte when Melissa left, and asked her if she'd like to sing backup for her. "This little voice inside me said *say yes!*," Charlotte recalls. "I was thrilled, really, because I wanted to break out of legitimate theater and go on the road."

Melissa worked with Charlotte for several weeks, teaching her the ropes. "She was very sweet to me. She 'passed the lineage' on to me. She said, 'It's going to be hard, but it's a lot of fun, too, and you'll survive.' Actually, it was much harder work and much more intense than I expected. But I took it all very seriously. The other Harlettes, it seemed to me, looked on it as a hobby, singing with Bette. My attitude was, this is a *profession*. There was never any conflict over it, but really I was the one who was usually in total alignment with Bette in terms of execution and presentation and attitude. I just placed my ego in a suitcase and said, 'I'm working for this woman and we're friends.' We got very close, and she could always depend on me. When you work with Bette you become her friend. She's interested in you, in what you feel about life. She's a real human being and she's sensitive to you because she wants you to be sensitive to her. And she'll go way out on a limb for you if there's any problem."

Charlotte found the creative atmosphere around Bette very stimulating. "We'd sit around and eat a lot of food and discuss concepts, and pull out old records and listen to music, old songs from certain eras that we liked and that had really touched us. And Barry was just a genius. He wrote beautiful charts, and they got along very well, creatively. We would come up with these ideas, then go into rehearsals and Barry could transpose all those ideas and really make them a part of the show, and add a lot of different musical color to them. He and Bette communicated well, because they liked the same things. Of course, there was a lot of other negative stuff going on with them, too. She really couldn't control him the way she could other men."

"We used to fight," Bette said several years after Barry had become a star in his own right. "Mostly because I would want to rehearse for hours and hours and I would never pay him! He got a salary, so I figured, 'Well, that's enough.'

"Barry and I worked so fast. It was two ambitious Jews in one room. Such *bitchiness*. We would bitch at each other all the time. He very rarely did an ar-rangement I didn't like. He's a much better musician than I. We would mostly bicker about which song should go where and how the show should be paced. . . and whether he was going to wear white tails or not. . . and would he *please* stop waving his head. . . and would he *not* sit on the phone books, if he didn't mind. He would always want to know how come I was always half a tone under and why I didn't come in on time. And it's true that he would insist on something that I would take to heart and get real spiteful about."

Norman Kean, who was the president of the Entertainment Division of Arts & Leisure Corp., which owned Mr. Kelly's in Chicago, remembers the impor-tance Barry Manilow had to Bette Midler during her 1971 stint opening for Mort Sahl. "I had signed Bette to a contract to work two weeks at Mr. Kelly's for $750 a week–but she had to pay her own airfare. I got a call from her one day and she said, 'Norman, I have a problem. I really think my act would be

OPPOSITE: Bette at home in her Greenwich Village apartment, 1973.

52

much better if I brought my accompanist, Barry Manilow, with me. But I don't have enough money. The $750 is fine, I'm not trying to renegotiate or anything, but I can only handle paying him, and he can only live with it, if you could pay his airfare.'

"I said okay, and when they arrived, the first thing Barry said after 'Hello' was, 'I need three phone books.' I said 'What? You've got friends in Chicago?' He said 'I need to *sit* on them.' The piano bench was too low and the piano too high, or something, so he had to sit on the books.

"Barry was just sensational for Bette, and I was grateful he was there. She stole the show from Mort Sahl, and Barry was important to the act. Bette is so musically inclined, she has antennas coming out of every point of her body. She needed a musical support to bring her up to her best energy level and mental level. Barry provided that for her.

"It was quite amazing, really. She could communicate with him by just waving her wrist or moving her shoulder or by a wink or an off-the-cuff remark—during rehearsals *and* performances. He would immediately know just what she needed. It was like his antennas were wrapped around hers. And he helped her feel confident just by being around—and that's why it was so sensational to see them work together."

Bruce Vilanch, who was writing free-lance comedy for Bette from his home base in Chicago, feels that Barry was highly instrumental as well in the formation of Bette's act. "Barry was the one who gave the act a beginning, a middle and an end. He placed the music and shaped the show. He's a terrific showman, Barry—no one knows how to construct an evening like he does. He does it the same way he constructs a chart—he starts slowly, he modulates, he builds, then he goes back small again. He was like Bette's director."

Bette, Barry and the Harlettes were preparing in January to embark on a cross-country tour of one night stands. It was Bette's biggest tour, and the situation was fraught with tensions. Melissa's departure had made matters worse, but Charlotte picked things up quickly. She remembers that the relationship between Aaron and Bette caused problems from the very beginning of her life as a Harlette. "I would sort of watch their relationship, you know. It was *nutty*. Continuous drama. We would be rehearsing at Barry's house, and if Aaron knew she was there, he'd keep calling again and again and they'd be *screaming* and yelling over the phone. I don't know how we ever got anything done. It was nuts. Unbelievably nuts.

"It was hard for us because Aaron wanted to be *it*. He wanted to be *the* one in her life. It was very painful for everyone around. He was so jealous of anyone close to her. When we got out on the road, one of the rituals we had was that we would come in and see her right before the show, and she'd see if we looked okay and we'd just be together to get our energies in sync because we had to go out there and kick ass on stage. He started locking her door because he was jealous of that, he couldn't have that—he wasn't part of it, he couldn't contribute to that the way we could. He felt very competitive with us.

"He was in love with her, and I think it was the first time in his life that he met someone who really *challenged* him, who pushed all the buttons on his emotional panel—ran their *elbow* across it, you know? He wanted to be doing something and she shared her dreams with him, and because he loved her he wanted to help make those dreams come true."

Bette's national tour began in Rochester, New York in February, and brought her to thirty cities in less than three months. "We did Buffalo, Syracuse, Ithaca, college towns," Charlotte says. "We were doing one-nighters, and they *kicked me in my ass.* It was very grueling for all of us."

The burgeoning gay liberation movement, which had given Bette Midler a chance to grow artistically, was now helped to expand by Bette Midler. In bringing her show to small cities and rural towns, Bette was making it possible for gay people to congregate in places other than bars—and more importantly, to be openly themselves in front of non-gay people, more and more of whom were attending Midler concerts. As writer Craig Karpel put it in *Oui*, describing Bette's concert in Buffalo, "The gaiety was contagious. I found myself laughing with relief as being privileged to relate to all that male pulchritude, flaunted shamelessly for the first time in a civic-auditorium lobby instead of some dank meatrack. Years, centuries of dissimulation, guilt, and blackmail would come to a symbolic end that night in Buffalo."

There were sometimes so many gay people in Bette's audiences that Bruce Vilanch used to say to her, "God forbid anyone in this town needs any emergency comb-out tonight."

While Bette always told her share of "in" gay jokes (usually referring salaciously to the infamous sex spots of whatever town she was in), that was only one part of her humor. No town was safe from her acid tongue. "We tried to make the audience feel that Bette really knew the dish about them," Charlotte recalls. "We girls would go out and look around and ask people what the scoop was, and Bette would take notes."

Bruce Vilanch was now a full-time part of the Midler entourage. There was some comment being made in the press occasionally about Bette's humor, questioning how much of it was genuinely spontaneous, and how much was written. Several critics expressed disappointment that Bette would use the same lines in show after show. But Vilanch stresses that Bette was anything but a line-reading machine. "Bette is quite witty," he says. "She's great with extemporaneous material on stage. But you can't leave it all to chance, you have to have a basic script. Bill and I would write up pages and pages for her, and then she'd sit there curled up in a little ball with her blue pencil and write 'No!' next to everything she didn't like, and then the three of us would rewrite together. She made *major* contributions. Then Bill and I would retype the pages and Scotch tape them to her mirror so she could see them, at a glance.

"An awful lot of what she did *was* extemporaneous, though, and she's a master at that. People who are shocked that she had writers just don't understand show business. But still, you can't be as good on stage as Bette Midler is and do nothing but read cue cards."

On March 10, Bette played the Capitol Theater in Passaic, New Jersey, where she set a house record with two standing-room-only shows. That Passaic was her mother's hometown did nothing to lessen Bette's ribbing: "Well, I missed my stop on the Seventh Avenue and wound up here in Passaic." Much primping of hair. "Passaic, darling, I do not *believe.* Honey, I never saw so many women in curlers in my life! I want you all to know we are embarking on a tour of the tackiest towns in America—and Passaic is definitely *numero uno!*"

Bette then turned the rapier on herself. "For those of you who haven't the faintest idea of what this creature is who is standing in front of you, my name is Bette Midler. My friends refer to me as the Divine Miss M—everything you are afraid your little girls—and your little boys, too—will grow up to be. Also known as the last of the truly tacky women."

Later, she introduces "Chattanooga Choo-Choo": "We are going to do for you at this point the Hubba Hubba. *Qu'est-ce que c'est* Hubba Hubba? I will tell

Wearing her "early usherette" outfit, Bette meets the press in Los Angeles before her Amphitheater concert, March 1973.

55

you what Hubba Hubba means. Hubba Hubba is a phrase that was very popular in the '40s. What it means essentially is 'hot shit.' This number was sung by the Andrews Sisters. Those girls could raise their eyebrows in unison – and often did.

"Actually, this number wasn't originally sung by the Andrews Sisters. Actually it was originally sung by the Bagelman Sisters – Theresa, Maria and Conchita – three Anglo-Saxon Protestant girls from the South who came up to New York to make it big in show biz. They failed miserably."

The whirlwind pace of the tour found Bette in Los Angeles a week later. She held a press conference in the Champagne Room of the Beverly Wilshire Hotel; there was a great deal of interest since Bette, who played the small Troubador Club less than four months earlier, was now back as a sell-out attraction at the 3200-seat Dorothy Chandler Pavilion. By now, her album was in the Top Twenty and there was tremendous excitement surrounding Bette Midler.

When she entered the room, the reporters didn't realize who she was. She walked over to a few and started to introduce herself. Flustered, a reporter tried to explain: "I've never seen you out of costume."

"But dahling, I *am* in costume," Bette replied. "This is *early usherette.*" Bette was asked if her act was one that would only go over in more sophisticated areas. "But they *adore* me in the Midwest!" she replied. "I don't understand, I really don't, but they like me. Out there on the great Plains. All the corn and the cattle. They don't see too many sequins, I guess."

Bette's show was a huge success, with her humor turned on fellow girl singers this time: "I can't believe I'm on the same stage where Karen Carpenter got her drums banged. That woman is so white, she's invisible" and "Ms. Reddy? Did you hear she got arrested . . . for loitering in front of an orchestra."

Even those put-downs which on paper might appear to be cruel were always delivered with such a twinkle, and followed by such a big smile, that they never became offensive. Bette's love of dishing, she says, comes from her father. "He's an old curmudgeon and he'll just lay you to filth. I picked it up from him, never realizing that it could be hurtful."

Los Angeles *Times* rock critic Robert Hilburn commented on Bette's astonishing leap to stardom. "In the midst of all this fanfare, there is danger that the person in the center of all this attention – namely Miss Midler – would begin listening too much to the applause of her audience rather than her own sense of standards; a danger that she would tend to coast on what she has seen work rather than dig deeper into her talent and imagination.

"Happily, she showed Saturday that she is still a vital, exciting, enormously entertaining performer; one who has been able to accept acclaim without letting it make her relax her own ambition and drives . . . Miss Midler, simply and surely, is a delight and there isn't a hall in Los Angeles big enough to hold all those who would benefit from seeing her perform. But hopefully she'll resist the basketball arenas and stick with more intimate facilities. She's too personal, too intimate, too valuable an artist to fall victim to the impersonal atmosphere of the larger rooms."

By the end of this early '73 tour, with her album now in the Top Ten and the "Do You Wanna Dance?" single in the Top Twenty, Bette Midler was being called "The Queen of Camp" and a "pop phenomenon." Reporters clamored for interviews with her, fans mobbed her wherever she went, her shows were sold out weeks in advance – and several national publications published exhaustive articles analyzing the popular success of Bette Midler. The two most notable of these were *Ms*, which in August gave Midler her first national magazine cover for their story "Why Bette Midler?," and *Oui*, which published Craig Karpel's "Notes on Bette," modelled after Susan Sontag's celebrated essay "Notes on Camp."

Ms asked influential women of all walks of life to analyze the appeal of Bette Midler. Marlo Thomas said, "Bette Midler's so honest, so totally herself. When she's on stage, she's really there—to rap, to be with the audience. You don't mind loving her because it's mutual. She'll sing till she's hoarse, not because she's a trouper, but because she's communicating."

Yoko Ono wrote, "I like her style. In the age when there is a question as to what sex comes first, she comes from that sex which is all sex."

Rosalyn Drexler, an artist and playwright, added, "Bette Midler reminds me of my mother if my mother could sing. She is an intelligent freak show. A triumph of brilliance over homeliness. I like her vigor—she's a hard worker. She's given camp back to women."

Several of the writers became very *deep* in their thinking. Dale McConathy, former literary editor of *Harper's Bazaar*, wrote: "As Mick Jagger and what he represents of the unsatisfied male fantasy life of the sixties fades, Bette Midler's importance as an expression of our sexual unconsciousness gathers. She is a final self-enclosing embrace of the Perseus-Andromeda myth that so intrigued the tortured sexuality of the 19th century and formed our own: the knight who saves the damsel from the dragon...the power of the man to make over the woman diminishes as the myth moves forward in time. Except in that magical realm exempted by our dreams—and show biz."

Karpel offered twenty-four "Notes on Bette," both pro and con, about everything from her looks and material to her audiences and costumes. He was particularly interested in the "camp" aspects of the Midler phenomenon. "Each Bette Midler concert is an Event. One dresses...the same individual who appears in a promotional T-shirt and a pair of shredded jeans at a Dead concert wouldn't be caught alive at a Bette concert without a bone linen suit, checked shirt and white collar and cuffs, brown-velvet batwing bow tie, high-heeled spectator shoes and slouch straw hat...Last New Year's Eve, one young man who went to both shows brought a second suit of clothes with him and changed in the men's room during the break."

According to Karpel, the attitude at sixties "happenings" was "we are going there because it is happening." The attitude at Bette concerts, on the other hand, was "It is happening there because we are going."

Discussing another aspect of the Midler appeal, Karpel wrote, "Her audience is deeply afflicted with nostalgia, so much so that they are not merely nostalgic for the Forties or early Sixties...but for last year or last spring or last month or last week, or for that matter, anything but the present or—heaven forfend!—the future...often Bette will repeat the socko ending of a tune three or four times. 'I just *love* reprises,' she sighs. So does her audience: *instant* nostalgia."

Bette herself was being asked more and more frequently to comment on her success—the reasons for it and its effect on her. "I try not to think about it," she replied at one point. "It's all very frightening." She told one interviewer that she was having nightmares about being pursued by autograph hunters and there is no place to hide. The star trappings and pressures of the business aspects of her life and the terror of having to live up to the inflated expectations all this attention was creating was putting her though "heavy changes." "I

After listening to news of the Gay Liberation Day parade on the radio, Bette makes an impromptu appearance before the Greenwich Village crowd, June 1973.

just don't know anymore. I just want to do it. I just want to wrap it up as a little present and give it to people. I can't stand it when I have to worry about what they think of it. . .I just want to give it to them. . ."

Bette's own analysis of the reasons for her spectacular acceptance were much simpler than the journalistic ones. "Look, I try to do what I can do. There ain't much I can do. I try to give people a good time, that's my big cause. These days, people are just not smiling, they are not amused and the sky is always gray. . .they don't understand why they're always miserable. I try to give them a little joy. There's something for everyone to like, that's the type of person I am. There's someone in everybody's family that everybody loves. I'm just one of those lovable people. I'm just like one of their family."

Perhaps it was for that reason that there was so much interest in Bette Midler's *personal* life. "Identity is a peculiar thing," she said. "Sometimes I don't know anymore who I am. I used to be Bette Midler and now I'm the Divine Miss M. When people don't know the Divine Miss M, when they only meet Bette Midler and they don't know what she does for a living or what books she reads or programs she watches or foods she eats or friends she has—when they don't know who I am, all they see is this person and this face. Like one writer said that I looked like the kind of girl who wouldn't be asked out on a Saturday night. . .When people meet me for the first time, especially if I'm not dressed up or don't have any goo on my face, they're not interested in knowing me. . .I know when I first started with this whole thing it was so that I would be asked out on Saturday night—now I'm too tired to go. I don't really care. I am content to be with people who don't care that I don't have any makeup on, and that's what you have to get to in your life."

But at another time she said, "I am lonely sometimes. . .sometimes I think I haven't got any friends left at all. I've traded in big friendships for the love of a great, huge number of people. But you can't take 10,000 people home to bed with you."

Bette was asked at one point about the comparisons being made between her and other performers. "Mae West? A great raconteur. Wish I could tell stories like she does. Judy Garland? I don't do that kind of performing. I'd love to, but I'm just a girl who sings and dances and tell jokes. Mick Jagger? Great. Him I can do. He's just a girl who sings and dances and tells jokes." The only comparison Bette said she resented was one to Tiny Tim. "I don't want people to think I'm an object of derision. I don't think of myself as anything like Tiny Tim, even vaguely, except that I occasionally pick a tune that is a little obscure and old. That's what labels like 'kookie' do to you. That word absolutely makes me nauseous. If they don't stop using that word, I don't know what!"

The off-stage Bette, she stressed, is nothing like the Divine Miss M. She described herself as bookish and shy—"I'm quiet. I don't bother anybody"—and, surprisingly, somewhat reserved. "I wouldn't be caught *dead* with a sequin on my body when I'm not working. How *tasteless.*"

Her success, she said, hadn't changed her life style much at all. "I have a small four-room apartment in the Village with a little garden, and I still ride the subway all the time."

The hardest part of all the attention she was being paid, Bette admitted, were the comments frequently made about her looks. "I hate it when they call me ugly, when they say I'm homely. I'm the one who's in the *body.* I'm the one who has the *face.* I can't have plastic surgery on my *heart.*"

In another interview, she treated the subject much more lightly. "It does

The Divine One is dressed
the part for another photo session in her
Barrow Street digs, 1973.

build your character. You're not as lazy as you might be if you were beautiful. Who was it that said, 'Beauty is only skin deep'? The Temptations. Well, really, who would want it any deeper, yunno? Unless you're a cannibal. . ."

In February of 1973, Bette made an appearance on a Burt Bacharach TV special, along with Stevie Wonder. According to Bette, he stole the show with his harmonica, but her appearance was memorable as well. She sang a beautiful version of "Superstar" sitting against a starkly-lit concrete backdrop with a shaft of light entering through a window. Then, singing "Boogie Woogie Bugle Boy," Bette appeared as all *three* Andrews Sisters. "They filmed all three, different outfits, different hairdos, and then they spliced me together. My mother saw it in Honolulu and she said, 'Gee, that's terrific. They found two girls who look just like Bette.'"

Eight

As Bette prepared to embark on a 35-city, four-month tour in the late summer, two more members of her "family" decided to leave, and Bette found herself having to audition over seventy girls to take the places of Merle Miller and Gail Kantor. Panicky, Bette sent a telegram to Charlotte Crossley, who was in Italy, to make sure that she would remain with her. Charlotte's return telegram read: "I love you. I miss you. Can't wait to work with you again."

To replace Gail and Merle, Bette and Barry chose "another dark diva," Sharon Redd, and a white girl, Robin Green. Robin had worked with Charlotte in *Jesus Christ, Superstar*, and Sharon had done *Hair* for a year in Australia, so the new girls had no problem relating to the veteran Charlotte. These new Harlettes, saucy and talented, in sync with Bette and each other, created a backup for the Divine Miss M that wonderfully augmented the Midler onstage magic.

Bette began the tour with an entourage which included Bill Hennessey and Bruce Vilanch. The tour was a smashing success, and everywhere Bette went she was the woman of the hour. Vilanch remembers one particular example of the lengths to which some people would go to get close to Bette Midler. "We get off the plane in Detroit, and this tastefully dressed man and woman meet us at the bottom of the ramp and say that the promoter of the tour has sent them to pick us up, and they bring us over to this Winnebago. Now we think this is really funny, because usually it's a limo, but we all climb in. They're driving, and I'm looking out the window and the hotel goes by and I wonder, *Where are they taking us?* We wind up at this restaurant, and it turns out that the two people own the restaurant and wanted to have a surprise dinner for Bette.

"We all think this is great, a free meal in a nice restaurant. In the meantime, Aaron arrives on another plane, and the promoter is tearing his hair out— 'Where are they?!' he's screaming—and Aaron's trying to explain that we were *on the plane.* So they find out about the Winnebago, and Aaron decides that we've been kidnapped and calls the police. They track us down and Aaron *bursts* into the room like Prince Valiant saving the damsel to rescue Bette from *who knows what?* He's absolutely crazed—Aaron always thinks the worst, and he was Bette's burly protector. When he's mad, he's like Ferdinand the Bull, he's ferocious.

"Now, we're all pretty bombed by this time, and we thought there was gonna be a terrible scene with the cops and all, so Bette, to break the tension, *heaves* this Baked Alaska that had just been served across the room at Aaron. He throws a *tray* of it at her. A major food fight breaks out, and this tasteful couple in this gorgeous restaurant with all their Guccis are *completely* covered with food!

"And it got to be that whenever we were in Detroit, real *weird* things would happen. And if they didn't happen on their own, we'd *make* them happen!"

Sometimes, it was Bette's audiences that made the weird things happen. As Craig Karpel had pointed out, Bette's audiences were frequently as much of a show as Bette herself. "Whenever we'd play some of the smaller cities," Bette said, "the people who came to see me were very far-out people, and when they all get together in one place they're amazed that there are so many of them." Bruce Vilanch recalls that it became a tradition for the first few rows of Bette's audiences to come in wearing raincoats, and as soon as she made her entrance on stage, they would stand, remove their coats and reveal that they were wearing only towels. Wild outfits–and *much* drag–were commonplace at Midler concerts.

Something that wasn't commonplace happened in Austin, Texas. Charlotte recalls, "It was at the Armadillo World Headquarters, or something, and we get out on stage and these people are *crazy*. It's festival seating, so they can go anywhere they damn well please, and all these good ol' boys are drinking Jack Daniels and Southern Comfort and smoking joints and passing bottles up to the stage. We'd never had an audience like *that* you know. They were *insane*, hootin' and hollerin' and carrying on. It was pretty scary, I'll tell you."

Another stop on this tour, in August, was a scary–and highly emotional– one for Bette: Honolulu. "She was a nervous wreck," Charlotte recalls. "It was very heavy for her, going back there for the first time to perform." She was close to complete panic when she walked out on the stage of the International Center, but the crowd gave her a standing ovation. And when the show was over, they gave her another one–this one lasting seven minutes. Bette stood before them and said, "I don't mind telling you I was scared shitless tonight." Then she looked up at the ceiling and cried, "God, if you only knew how happy you've made me!"

The second night, most of Bette's Radford High graduating class attended, presenting her with a flower *lei*. At both shows, Bette's mother, Susan and Danny sat in the third row to cheer her on. Her father did not attend. "It was heartbreaking for Bette that her father didn't come to see her," Charlotte remembers. "It was *real* tough for her." Bette explained, "My father is very, very conservative. He's read some things about me, you know, and he likes Lawrence Welk. If he saw my act, my father would *die*. He would kill himself, he would jump off the roof. . .He doesn't like too much cleavage. In fact, every time I went over there to dinner, he made me safety-pin my dress together. I was glad my father didn't come to see me perform. I would have been afraid to be dirty or gross, afraid that he would walk out or start yelling at me."

Mrs. Midler, however, thought her daughter was indeed divine. "My mother got a charge," Bette said. "She kept screaming, *faaaaabulous, faaaaabulous!*'" "We always thought she was witty," Mrs. Midler said, "but we didn't know she was *that* witty."

There was a luau in her honor (which her father *did* attend) and Bette joked characteristically, "Well, now I'm going to a reunion of all the people who couldn't stand me." But when the party came to an end, she wept openly. "I didn't want to leave so early. I didn't get a chance to say good-bye to Judy and Jane and. . .Oh, I just wish I could stay."

But the tour had to continue, and the next stop was Los Angeles. When the troupe got to Hollywood, the first thing the girls did was visit Frederick's. "There were *hundreds* of pairs of shoes in that place, honey," Charlotte relates, "and the four of us would have *so* much fun. We'd buy and buy. And later Bette used to say onstage, 'This is a show about shoes.' And it *was*." Bette later said, "I have *thousands* of pairs of shoes. I don't know why. I guess because I only had one pair when I was growing up."

Bette's engagement at the Universal Amphitheater in Los Angeles was a triumph. The show was standing room only, including a great many Hollywood celebrities. The two remaining Andrews Sisters, Patty and Maxene,

Camping it up
in her dressing room during her
Fall 1973 tour.

were in the audience, and joined Bette on stage for "Boogie Woogie Bugle Boy" to thunderous applause. (Bette's single of the song had risen to #8 on *Billboard* magazine's Top 100 Singles chart.)

Los Angeles *Times* critic Robert Hilburn wrote, "I'm supposed to write about rock music and I keep finding these nonrock performers with such impact and power that I find myself occupied a lot with them these days. First, there was Harry Belafonte and then Liza Minnelli and now Bette Midler. I mean what are my pals going to think?...She's a strikingly original, vital, even thrilling performer who is able, on her best nights, to touch your emotions with both her music and manner...Her show drew one of the strongest ovations of the season, greater even than Liza Minnelli's opening at the Greek Theater."

While she was in Los Angeles, Bette made another appearance on *The Tonight Show*. Johnny Carson introduced her by saying, "One of the great kicks of doing this show is seeing people who come on and make their initial television appearance, and then seeing what happens in their career. This young woman was appearing in a men's turkish bath in New York—very strange—but as soon as you heard her sing, you knew there was a very unique talent there, and this year she's been hailed as the first star of the seventies."

Bette, Barry and the Harlettes did "Lullaby of Broadway" and a *hot* live version of "Boogie Woogie Bugle Boy" which left the audience on their feet cheering. Comic David Steinberg, set to follow her, turned to the person next to him and said dejectedly, "She's the worst thing that can happen to you in show business. It's like following a moonwalk."

The reaction of her audiences in San Francisco two weeks later was even more enthusiastic. But a critic for that city's top newspaper, the *Chronicle*, gave Bette—and Barry, who did a solo turn on this tour—a devastating review. Under the headline "Mass Mince-In for Midler—Every Gay Blade's Fantasy," John Wasserman wrote, "Well, my dear, you hadda been there. People bounded about as if on pogo sticks, terrifying shrieks, yowls and bellows rent the auditorium, mascara ran unashamedly and mothers swept up small children and ran from the auditorium in horror. The blind saw, the halt leapt from wheelchairs, and 300 closet drag queens stripped off their false moustaches and began a mass mince to the tune of 'La Cucaracha.'

"It was amazing. The Divine swept from one end of the stage to the other, waving giant fans of pink feather and hurtling along like a rag doll on speed, her various appendages sprawling in four directions simultaneously, her eyes rolling like marbles in a vacuum, her bountiful breasts, which resemble ostrich eggs dropped into a pair of panty-hose, springing up and down like yo-yos. 'Oh,' she cried in mock melodrama, throwing her hand to her forehead, 'Gross us out, Miss M, *gross us out!*' And so my children, gross us out she did for the ensuing two hours."

Wasserman's cruelest comments were reserved for Barry. "His opening number guaranteed instant obscurity and he went downhill from there. The second tune was, incredibly, 'Cloudburst,' accompanied by the Harlettes. 'Cloudburst,' is, of course, the Pointer Sisters' hit. For a third-rate singer to come into the Berkeley Community Theater and render 'Cloudburst' is approximately equivalent to peddling near-beer in Munich. The third tune was pathetic. The fourth was titled, apparently, 'Mama, Can You Hear Me?' Which needs no comment, save Mama's, which is 'Yes, son, and you should wash your mouth out with Black Flag.'"

Bruce Vilanch recalls, "Barry had just cut his first album and he sent me a

Bette is all eyelashes at a
press conference prior to her second
1973 Los Angeles appearance,
at the Dorothy Chandler Pavilion,
September 1973.

OPPOSITE: Chatting with
Johnny Carson on "The Tonight Show"
after performing "Boogie
Woogie Bugle Boy," September 1973.

demo of it. I loved it, and sent him a note to San Francisco. It arrived on the day of this review. He called me and said, 'Thanks, Bruce, your note was the only thing that kept me from the gas pipe.'"

Considering the futures of Bette Midler and Barry Manilow—and the soon-to-be political prominence of San Francisco's gay population—one can only guess that Mr. Wasserman did not remain in the employ of the *Chronicle* for very long.

Bruce Vilanch does say, though, that ironically, gay audiences were often the hardest ones for Bette to play to. "They had heard about her, and they'd heard that she was theirs—and they were going to be there the night she was *fabulous*. If she wasn't fabulous, they'd be fabulous *for* her. So we could never gauge what was working, because *everything* she said would get roars and screams, and often the roars and screams would be more about *them* than about her."

Whatever the reasons for her audiences' ecstacy, Bette Midler was clearly on an inexorable climb to superstardom. But the day-to-day grind of touring was a sharp contrast to the rapturous receptions Bette was receiving in city after city. "I get very irritable on the road," Bette says. "Tours get me down. I feel torn away from all the things I love, like the rug has been pulled out from under me."

And all was not always rosy in the Midler entourage. "There was a lot of backbiting in my camp and I couldn't put my finger on it. I didn't know who was telling the stories. Gossip, gossip—it's deadly in this business. I used to get stories from one guy and then somebody else would come in and tell me the same thing with a different slant on it. I didn't know which end of the stick was up."

"That was Aaron," Charlotte says. "He was so jealous of anyone getting close to Bette that he would always tell her things about people, you know, tell her that no one cared about her and he was the only one she could count on, things like that. It was very tough on all of us."

"Bette was having an affair with one of the band members," Bruce Vilanch recalls, "and Aaron didn't like that one bit. So he made things particularly unpleasant."

Bill Hennessey was the next of Bette's original entourage to leave. "Aaron came into the picture and became, to be kind, *overbearing*," Hennessey has said. "In terms of being the kind of manager who closes the door and locks Barry and I out [of her dressing room] so we couldn't even get in half the time to discuss what was going to go on before the show."

Despite the backstage problems—and they would get worse—Bette Midler's climb to superstardom was about to take a giant leap. Her entire four-month, 35-city, $3 million cross-country tour had been but a rehearsal for her anxiously awaited Broadway debut at the famed Palace Theater. When tickets went on sale in mid-October, Bette Midler set the all-time Broadway record for one-day ticket sales ($148,000). The anticipation among Bette's New York fans grew to a fever pitch, and the show she put on disappointed no one.

Bette was out to make the biggest splash she ever had, to make all her other shows pale in comparison, and she did just that. There were more production values in this show than ever before—but it was Bette *herself* who was at an absolute peak at the Palace. She had, in the past year, perfected an awesome ability to charm, excite and mesmerize an audience, to make 3,000 people feel as though they were sitting in her living room. Her comic delivery had developed into something wondrous in its mastery. She could alternate be-

OPPOSITE: A dramatic moment during a sold-out concert in Los Angeles.

tween a Jewish mama, a tough Philadelphia *shiksa*, Sophie Tucker, Mae West and, of course, the Divine Miss M. Her musical numbers were virtually flawless, delivered with passion, pathos and humor. Bette's show at the Palace, sold out for three weeks, was the talk of New York for a year-and-a-half –until her *next* Broadway show supplanted it.

The show opens with a tropical motif, accompanied by pseudo-Hawaiian music conjured up by Barry Manilow. Then, Bette saunters out, covered front and back by two huge pink Josephine Baker fans. She reveals her glowing smile to the rapturous cheers of the crowd and, in white pants and a colorful Hawaiian shirt, rips into "Friends," running across the huge stage where Sarah Bernhardt, Sophie Tucker, Mae West, Fanny Brice and Judy Garland had trod before her. At the point in "Friends" where the lyric says, "there is no one to deride me," Bette changes it to "there is no one to *describe* me"–and how right she is. After the number, on opening night, she looked out at the celebrity-studded audience and said, "Oh, my God. I can't believe it! There is not a star left in the firma*ment*! They are all here at the *palazzo* tonight!"

After opening night, Bette took to dishing her first-night audience, which had given her jitters. "It was all so *heavy* my dears. Puccis and Guccis everywhere. The smell of *nouveau* leather everywhere. And lots of people with sucked in cheeks and small mouths. I tell you, *we were not pleased!*"

She introduces the Harlettes as "three chorus girls from *Rachael Lili Rosenbloom*," a reference to a much-publicized Broadway disaster by Paul Jabara about a Midler-like young girl who idolizes Barbra Streisand. Bette had reportedly turned down a half-million dollars to play the role. Then she discusses the tour which led to the Palace. "We set out to see America and the thing *disintegrated* before our very eyes! It was an amazing tour–the kind Martha Raye would have given her eye teeth for."

After singing "Delta Dawn" ("one of Ms. Reddy's greatest hits"), she looks out at the audience with an expression of utter befuddlement. "Isn't this the most amazing time you've ever been through in your life? I'm *freaked out*. I don't know *what's* going on. Do you know what's going on? *Who's Jerry Ford?* I never heard of him. I don't want to be rude before he even gets started, but have you *ever* had a Ford that didn't break down?

"And *Rose Mary Woods!* What do you suppose *she's* thinking about? You don't suppose Nixon's sockin' it to her, do you? Couldn't be. He doesn't sock it to anyone. He only socked it to Pat twice, and look what a botch he made of *that*! Did she really *say* that? I can see what kind of night *this* is going to be. I can tell from this audience. This is an A-200 crowd if I *ever* saw one!"

She then does a number she's never done since. It begins with a sexily described pickup. Then Bette sings, "and when I got you home it was *bad sex*. I *swear* I've never had such *bad sex*." The audience is still roaring as Bette begins "Empty Bed Blues."

Every song Bette sang at the Palace was introduced with some witticism or other. Introducing Hubba Hubba, she said, "This was popular in the Forties. I wasn't there you understand"–she scowls at the audience–"I *wasn't there*–but I *heard* about it. Oh, it was a fabulous decade, filled with wars and revolutions and floods and plagues. But it also had this great music. Now we're gonna do a song that was originally an instrumental, 'In the Mood,' only we're gonna add a vocal to the instrumental." She pauses. "It's called *singing*."

Next, Bette goes into a long monologue about the history of the Palace (this show was just as much stand-up comedy as music). "There was this guy George White, who used to put on these shows called *George White's Scandals.*

OPPOSITE: The triumphant Palace Theatre show opens with "Friends" and a Hawaiian motif, December 1973.

66

Midler clowns
during the Second Act
at the Palace.

Now, he was in competition with Ziegfeld, so they were very *extravagant*. And one year he put on a vegetable ballet–there were all these rutabagas and celeries walking around. The next year, he had to top himself, so he did a *fruit* ballet. All these lovely chorines were dressed as very large fruit trees. And there was this one girl whose first show it was, and she had to wear this very heavy orange tree on her head. Well, she had a *real* hard time maneuvering this orange tree, and by the time she got to the bottom of the staircase, she and the orange tree were in a *heap*, honey!"

A hilarious impression of this unfortunate girl follows, after which Bette looks down at the front row. "You people better get hot. 'Cause the people in the balcony would *kill* for those seats!"

Bette's next number, the last of the first act, is a powerful version of "I Shall Be Released" that leaves her audience on its feet roaring. After intermission, Barry Manilow, in white tails, performs four songs, then the Harlettes return wearing pink waitress outfits, singing "Optimistic Voices" from *The Wizard of Oz*. The curtains part to reveal a spectacle that was talked about around the country for months: a gigantic silver lamé platform high-heel shoe that fills the entire stage. Bette's voice joins the Harlettes for "Lullaby of Broadway" as she begins her descent down the shoe, wearing an iridescent pink-and-lavender sequinned gown. The crowd is beside itself as Bette camps and vamps her way down the shoe. The Harlettes open up their waitress costumes and turn them into American flags as the foursome break into "Boogie Woogie Bugle Boy." Bette Midler was determined to leave her mark on the Palace, and leave it she did.

The second act was more musical, with Bette doing breathtaking versions of "Do You Wanna Dance," "Surabaya Johnny" and "Hello, in There," as well as a blazing rendition of "Higher and Higher." At one point, someone calls out from the audience and Bette says, "Oh, no, I can't do *that* joke." The crowd roars its encouragement. Bette looks up suspiciously. "It's the guys in the balcony, I knew it. That's real trash up there–I know the type. All right, I'll tell the joke–but remember, you *made* me do it. I'm real ashamed to be an American telling this joke. Oh, it's so embarrasing. Well, here it is: Did you hear that Dick Nixon bought a copy of *Deep Throat*? He's seen it ten or twelve times. He wanted to get it down Pat."

The crowd goes crazy. "You're cheaper than I thought you were. Oh, you're all *trash*!"

As the intro to "Chapel of Love" begins, a huge valentine heart descends on to the stage and Bette tells the audience to sing along, which they do with infectious delight until everyone is swaying back and forth to the lilting melody. As the song ends, the house lights come up and Bette begins a reprise of "Friends," grabbing on to the hands of the people in the front rows and accepting dozens of bouquets–and the deafening cheers of the rapturous crowd. Bette Midler's mass love-in has entered the Broadway history books.

All during her Palace run, Bette was the toast of Broadway. Every celebrity in town came to see the show, and most came backstage to meet this wondrous new star. Bruce Vilanch recalls one memorable evening: "Paul McCartney had been denied entrance to the United States for more than a year because of a drug bust. Finally, they let him into the country and his first day here, he comes to see Bette at the Palace. After the show, he invites me and Bette to Linda's brother's apartment, and we just sat and schmoozed, and he was absolutely delightful. He kept calling her 'Betty' and thought she was just wonderful. There were other people there, his coterie, you know, and at one point he sprang up and said, 'I want you all to hear this new record we just made in Jamaica, Linda and I sing it.'

"So he puts this record on, and it's the Andrews Sisters singing 'The Hawaiian Christmas Song.' Well, Bette and I just looked at each other and giggled, but the rest of the people are sitting there very silent, then they say, 'Gee, Paul, that's really good.' And he's looking around the room and he says, 'You all *believed* me! This is incredible. What do I have to do? Anything I say you people *believe*.' Then he looked at me and said, 'You believed me for a minute, too, didn't you?'

"I said, 'Yeah, *sure*, Paul, I believed you. I also believe that you're *dead*.' So we all just had great fun that night."

One week after her Palace opening, Bette made the cover of *Newsweek*. It was the final, bona-fide, official, authenticated certification that she had *arrived*—she wasn't a freak, she wasn't a gay cult object, she wasn't a flash-in-the-pan—she was a *star*. As Charlotte puts it, "We were all blown away by that *Newsweek* cover. There weren't very many rock stars who'd had the cover of *Newsweek* at that time." The Midler issue became the biggest-selling issue of the magazine to that date.

Singing "Superstar" at the Palace.

The article, by Charles Michener, amounted to a valentine. "It's safe to say that not even Garland's legendary appearances in the great old house ever aroused so much anticipation as Bette Midler's Palace debut. . .and [the audiences] were not disappointed. In this age of pseudo-phenomena, Bette Midler is the genuine article. . .few performers since the Beatles have been so heralded as the harbinger of a 'new era'—or analyzed so seriously by the media."

He mentioned *Ms* magazine's piece "Why Bette Midler" and wrote, "Why indeed? Is she brilliantly exploiting the nostalgic craze for old songs, old movies, old chic—with dashes of contemporary irony and funkiness thrown in? Is she, like Alice Cooper, Elton John and David Bowie, capitalizing on the trend toward sheer spectacle in rock? Does her parodistic bawdiness feed our lingering hunger for the risqué—as opposed to the pornographic? Is her affectionate, welcome-all style an antidote to the angry, divisive music of the '60s? The answer is yes—to all the questions."

Bette Midler was indeed the biggest star in the country as 1973 drew to a close. And further certification of her stature was to come shortly—a Grammy Award as "Best New Artist" in March and a special Tony Award for "superior concert entertainment on the Broadway stage" in April. But with all her success, there was that dark undertow, the negative side of the stardom coin. Ellen Willis, reviewing the Palace concert in the *New Yorker* magazine, seemed to sense the pressures Bette Midler was under: "It was obvious that the Divine Miss M had not emerged as Bette Midler, Superstar, without a strain. As an ambitious artist in every sense, she was facing familiar contradictions: how to remain 'the last of the tacky women' and preserve her special relationship with her 'real' fans while playing the Palace at fifteen dollars top; how to make the mass audience love her while resisting subtle and not-so-subtle pressures to pander. Her uneasiness and her need to assure herself of our complicity came through in a running putdown of the celebrity-ridden opening-night crowd."

The strain Bette Midler was under was far greater than anyone but her closest associates could have imagined: "I was tired. And I was scared to death. I was so battered emotionally and physically that I thought I would break down."

As the Second Act begins,
Bette descends a giant high-heeled shoe
and sings "Lullaby of Broadway."

Nine

With hindsight, it seems predictable that the incredible year Bette Midler had been through in 1973 would take its toll on her. Midler is such a passionate performer, her shows are such an intense experience for both her and her audiences, that doing them night after night almost continuously for a year would leave the strongest person exhausted.

Bette Midler isn't the world's strongest person, and there were so many other problems and pressures which had nothing to do with her performances that it seems astonishing that she was able to get through the year at all.

The atmosphere in the Midler camp during the 1973 tour was a highly charged one. Her creative nucleus—the Harlettes, Barry, Bill Hennessey, Bruce Vilanch—are all emotionally high strung people who were working under a lot of pressure. And none was more emotionally highstrung, or under more pressure, than Bette.

There was constant fighting, frequent screaming matches—between Bette and Aaron, the Harlettes and Aaron, Barry and Bette, even Bette and the Harlettes. Charlotte recalls, "We would scream back and forth—Bette is a very *confront* kind of person. That's her way of communicating. And there was so much responsibility on her shoulders. If she raised a lot of hell, things would get done. The more I got to know her and see the much more temperamental sides of her, I kind of understood where that came from—she grew up in a family where there was constant fighting, and you couldn't get any results from being nice—it was only when you screamed and yelled and got everything to a crisis point that anything got accomplished. And that, unfortunately, spilled over into her work. And what happened was that in her relationships creatively with people, it was just too much for them. It really pushed a lot of people over the edge and away from her."

Bette's emotionalism centered around the enormous pressure on her to be *wonderful*. Her press was so ecstatic, her audiences so worshipful, that she frequently found the entire thing impossible to handle. "I was afraid of having to pull myself up into something I'm not. I can *pretend* to be a star. I can be as grand as the next lady. But to have to do it every day—that isolates you. I was afraid all the things that make me a human being would be lost."

Sometimes, Bette would even be afraid for her life. Some of the people in her audiences occasionally got out of hand. Robin Grean recalled, "One night some gentleman dressed in long underwear and carrying a bugle came streaking down the aisle and leaped on the stage and grabbed Bette and planted a kiss on her. I got very apprehensive. We're supposed to have some sort of security. You don't know what people will do. He obviously only wanted to do that, but people are strange, you know, and that really shook her. Because he really grabbed her. I was ready to hit him with a chair. I didn't know, he could have had a knife or something. He might be crazy."

One of the problems, of course, was that there was liberal drug use among many of Bette's audiences, and in the supercharged atmosphere of a Midler concert, there's no telling what a drugged fan might do. Several times during the Palace engagement, Bette ran under Barry's piano to get away from people who jumped up on the stage.

The day-to-day tensions sometimes manifested themselves on stage. Occasionally, Bette would be in a foul mood, and take things out on the audience. "She'd be saying the same kind of things, you know," Charlotte recalls, "dishing people and all. But sometimes it would come out really *vicious*, and we knew that Bette was getting real close to stepping over the line. She'd cut into people, chew them up and spit them out. Some people couldn't tell the difference, but we could – and a lot of her fans could – and they'd get offended."

Not only would Bette goad the audience occasionally, but Barry and the Harlettes as well. Several times during the Palace engagement, she'd stop, turn to Barry and say, "Oh, Mr. Music. Let's not do 'Surabaya Johnny' tonight, let's do 'Superstar.' Barry would coldly hide his fury on stage; afterwards there would be a screaming match backstage, with ashtrays thrown and threats of strangulation from Barry. But always, just to provoke him, Bette would pull the stunt the next night or a few nights later. "The woman provokes people," Charlotte says. "She provokes people on stage and off, and sometimes it's good provocation and sometimes it's bad."

The biggest source of tension in the Midler entourage throughout 1973, not surprisingly, appears to have been Russo. There was already the resentment against Russo simply for having *moved in*, but his hardcore business practices and his abrasive personality aggravated the situation considerably. He paid the Harlettes union minimum, and tried to pay everyone else as little as possible.

What was much worse, though, according to Charlotte, was that he would try to pit Bette against her friends. "We were a support system for her. But he made it very difficult for us to be. He would try to create a gulley between her and all of us. He would go into her and say, 'They're all against you, they don't give a shit about you. I'm the only one who really cares about you.' He would just stir the shit up whenever possible. And it used to drive us crazy.

"It was *heartbreaking* to watch him manipulate her. If Bette was down about something, or felt isolated and that no one cared, Aaron would always be there to reinforce that feeling in her. It was real weird, he was like this suppressive person with her, he felt powerful when she was down, because he was then able to bring her back up. Then he'd have more control over her.

"And then when she was bright and feeling good and could get things done on her own, he'd sink down and she'd go, 'What's the matter?' and he'd say, 'You don't need me anymore.' I mean, it was a *very sick* thing.

"Then he would take anybody he could aside and try to get them to rally to his side. But nobody would for long because our allegiance was to her.

"He would do all this stuff without her knowing it, you know. He would offend people, and it would reflect badly on her. And she just let him have his way. She didn't want to know. She opted not to know certain things, so he would go around and create all these scenes in her name. He'd create trouble and crisis all the time. Then the shit would come out and people would say to her, 'I'm not gonna work for you, because of blah-blah-blah,' and she had no idea of what had gone on, and she'd go back to him and scream and yell.

"So she *had* to deal with it ultimately. She'd say to me, 'It's too much for me to handle,' and I'd say, 'I know it's too much for you, but it's better that you know what's going on in your business.'"

Things would sometimes get so bad between Bette and Aaron, Charlotte says, that she would feel compelled to tell Bette, "I'm not going to let anything fucked-up happen to you, and if that guy fucks with you, if the shit gets real bad, I'll call the police on that guy – and I'll kick his ass, too."

"I had that very South Side of Chicago kind of loyalty – if you call on me to help you, I'm not going to desert you. He tried to cut her off from her life sup-

Aaron Russo escorts
Bette to the 1974 Tony Awards,
where Midler won a
special award for her Palace show.

OPPOSITE: Johnny
Carson congratulates a thrilled Bette
after she was given her Tony.

port systems, and it took its toll on every one of us. She was a wreck. I saw some very heavy things go down, not very pretty things. It was so deep, I'm telling you. I went back into therapy for awhile. But she depended so much on us, we couldn't say no to her."

Sharon Redd agrees: "The reason everyone puts up with it," she said, "is because we all love working with Bette."

Bette has referred to all of this, rather succinctly summing things up: "Aaron loved me, hated me, fought for me and tried to destroy me. He brought me to the heights and he put me in the pits."

With all the trouble Aaron Russo seemed to cause (and things got worse), why did Bette keep him around? "Business-wise, she needed him," Charlotte says. "He threw his weight around and made deals, and he was able to pull off a lot of stuff. She stuck with him for so long because of his obsession with getting the best for her *always*.

"Basically, I think she trusted him," Charlotte continues. "You know how we sometimes get into relationships with people and all of our friends don't understand what we see in that person? And it's because we're dealing with that part of them that is a pure, vulnerable, scared soul. You see right through the bad stuff and you love them. It doesn't matter if they're beating you over the head with a frying pan. But then after a while you realize you're tired of getting beat up, tired of all the crisis. But Bette loved things in Aaron no one else could see, and I think that's why she kept giving him chances over and over again."

In an interview for a *20/20* profile of Bette in 1983, Aaron spoke briefly but tellingly of this period. "I guess we fought principally because here I was sort of dominating her career in one way, and in another way, in our personal life, I

was very insecure..." On the same show, Bette said, "Aaron really loved me. He *really* loved me."

Whatever the reasons for it, the toll all this "constant drama"—as Charlotte calls it—took on Bette was enormous. She was in such a fragile emotional state early in 1974 that a viciously negative review of her second album made her feel "as though I had no worth as a human being" and led her to flee to Europe and become incommunicado for the rest of the year.

The album, *Bette Midler*, was, for most listeners, on a par with—if not better than—*The Divine Miss M*. Her version of "Skylark" is quietly affecting, "Drinking Again" is a patented Midler demonstration of her ability to act a song, "In the Mood" is just as much fun as "Boogie Woogie Bugle Boy," and "I Shall Be Released"—although not nearly as impassioned as she had performed it live—is a stirring cut. "Twisted" is a hilarious novelty number, "Higher and Higher" a pounding rocker that amply demonstrates Bette's versatility. But her performance of "Surabaya Johnny" is the highlight of the album and unquestionably the most moving, theatrical and dramatic song ever performed on a pop album. There is resignation, anger, melancholy, devastation in her voice and the effect on the listener is numbing. On this one song, Bette justifies all the superlatives heaped at her over the prior three years.

Bette Midler was a hit album. It rose to Number 6 in *Billboard* magazine's Top 100 Albums chart (Bette's first album had peaked at #9) and received generally favorable notices, including positive comments in the *Newsweek* article. But Bette was devastated by the cruelty of *Rolling Stone*'s notice, especially since the magazine had given the first album a good review.

"*Bette Midler* asks the question," Jon Landau wrote, "what were co-producers Barry Manilow and Arif Mardin thinking about while Bette Midler was singing 'I Shall Be Released'? It's hard to believe they were listening to Bette, for they are too knowledgable and sophisticated to have approved of any singing so unmusical, so embarrassingly flat, so brazenly insensitive...Bette Midler's recorded performance of 'I Shall Be Released' is the worst performance of a Bob Dylan song I have ever heard. [The album] contains the artifacts of style without nuance, content or intelligence...Onstage, she doesn't so much sing as she acts. But, in the studio this time around, she barely sings either...even her most devoted followers will inevitably be confused by the emptiness of her interpretations of things like the beautiful Johnny Mercer ballad 'Skylark,' Kurt Weill's mysteriously foreboding 'Surabaya Johnny' and the standard 'Drinking Again.'

"In her lust for applause, there is nothing so degrading that she won't use it to get it...and when a performer merely wallows in negative qualities as part of an act, it's only to ask for (or, in Bette Midler's case, demand) sympathy, or worse still, pity. To degrade oneself as a means of attracting and establishing rapport with an audience is not only to diminish oneself but to diminish all those who come to enjoy the performance."

That Landau had quite clearly missed the mark in his perceptions both of the album and of Midler as a performer didn't make Bette feel any better about the review. She was deeply upset by what she saw as a larger pattern. "I was on the way up," Bette said later, "and I didn't know that when you're on top people take it upon themselves to shoot you down. I thought I would be beloved. I was a very frightened person. I felt as though someone was trying to pull the rug out from under me. It was like my baby [her career]. It was like someone was trying to mash its head in. I was very insecure..."

Her distraught state resulted in several public scenes, including one at an

OPPOSITE: Bette introduces Lucille Ball as the 1973 winner of "After Dark" magazine's Entertainer of the Year Award, 1974.

After Dark magazine party. As the winner of their "Entertainer of the Year Award" for 1972, Bette agreed to present Lucille Ball with the 1973 citation. After the presentation, Bette was mobbed by fans who pushed and shoved her frighteningly. She wasn't able to handle it. She fled to the kitchen of the restaurant and refused to come out for pictures. There was a screaming match with one of the *After Dark* staffers, who slapped her. She collapsed into tears. Lucille Ball went into the kitchen and took Bette to her car, where they spent the rest of the banquet drinking whiskey in the back seat.

All of this convinced Bette that "I might as well pack it all in. When I finally took a step back and a breath, I almost fell down. I almost had a breakdown from it. I was at my wit's end. I was very, very irritable and desolate, mostly from exhaustion. I became pretty nasty. So I took the year off and I was miserable, just miserable. I went to Paris and I gained a lot of weight. I ate like a pig—*like a pig*. I was so tired I spent twelve, fourteen hours a day sleeping. I didn't even see the city. I just slept and called room service."

Ahmet Ertegun was worried about Bette, especially since her traveling companion, Lesley Ann Warren, had to return after a few days because her son fell ill, leaving Bette alone. Ertegun asked the Atlantic Records Paris office to have someone look after her. She had an affair with the French gentleman Atlantic sent, Benoit Gautier; seven years later they would rekindle their relationship and live together in Hollywood.

Bette returned from Europe after several months, but she remained underground, making almost no public appearances and turning down scores of concert, television, Broadway and movie offers. By early 1975, people were asking, "Whatever happened to Bette Midler?" One of her former agents was quoted in a magazine piece about her "disappearance": "a vacation is one thing, but complete oblivion for a year and a half is another. She had this business kissing her feet; we were getting offers from everybody. Every director, every network—they were falling over each other. Now a lot of the people in the business think her whole thing has cooled, that she had her star shot and blew it."

Aaron Russo, of course, knew better. He knew that if he could just get Bette back to work, she'd be back on top, too. They had talked about a project for months, but Bette was noncommital; she didn't seem motivated to do *anything* professionally. So Russo did something typically brash. He called her on the phone and said, "We're going back to work. I booked a Broadway theater and the ads are breaking next week."

"What do you mean *next week?!*" Bette screamed at him. Aaron understates, "She was forced, in a sense, to go back to work." And so the stage was set for another whirlwind round of fabulous success, backstage crisis and unparalleled entertainment with the Divine Miss M.

OPPOSITE: With Karen and Richard Carpenter after winning the Grammy as "Best New Artist of the Year," March 2, 1974.

PART THREE

SUPERSTAR

(1975–1978)

Ten

A lthough Bette Midler was, in the words of *Rolling Stone*, "missing in action" during 1974, there was a good deal of activity going on behind the scenes. Before she left for Europe, she met with celebrated director Mike Nichols (*Who's Afraid of Virginia Woolf?*, *The Graduate*) to discuss his desire to have Bette make her movie debut in his next film, *The Fortune*. Nichols was one of the many film directors and producers anxious to transfer the Midler magic to the big screen. The meeting, as was widely reported in the press, was a debacle.

The account which made the rounds was this: Bette arrived an hour late for the meeting in her suite at the Beverly Wilshire Hotel after being delayed by a massage. When she got there, she insulted Nichols by asking, "And what are your credits?" As Bette put it, "He wound up storming out of the meeting, absolutely furious. He told everybody what a cooz I was and how I had no business in the business."

Years later, Bette explained why she had treated Nichols that way: during her massage, she had been molested by the masseur. "He threw me into the shower and started soaping me up...I was terrified he was going to whip it out and whip it on me at any minute. I couldn't get away..."

Bette did get away without being raped, but "by the time I got back to the suite, I was a nervous wreck. I sat down and I didn't know where I was or who this guy was. I looked at Nichols, and all I thought was, Who is he?"

Needless to say, Bette did not get the role in *The Fortune*, that of a befuddled heiress who is kidnapped by two con men who are after her money. The male stars were set to be Warren Beatty and Jack Nicholson, and Bruce Vilanch feels Bette was frightened by the prospect of working with stars of their stature. "She had never made a movie before, and she was intimidated."

Aaron Russo has said that he didn't want Bette to do the movie because "anybody could have played that part. Bette's first role should be in a film with a role only she can play."

Whatever the reason (or combination of reasons) Bette failed to do *The Fortune*, it was fortunate that she didn't: the film, which co-starred Stockard Channing, was one of Nichols' least successful pictures.

Bette's fans (especially those who were closely following her career and were aware of her inability to find a "suitable" movie role) were surprised in May of 1974 to see an advertisement which proclaimed: "Bette Midler in her film debut." The movie was entitled *The Divine Mr. J*, and the ad featured a caricature of the famous Richard Amsel rendering of Bette which had appeared on the cover of her second album, along with a sampling of reviews from critics and magazines about how wonderful Bette was, supposedly in this movie.

Bette, as she would put it, *was not pleased*. The truth of the matter was that in 1971, for $250, Miss M had filmed a twelve-minute part as the Virgin Mary in a *very* low-budget 16-mm religious satire to be called *The Greatest Story Ever Overtold*. Its writer/director/producer/editor Peter Alexander McWilliams (Peter Alexander *professionally*) hoped to enter the film—which cost him $30,000 to make—in the Ann Arbor, Michigan, film festival. Instead, it remained in the can for four years—until Bette Midler became a star, and

OPPOSITE PART THREE:
Bette sings "Oklahoma" as she emerges
from a giant clam shell to
open her first network TV special, 1977.

82

NATIONAL ENTERTAINMENT CORP.
Presents

BETTE MIDLER

IN HER FILM DEBUT

'The DIVINE MR. J
IN COLOR

A RELIGIOUS SATIRE

MORE THAN A MOVIE...
it's a Happening

"In the tradition of Lenny Bruce and Woody Allen"

a film by PETER ALEXANDER   [R]

WORLD PREMIERE
NOW

THE Festival
A WALTER READE THEATRE
57th St at 5th Ave · LT 1-2323

The advertisement for "Bette Midler's first movie," 1974. She had actually made just a brief appearance in the low-budget religious satire several years earlier, and the producers tried to make Midler fans think it was a starring vehicle for Bette.

McWilliams and an associate, Stuart Gorelick, smelled a goldmine.

McWilliams went to Hollywood, raised another $40,000, transferred his film to 35mm, added titles, music, animation and stock footage from earlier Hollywood biblical films and changed the title. He then took out ads in newspapers and gay publications, as well as radio spots featuring music from Midler's albums, and booked the film for a May 24th opening at the Festival Theater in New York.

Aaron, who had heard reports that the film's release was imminent, was unsuccessful in his attempts to dissuade McWilliams from opening the film. While court action pended, Russo and an army of volunteers passed out leaflets in front of the theater warning Bette's fans that this was not a starring role for her and that they were being ripped off. One of the leaflets contained a statement from Bette: "In my opinion, the movie is dreadful. However, I did it and there's nothing I can do about it except advise you of the true facts. If you still wish to see me in the film, c'est la vie."

In the movie, Bette sings a snippet of "I've Got a Date with an Angel" just before the immaculate conception, and, as her pregnancy starts to become apparent, "It's Beginning to Look a Lot Like Christmas." In one scene, Joseph and Mary are trying to decide on a name for their baby as Joseph is working on one of his inventions, a roll-top desk. He slams the desk top on his fingers and exclaims "Jesus Christ!"

"Yes, I like it," Mary responds thoughtfully.

At one point, two of the three wise men are discussing following stars –the Hollywood variety. One mentions an actor and his companion asks, "Who's that?" The first man looks at him in disdain. "The next thing you'll want to know is, 'Who's Bette Midler?'" It was an ultimate in-joke that no one could have predicted would become *really* funny.

Russo's court action resulted in an agreement that the caricature of Bette would be removed from the advertisements; the word "divine" would be removed from the title; and Bette's name would not appear larger than any other actor's. This and Aaron's leafletting of the theater helped to keep the box office receipts almost non-existent, and the film quickly faded from view.

In February of 1975, Bette appeared on a Cher television special with Elton John and Flip Wilson. When Cher, a friend, first asked Bette to appear with her, Bette was to be the only guest. Producer George Schlatter, however–true to television wisdom–decided to pack as many guests in as possible to assure high ratings. Bette was promised a good amount of time on the show, though, including a solo spot.

When she arrived for the taping, Bette says, she had just had a permanent and "I looked like death. For the whole two weeks of rehearsals my hair was frizzed out and I wore no makeup. Well, they all looked at me like, 'Oh, holy shit. What did Cher drag in from the East Coast?' Then, when I showed up on the set looking like a human being, I swear there was an audible gasp from the control room. They were *so* relieved."

Bette looked quite glamorous in one segment of the show, wearing a Bob Mackie gown designed just for her which she later wore in her "Vickie Eydie" lounge act lampoon. During a tribute to the "trashy ladies" of history, Bette and Cher pulled out all the stops.

All four stars then got together for a hilarious sketch in which they played ancient residents of an old folks home. "I had a good time doing that," Bette said. "That was Elton's skit all the way. We were hysterical at him absolutely all the time. I really adore him. . .he loves to laugh. And he puns all the time."

Bette taped her solo spot, but it was never aired, a decision of Schlatter's that upset Bette considerably. She did nothing about it except dish Cher on stage a little later on; Raquel Welch, who had had the same problem, sued Schlatter for $100,000.

As Bette was preparing for a return to Broadway, she did so without the presence of Barry Manilow, who had ventured out on his own after the Palace engagement and was becoming a major star. It was difficult for Bette to lose Barry. Don York, who took his place, admitted, "They had a strong communication worked out. It was hard for Bette to accept someone else's presence." Bruce Vilanch adds, "When Barry left, she was very much at sea musically. He gave the ballads a texture that was missing after he quit. She's had wonderful people who've worked with her, but she hasn't had anybody who's given her what Barry did–she has had to do it for herself. Of course, she learned a lot–she's the world-famous *sponge*. She absorbs *everything*."

Around the time Manilow left, Bette said, "I miss Barry. I *really* miss Barry. . .but I think his success is fabulous. . .I was a little surprised. . .in fact I was *very* surprised because there were times when he was working for me–working *with* me–when he would bring me some of his songs that I

The chef makes sure Midler enjoys his mollusks as Bette announces her new Broadway show, *Bette Midler's Clams on the Half Shell Revue*, February 1975.

didn't like. I would say to him, 'Why are you singing "Come to where the stallions meet the sun?" I can't *stand* that! Don't sing that! I must have thought, of course, that I was the final arbiter of taste. Obviously I wasn't, 'cause he had a big hit with that song.

"His audience and my audience are not the same . . . I would have thought, 'He's gonna steal my audience,' but he didn't . . . he has young girls who think he is *it*!"

Bette not only feared that Barry would steal her audience, but her backup singers as well; and the last thing she wanted was to lose some more of her "support system" on the eve of a major Broadway production. Charlotte explains what happened: "Sharon, Robin and I went out with Barry while Bette was in Europe. Later on, Barry was putting together another backup group of his own and he wanted me to join it. Bette was putting together her new show, and she wanted me, too.

"Barry said, 'I really want you, but I know that she's gonna offer you a lot more money. I respect that—and I know that you love her.' I told him I'd let him know in the next ten hours.

"I get back home and my soon-to-be-ex-husband tells me Bette's called six times. When we talked on the phone, I sensed that as soon as she found out Barry wanted me, her attitude was, 'I'm not gonna let her go!' She wanted my answer over the phone and I said I'd come down to see her and she said, 'Why can't you tell me over the phone?' All I told her was 'I'll see you in a little while.'

"When I got to her place the woman was just *insane*. She was screaming 'Are you gonna go with that so and so? What are we gonna do? How much do I have to pay you?' I said, 'We can come to an agreeable figure. I want to work

OPPOSITE: With Stevie Wonder at the 1975 Grammy Awards. Bette created a sensation with her platter hat. "It's 'Come Go with Me' by the Del Vikings," she said. "A great record, but a better hat."

with you.' She said, 'Well, Aaron doesn't seem to think so.'

"Aaron had put all this stuff out to her—'Charlo isn't gonna come back—she's working for Barry,' and he just created all of this doubt in Bette's mind about my commitment to her. I said to her, 'That's not true, Bette. I love you and I love working with you, and it's not just the money.' I really resented the shit that Aaron was putting out, but I decided that I was just not gonna let it get to me, that I would have a whole new attitude, and we started rehearsals right away."

Bette's Broadway show, *Bette Midler's Clams on the Half Shell Revue*, evolved from a much different concept. Late in 1974, Bette went to Chicago, and she and Bruce Vilanch discussed ideas for her return to Broadway. "We had a whole different idea," Vilanch says. "The show was gonna be at a small house for six months. There would be Bette and a group of sketch players—and Benny Goodman. She wanted to act and do something quite different. She was afraid to do something too much like her old shows.

"I brought her to Second City, and we went out to dinner with the kids in the company. We decided to hire Gilda Radner, Eugene Levy, John Belushi and Brian Doyle-Murray as the sketch players, and Benny Goodman was going to be the bridge between the 'hubba-hubba' and the rest of the show.

"But then things began to fall apart. Benny Goodman didn't want to do six months, and Aaron said we were crazy—'look at the kind of money you can make in six *weeks*, why do you want to prolong it into six months?'—and so we couldn't do it. But from that came Lionel Hampton in *Clams*, and some of the sketches—we had a lot more sketches, but the show just got too long and we had to cut most of them."

Barring anything as different as Bette and Bruce had envisioned, the logical step was to present a show with as much genuine theatricality as possible. The decision was made to treat *Clams* as a legitimate Broadway production. Aaron hired a director, Joe Layton, who had guided Streisand through her television specials in the 1960s, a set designer, Tony Walton, and a choreographer, Toni Basil. Charlotte recalls, "For us, *Clams* was what we were all used to—Bette included—because we had all come from Broadway beginnings. And this whole thing was mounted like a Broadway show. I remember Bette saying to me, 'Charlo, here we are—back on the boards, honey.' Of course, it was overwhelming for her because the entire thing had her name on it."

"I never imagined it would turn into this epic of death," Bette said. "*The* most mind-boggling, stupendous production ever conceived and built around one poor small five-foot-one-and-a-half-inch Jewish girl from Honolulu. All of a sudden I'm a whole industry. People run, they fetch, they carry, they nail, they paint, they sew . . ."

By all accounts, the addition of a true director, especially one of Joe Layton's talent and stature, was extremely important to the formation of what was to be Bette's greatest triumph to date. According to Bruce Vilanch, both Bette's entrance inside the clam shell and the King Kong sequence were Layton's ideas. "I remember him saying that he wanted to make the opening a great big joke, a take-off on all the *other* great Broadway shows in history—'We'll open with *Oklahoma*, then go into the first act of *Show Boat*, then into *South Pacific*.' And Joe was watching *King Kong* on TV one night, and he had been looking for something intrinsically New York for her to do, and that gave him the inspiration."

Needless to say, however, the basic concept of the show was built around what Bette wanted to put out. "Joe Layton is perfect for that," Bruce says.

OPPOSITE: The opening number—Bette is revealed as the giant clamshell opens.

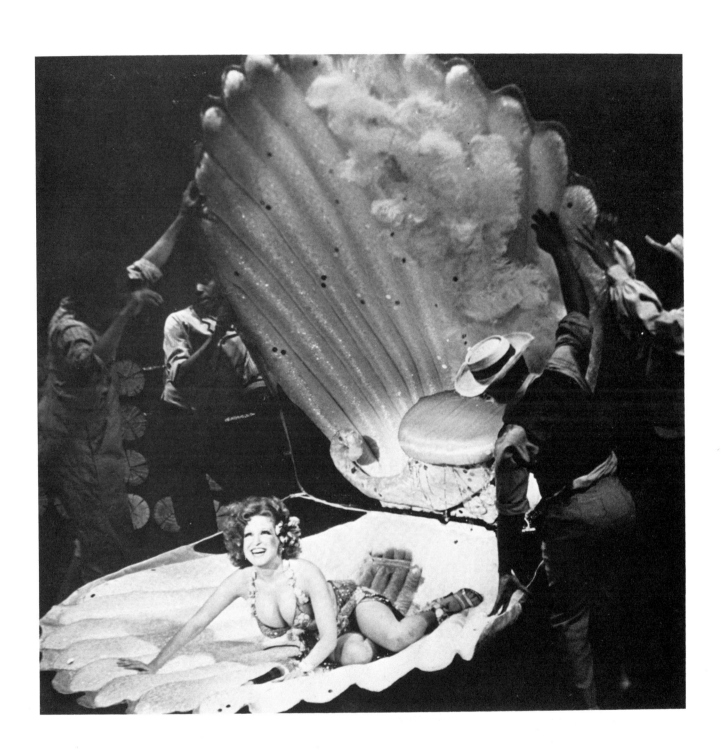

"What he does best is put something together for someone in particular." Bette had two main requirements aside from "stupendous" production values—that the show contain a tropical motif and that she be allowed to act in a sketch or two. The opening filled the first bill, and during rehearsals Layton noticed poi balls and asked Bette what they were. She explained that everyone in Hawaii uses them, and demonstrated how they are spun around on long strings. He was astonished by Bette's skill and knew that the audience would be delighted. From that point on, Bette usually had a poi ball demonstration in her show.

The show's "Nanette" character developed from Bette's desire to do some acting in her revue. Vilanch: "Joe Layton convinced us that she could show off her acting in a mosaic of different songs in a bar, where she could play a character. It became the 'Drinking Again' segment, and in later shows, Nanette became the bag lady."

Bette wasn't used to taking direction in her shows, but things seemed to go fairly smoothly. As Vilanch recalls, "It was a good collaboration. They had fights, but he gave her a lot of leeway, and she took direction well."

Layton said, "What I like about working with Bette is that she wears her whole presence on the outside. If she's mad at you, she comes at you with a knife. If she loves you she gives you a smile. You never have to worry what she's thinking. It makes it much easier to deal with and gets the work done with great efficiency."

Despite the production exigencies, there were fewer problems with this show than any Bette had ever put on. Ironically, things went *so* smoothly that Bette worried that perhaps it was a bad omen. "My big question," Bette said a few weeks before the opening, "is whether the lack of friction that usually existed in rehearsals will affect my creativity. Do I really need to pump myself so full of anxiety and fear and loathing and negative things in order to release it during performance? It's extremely frightening. I was relatively calm until last week and then I think I psyched myself into a fit. I had two or three days that I literally bit people and called them horrendous names. I also started dreaming. I had a nightmare that David Bowie opened up across the street from me and had the same sets and he was wearing my costumes."

Bette needn't have worried—even if her nightmare had come true, it wouldn't have made any difference. The night before tickets for the show went on sale in February, people started lining up at the box office; by 3 a.m. the line was around the corner, and by the time the tickets went on sale at 10 a.m., 800 people were standing in the rain. By the end of the day, Bette Midler's Palace one-day ticket-sale record of $148,000 had been broken—this time, the take was $200,000. The show was extended from four weeks to ten, and grossed nearly $2 million. The stage was set for Bette Midler's Broadway comeback.

Opening night was a triumph for Bette. The crowd was warmer than most first-night audiences, because Aaron had limited the number of tickets distributed to "industry people" and "media types"—notoriously reserved audiences—and made available far more tickets for the Midler faithful. After her high-camp entrance in the clam shell was uproariously received, she said, "You're such a wonderful audience, much nicer than most first-night audiences. Really, you're very sweet...I better stop before I make myself *nauseous*."

Bette set the comic tone for the evening early. "We have reached a new level of taste. We are now *taste free*. Well, we gave you a year off—and now you

OPPOSITE: Singing "Do You Wanna Dance?" during the barroom segment.

are going to *paaay*. We busted our buns for you this time. We had our hair dyed, we had our teeth capped, we shaved. Some of us even douched—and if that isn't an act of love, I don't know what is!"

Her jokes were the usual top-notch comments on the people and foibles of the day: "Gerald Ford—*puh-leeze!* I want a *rebate!* That man is not only dull, he is the *cause* of dullness in *others*. And I've got news for you—I ain't never gonna vote for him again!

"*And where is Patty Hearst anyway?* I recently found out where she is. On the corner of 53rd and 3rd—*working*, honees. Oh, listen, you must all rush out to McDonald's—they're featuring a new item on the menu. It's called the Hearst Burger—there's *no patty!*"

Bette then told the audience of her future career plans. "I have agreed to do the sequel to *Emanuelle*—it's called *Temple Emanuel*, and it's about a nice Jewish girl who's appointed Ambassador to Great Neck. There's not much sex, just a lot of kissing mezuzahs. There's a subplot, though, in which she becomes involved in an unnatural relationship with a kreplach. Now I know there's one or two of you out there who haven't the vaguest idea what the hell is a kreplach. A kreplach is a person from Kreplachia."

In addition to the new humor and lavish sets, the most impressive thing about Bette's show was the large amount of new musical material, more than she had ever used in a show before. "We learned *so* many songs," Charlotte recalls. "We loved all of them and we had to drop so many of them. But we did get to do a *lot* of the new stuff, too."

Bette sang contemporary material like David Bowie's "Young Americans;" Paul Simon's "Gone at Last;" the Beatles' "A Day in the Life;" "When a Man Loves a Woman;" and Elton John's "The Bitch Is Back," as well as older songs she'd never performed before: Billie Holiday's "We'll Be Together Again;" "If Love Were All;" and "Sentimental Journey."

At the end of the first act, the Harlettes begin to sing a medley of "Lullaby of Broadway," "I'm Wishing" and "A Dream Is a Wish Your Heart Makes." The New York backdrop behind them begins to lower, and we see the Empire State Building. As the set continues to lower we scale the heights of the building until we are looking at the top—and an enormous King Kong. Slowly, the left arm of Kong swings around to the front of the building—and Bette Midler lies passed out in his huge hand. The audience is in a frenzy as Bette stirs and looks at her captor with horror. Then she sings "Nicky Arnstein...Nicky Arnstein!" before breaking into "Lullaby of Broadway" and bringing the curtain down to the disbelieving, delighted audience. Said Bette later, "You just can't imagine what true joy is until you sit in the hand of King Kong! What power! What freedom!"

The second acts opens with a gorgeous set: a huge revolving record with a dazzlingly lighted juke box atop—and Lionel Hampton on the vibraharp backed by his big band. Bette and Lionel proceed to really cook on "In the Mood," "Boogie Woogie Bugle Boy," and "How High the Moon." In a newspaper piece the day before the opening, Joe Layton talked about the teaming of Midler and Hampton: "Now that's a nice meeting of the minds," he said. "Bette does nostalgic stuff, music of the '30s and '40s as well as the '60s and '70s. We're extending her, putting her with an all-time great who lived those years before she was born. They both love jazz, and he's reaching forward, and she's reaching backward. They're stretching."

Robert Wahls, who wrote the piece, described a rehearsal: "Hamp was stretching until it looked as though that red-haired woman was gonna make a

OPPOSITE: "Nicky Arnstein . . . Nicky Arnstein!" At the close of the first act, Bette sings "Lullaby of Broadway" in the clutches of King Kong.

The "Drinking
Again" barroom segment.

OPPOSITE: Bette and
Lionel Hampton get down to the sound
of the vibraharp.

freight train leave the track. The sweat is pouring off Hamp's forehead, and Bette is swaying her butt and tossing that red mop like a buoy in a high sea. Then they were into Hamp's composition 'Flying Home,' one of Bette's favorites. Where Hamp went on the vibes, Bette followed. And where she went with her kaleidoscope delivery, Hamp followed. They were a couple of pros, each hearing with the other's ears."

On stage, it was a magical moment in a show filled with them. The Nanette "Drinking Again" segment was also quite affecting, with Bette combining desolation and loneliness with hope and optimism, telling jokes and singing "Strangers in the Night" and "Do You Wanna Dance?" to mannequins positioned throughout the bar.

Another highlight of the show was a medley performed with the Harlettes. Bette had joked at Carnegie Hall that all she could scrape up for a medley were two songs, and she seemed to want to make amends—this medley contained more than a dozen tunes, including "Why Do Fools Fall in Love," "Papa-Oooh-Mow-Mow," "Chain Gang," "He's So Fine," "Under the Boardwalk," "I Will Wait for You," and "Fun-Fun-Fun."

On opening night, April 14, Bette seemed to take forever to introduce what she called her "toilet medley." Charlotte says it was a common occurrence: "Miss Thing *loves* to chat. She would get on her platform and she'd be talking for ten minutes before a number. We'd be standing back there waitin', and I'd be goin' 'Uh hunh,' and the stage manager's looking at his watch...but it was something she needed to do sometimes. A lot of times she had important things to say to the audience, and there was no other female performer doing that at the time. She'd say, 'You guys are hurting each other out there. I don't want you to do that'—she'd take a *stand* about something, you know? And she really touched a lot of people."

Bette Midler's Clams on the Half Shell Revue was a critical as well as financial success. Although she had the usual amount of trouble from stuffy establishment critics like Clive Barnes of the New York *Times* and John Simon of *New York* magazine, two reviews in particular reflected the general consensus. Jack Kroll in *Newsweek* wrote, "At long last a truly exciting musical exploded on Broadway last week—Bette Midler was back...like all great parodists, Midler is an artist-critic who both loves and sees through the things she parodies. Like Lenny Bruce, but more sophisticatedly and more benignly, she has absorbed the paradoxes of pop culture and plays them back for us in a powerhouse catharsis of eclectic energy."

And Rex Reed enthused, "I love Bette Midler, and her star-spangled revue is full of the reasons why the romance just might go on forever...Giant phonograph records whirl behind a vintage jukebox with Bette swinging 'In the Mood' on the whirling turntable. Ken Russell would lose his mind. And I can't describe to you the thrill of sitting in an audience that is screaming 'Hey Ba-Ba-Re-Bop' in rhythm with Lionel Hampton's big band and the Harlettes. It's raunchy, it's riveting, it royally welcome. Dear Bette, with the flamboyant fanny and the hair by General Electric, is it clear that I love you?"

Once again, Bette Midler was on top of the show business world—and had a *People* cover to prove it. The story referred to her self-imposed exile: "Show business minds boggled. Was she going to blow it all—the record deals, the TV specials, Las Vegas, the movies?...Midler has confounded the industry again, coming back to triumph. Packed audiences rolled over and begged. In the past Midler's devotees were largely the gaily liberated; this time they were as broad as her repertoire, spanning four decades."

Bette is lost in her thoughts as she waits in her dressing room to go on.

One of the members of her audience during *Clams* was her mother, who came to New York to see her. Charlotte recalls that Ruth Midler was "a really wonderful person, and she really loved Bette. Bette was her hope, she contributed so much to Ruth. And Ruth treated us all like we were her daughters."

Along with the stunning success of *Clams* came some problems. Charlotte recalls that on opening night, "Aaron Russo gave Bette a real expensive ring, and I think he asked her to marry him. She said no, and they had a *huge* fight. And a little while later, Bette's apartment was robbed. Her road manager, Patrick Cochrane, was staying there, and they tied him up and took her jewels. It all seemed pretty suspicious to me, but I have no proof of anything."

Although Bette at first enjoyed the fact that having this show structured for her allowed her more freedom during rehearsals, she found things to be just the opposite during the run. "The trouble with the *Clams* show," Bette said, "was that there was no room for spontaneity and I saw that spontaneity has a lot to do with the innocence that I felt had been slipping away. Every night you had to go out there and be very loud and very vulgar, even if you didn't feel like it. There was no room for me. I dealt with my lines and my costumes and my songs in that show. I was amazingly 'professional.' And it was a fabulous show. But I had become separated from that character. And that depressed me."

On May 18th, Bette made an appearance at a telethon for the benefit of the United Jewish Appeal. After singing "Sentimental Journey" and "Boogie Woogie Bugle Boy," Bette said, "What could be more wonderful? My first telethon—and at the Ed Sullivan Theater. Oh my dear, it gives one pause. The great, the near great and the lame have played here. Some as recently as this evening. But, we did not come here to dump, we came to ask for your dough. You know, this cause means so much to me that I am prepared to *drop my dress for Israel!*

"Out there in television land, I know there is someone who wants to see it.

OPPOSITE: Bette beams as she accepts cheers after "In The Mood."

Someone who wants to be responsible for allowing all of New York to see the end of my reputation, the end of my career—and my legs, which are the most beautiful in the business. Thank you, thank you—and *kiss my tuches!*"

After "Hello in There," Bette asked expectantly, "Did I get it? Did I get my pledge? I got it?! I got it?! Oh, I'm so excited!! Are you ready?!"

Applause, drumroll—and Bette did a slow bump-and-grind strip-tease to remove her dress, revealing the satin slip with the heart on its front which she wears in her show. "I hope you all aren't too disappointed. I hope you all weren't expecting to see the whole thing. I mean, you're gonna have to pay a lot more than five grand to see the whole thing!"

Bette introduced the Harlettes as "three prime examples of non-kosher meat," sang "Friends" and an announcement was made that the $5,000 pledge has put the campaign over the $1 million mark.

Bette took another long rest after *Clams*, but spent a good deal of time recording tracks for what would be her first new album in two years. She also did some recording with an unlikely new beau—Paul Simon. Rumors had circulated about Bette and Paul necking at parties, and much was made in the press about their collaboration: a duet on Simon's song, "Gone at Last."

Fans of both eagerly awaited the single. "One day the record came out," Bette said, "and I wasn't *on* it! And there *had* been a certain amount of advance publicity. I was very hurt, it took me a long time to get over it."

Phoebe Snow sang with Simon on the released record, and Bette never did hear from Paul with an explanation. One night a few months later, Bette went to a party in the Hamptons on Long Island, not knowing that Simon would be there: "I got very drunk, 'cause I was *real* hurt. . .I musta put six gin and tonics into my system, and the more gin, the *louder* I got. . .We went into the kitchen and it wasn't a chat for very long, I did all the *yelling.*"

Simon has said that the biggest problem was negotiating terms between his label—Columbia—and Bette's. Aaron Russo hints that he didn't do much to facilitate things. "I think Paul and Bette were having a little bit of an affair, which didn't sit too well with me. . .I'm the jealous kind of man. . .The lack of my enthusiasm in putting the deal together sort of killed it. . .I have no use for Paul Simon. . .if I never saw him for the rest of my life it would suit me fine."

"Paul's a very private person," Bette said, "and he doesn't like airing his dirty laundry in public. In fact, I venture to say that he doesn't like doing his laundry *at all*—'Oooh! Did she really say that?'"

Bette with her
mother Ruth after a performance
of *Clams*, 1975.

OPPOSITE: Bette strips
down to her slip for a donation of
$5,000 during a United
Jewish Appeal telethon, May 1975.

Eleven

While Bette was finishing up her album and preparing for a new cross-country tour, she took time out on November 16 to sing at a tribute to celebrated lyricist Ira Gershwin at New York's Avery Fisher Hall. As Bette looked out at the black-tie audience she said nervously, "This has got to be the most tasteful event I've ever been associated with. And you know I know about things like that!"

Bette was easily the biggest draw on the bill, which included Elizabeth Ashley, Chita Rivera, Bobby Short, Barbara Cook, Jerry Orbach and Larry Kert, and her presence guaranteed success for the event, held to benefit the American Musical and Dramatic Academy and the George Junior Republic. Still, certain observers felt that Midler's presence was inappropriate: Arthur Bell, the churlish *Village Voice* critic who hurls vitriol at Bette (and practically everyone else) whenever possible, said that having her at a tribute to Ira Gershwin was like "dumping ketchup on caviar."

His comments didn't bother Bette too much, though: she had little respect for the man after he once came backstage, showered her with compliments, then wrote a review trashing her. In a May 1979 "interview" with herself in *After Dark* magazine, Bette *did* have the last word with this exchange:

Bette: It has been said that the seventies is the age of asexuality. Do you agree?

The Divine: Who said that? I bet it was Arthur Bell.

Bette: How did you know?

The Divine: Because only someone who can't get laid would say a thing like that. You know there's nothing worse than an ill-tempered little snake with a brain.

Bette: What a horrible thing to say.

The Divine: You're right. Leave out the part about the brain.

Late in 1975, Robin Grean decided to retire as a Harlette, and Bette was once again in the position of auditioning half of New York to find a replacement. Ula Hedwig had been doing *Godspell* in Chicago, and got a call from a friend telling her about the auditions in New York. Ula called Moogy Klingman, who was working on Bette's new album, and he set up an audition for her.

"I had cracked a rib in *Godspell*," Ula says, "and I was wrapped up in this Ace bandage, but I hopped on a plane because the audition was the next day. I had no music, I was totally unprepared—I just figured I'd do whatever she wanted. I was real nervous, but when I saw Charlotte, I felt a little more at ease—we'd done *Hair* together in Chicago. Then I saw Zora Rassmussen, who'd been a friend for years—she was auditioning, too.

"She'd brought this stack of music, and I said, 'Zora, you go first.' She sang 'Wedding Bell Blues,' which I'd sung as my *Hair* audition, so I figured it was a good luck song. But I couldn't sing the same song, and I had nothing else prepared, so when Bette asked me to sing, I said, 'Tell ya what—why don't we all three sing 'Wedding Bell Blues' so we can see what we sound like together?' Well, Bette thought that was a good idea, and we harmonized and improvised, and that's all she needed to hear, I think.

"This was a Friday, and all weekend long I heard from friends that Bette was

OPPOSITE: Resplendent in a babushka, Bette rehearses the opening number of her "Depression" concert, December 1975.

100

auditioning *everybody*—she even had *guys* trying out. On Monday, I get a call from Bette and she says, 'So, you want to work for me?' And I said *'absolutely!'*"

Bette began rehearsals the very next day; this twenty-city tour—which would turn out to be stunningly eventful—was set to begin in less than a month. Dubbed the "Depression Tour" after her upcoming album, *Songs for the New Depression*, it required some of the most intensive rehearsals Bette had ever had. There was a lot riding on this tour; it was her first in two years, and there was the album coming out in connection with it.

"She was *very* hard on us," Charlotte says. "We'd work and work and she wouldn't be happy. She'd change her mind all the time. She was always looking for something fresh, something different. We'd be rehearsing wildly, putting in long, long hours, and then we'd call it quits, and she'd have insecurities in the middle of the night and call me up and say, 'Charlo, we have to change this and that,' and I'd say, 'Okay, let's deal with it tomorrow, when we're fresh.' Once we got on the road, she'd call me up every night until I had to tell the hotel not to put the calls through—but they'd always put *her* through. This went on *all the time*."

Bette's insecurities caused her to work herself and everyone around her to a breaking point. Aaron said, "She's still a scared, confused girl. . .always saying, 'My career's going downhill! Nobody loves me anymore! Nobody cares! I don't know how to sing! I'm not a good actress!' You know, constantly putting herself down—that's the fuel that feeds her."

"Toni Basil would come up with some choreography," Charlotte says, "and Bette would want to edit it—which is her right—but then she'd change it totally after we'd learned it and we'd have to go back to square one. That's when it was really tough.

"Sometimes we'd *love* something, and she'd want to drop it. We'd fight, we'd walk out. One day, we had been rehearsing for *ten hours* straight, and she was under a lot of pressure, and she got mad and called us *amateurs*. We were *furious*. When you rehearse that long, you get tired and you make mistakes—but that doesn't make you unprofessional. Ula cut her hand, I had blisters on my feet, I was hoarse, we were all getting the flu. I was dead tired, and I couldn't sleep because she kept calling me and calling me in the middle of the night. And we'd get up early in the morning for costume fittings, then work late into the night. We would get so beat.

"Then there was Aaron, just to throw his shit around. Whenever things were *really* tough, he'd show up to throw a little barb in about something, and she'd go off. She'd scream, 'You get the hell out of here! You're a fat fuck and get the hell out of here'—in front of the whole company. And we'd just go, 'Oh, no. . .'

"So the night that Bette had her appendicitis attack, I felt worried and sorry for her, but I was so *relieved*, because we were some tired, tired people."

Bette's emergency appendectomy was performed, as she later put it, "in a plush Beverly Hills Medical Center." "I remember going to see her," Charlotte says. "It *was* very plush and quiet. The nurses were quite tasteful—'Oh yes, Miss Midler is looking forward to seeing you'—and we all went in. I was crying, and we helped pull her hair back off her face. It was all very emotional, really—it was like our mother or our sister being in the hospital, you know?"

Bette's room was full of flowers and gifts. "I really got a sense of just what a huge star she is, how much people love her," Charlotte says. "There were *tons* of flowers from every star, everybody sent her things—Elton John sent her this

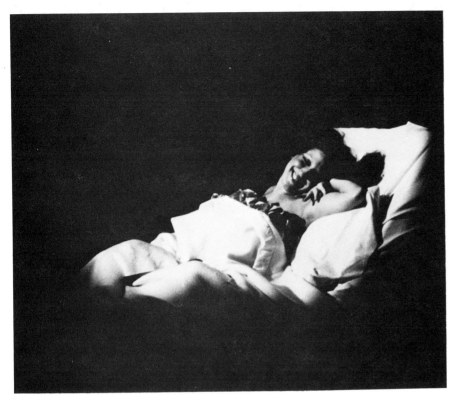

"This hospital motif
was suggested to me by my recent
stay in a very plush
Beverly Hills medical center."

huge Teddy bear, there were literally hundreds of bouquets."

There were reports in the press that even while hospitalized, Bette held rehearsals, but Charlotte says it wasn't all that elaborate. "We did some vocal stuff. She'd say, 'Let me hear how this sounds,' so we'd sing a few things for her and she'd say, 'That's good. . . .' That's all it was, really."

Bette returned to full-scale rehearsals as soon as she was released from the hospital a week later. "But it made her slow down," Charlotte says, "and that was fine with us, because a lot of good stuff got done, quickly."

"The Depression Show" was a pared-down version of *Clams* with only the King Kong set included because of the travel difficulties. An ingenious convertible set was devised, principally to accomodate the major new element in the show: Vickie Eydie's Global Revue, "Around the World in 80 Ways."

The addition of Vickie Eydie to Bette's show was an inspired stroke, allowing her to spoof "lounge acts" while performing campy, funny musical numbers and looking fabulous (she wore the white sequinned dress Bob Mackie designed for her Cher show appearance).

Charlotte recalls how the idea of Vickie Eydie germinated. "Bette took me to a club in New York for my birthday, and we saw Joey Heatherton. Well, honey, we were *screaming* with laughter. I mean, it was *total cheese*. We both said Bette *had* to do a take-off on her in her show."

Bette originally planned to open the show with "I Sold My Heart to the Junkman," but her appendectomy gave her an idea: she'd begin the show in her hospital bed, singing "Friends" ("And I am all alone. . .there's nobody here beside me") and "Oh, My My" ("I called up the doctor, to see what's the matter. . .")

The first show was in Berkeley, California, and Ula Hedwig remembers it vividly. "It was my first show with her. I was standing there waiting to go on in my nurse's uniform, with my little I.V. bottle, and the curtain went up and I'll never forget that incredible *cheering*. I'd never heard anything like it before. I had tears in my eyes and I got the chills."

The next stop was Los Angeles, where Bette's jokes were particularly appreciated: "You might have heard that I was stricken with appendicitis. But I am here to tell you the truth, *El Lay*—in a spasm of sisterly generosity, I donated my tits *to Cher*. And she was *so* glad to get 'em, I can't even begin to tell you. By the way, have you heard—Cher is *preggie* by *Greggie*.

"I want you all to know that I am making the sequel to *Jaws*—in which a shark is attacked by a great white woman."

At one point, Bette announced that she was now going to do her impression of Shelley Winters in *The Poseidon Adventure*. She took her stool, placed it in the middle of the stage, walked to stage right, turned around, ran toward it and plopped herself onto it in a prone position. She mimed swimming for a few seconds, then let her body fall limp and hang over the sides of the stool.

"When she would do that," Ula says, "I could *feel* it in my stomach. She wasn't even supposed to be *working* after her surgery, much less throwing herself stomach-first on a stool!"

Another addition to the show was the finale, in which Bette put her head through a giant sheet depicting the Statue of Liberty. "You didn't think we'd do the whole show without a tribute to the bicentennial, did you?" She begins "Friends" and sings "And I am all alone, there is no one here beside me. But my problems have just begun—what if Reagan is to guide me?"

The show, needless to say, was a smash, and Bette was once again the toast of Los Angeles. Jane Fonda bought a thousand tickets to benefit her husband Tom Hayden's campaign; and practically every movie star living or working in Hollywood came backstage to pay their homage to Bette. But the highlight for her was meeting Sir Laurence Olivier, one of her idols. He had come to the show twice, and the second time he went backstage, where he and Bette sat on the couch in her dressing room holding hands and trading flatteries. Later, he escorted her to a Hayden rally. Dustin Hoffman remembers, "I could see right away that he was, well—there's no other way to put it—he was sexually attracted to her. I kept kidding him about wanting to get into her drawers, and he kept putting his hand up in horror and saying, 'Nasty, nasty.'"

Bette's reviews on the Depression Tour were among the best of her career. Blair Sobol, in the *Village Voice* (not often kind to Midler), wrote, "Bette is the kind of performer who needs an alive audience. Matter of fact, it's the reason why so many people can go back and see her night after night. Not only because she changes her material but because of the change in crowds. Her spontaneity is her genius. And though she's been criticized for being crude on occasion or out of control, I adore her for being just that. Bette takes chances onstage... [but] there is less of the hysterical Divine Miss M in this show. You could say that Bette is no longer the transvestite performer she used to be. This time there is a sense of reality about her patter and less shtick."

Robert Hilburn, reviewing the show in Los Angeles, said, "Bette Midler is *back*...she has recaptured the spirit, purpose and innocence that made her such a captivating force in pop music when she arrived on the club scene in 1972. Her concert was, in fact, a more varied, accomplished and endearing performance than the one she gave in her Troubador debut. It was simply a stunning tour de force that left little doubt about who is the new queen of the concert-cabaret field in America."

After discussing the freshness of Bette's Divine Miss M in 1972, Hilburn said, "The problem that surfaced as Midler's career progressed was that the

OPPOSITE: Singing "Shiver Me Timbers." With a few pulls of a zipper, Bette's odd ruffled outfit revealed the clinging, sequinned Vickie Eydie gown.

Divine character began to smother Midler's own stage personality. Perhaps, it seemed for a while, Midler's main contribution would simply be the creation of the Divine. The triumph of Friday's show was that Midler has re-established her own identity. She has once again become the star of her own show. And she is more confident and daring a performer."

Bette's final Los Angeles performances were New Year's Eve. "Lord, what a night that was," Bette has said.

The day started out well. The California state legislature had passed a bill making possession of marijuana a misdemeanor instead of a felony, and the new law was set to go in effect at 12:01 a.m. January 1st. Bette wanted to do something really special for New Year's Eve, and she hit upon the idea of putting a joint under every seat in the house: at midnight, she'd wish everybody a Happy New Year and tell them to look under their seats. Bette and her entourage sat around for most of the day rolling joints, and they were up to 1,800 when they got the word: someone had leaked the story to the press, and the police made it quite clear that *that* was not going to be Bette's New Year's Eve surprise. "I was devastated," Bette said. "I kept hoping until the last minute that somebody would come up with an idea as marvelous as that, but when push came to shove, I realized it was up to me . . ."

At the stroke of midnight, Ula remembers looking up as the Harlettes were singing "Lullaby of Broadway": "By this time, the audience was pretty loaded and so was Bette. I noticed she didn't have her nylons on, and the straps of her dress were down, and I thought, Oh, God, what's going to happen next?!"

Bette, sitting in King Kong's hand, yelled "Happy New Year" and "duh-ropped my dress and exposed myself to 3,600 people."

The audience went insane, flashbulbs popped in a blinding burst, and everybody stood, cheered and kissed each other as the curtain came down. Aaron Russo, however, was beside himself with fury. During the intermission, there was a dreadful fight during which Aaron screamed that what she had done was "stupid and self-destructive." Things got so bad security men had to be called in. Aaron left the theater. "I went through the rest of the show under this rotten cloud of ghastly doom," Bette said, "and just sort of dragged myself to this big party in my behalf afterwards."

Bette went to the party with Hamish Stuart of Average White Band, whom she was dating–but it wasn't the kind of party she expected. "I had come to a party that I didn't know was a company party. I thought it was a party for my own cast and crew. I had no idea that I was going to have to face anyone in the business because I was so exhausted. I was really in no condition . . ."

Atlantic Records executives, and important radio people, were there–including Paul Drew, head of programming for more than 300 radio stations across the country, a man very instrumental in the success or failure of singles. Bette began talking to Drew, who had a copy of a new Midler single, "Strangers in the Night"–a record which, according to Bette, she was completely unaware Atlantic had released.

What happened next has had many different versions, but the best reconstruction goes like this: Bette asked Drew what he thought of the record, and he replied "Happy New Year." She asked him again, and he tried to avoid a reply, explaining that Elton John had said she was paranoid about her recording.

"Elton says I'm paranoid about my recording? When did Elton ever say that?" Bette asked, taken aback.

OPPOSITE: The fabulous Miss Vickie Eydie introduces her global revue, "Around the World in Eighty Ways."

"He says it in 'Playboy' magazine," Drew replied.

Bette was shocked. "'Playboy' magazine! Elton said that I was paranoid about my recording in 'Playboy' magazine!"

"Elton says you're paranoid, so I don't know what to answer you."

"I don't know what that means."

Finally, Drew had to respond. "It means I didn't like it."

"Oh, I see," Bette replied. "Well, that's number four . . . Happy New Year to you, too."

Bette walked away, and began to dance with Hamish. But, she says, "I sulked about it until I was in a perfect frenzy and then I marched up to him and said, 'You don't like it, *don't play it!*,' and I slugged him and smashed the record and threw it in the fireplace and stalked out of the joint on my spiked heels . . ."

The result was that Bette was banned from Drew's RKO chain of radio stations, a serious blow to her singles sales. But the evening wasn't over yet. When Bette returned to her hotel, she went to Aaron's room and didn't get a response from her knocks at first. Then she heard moaning. She went for the concierge to let her in, and found Aaron on the floor. "He'd taken a bunch of pills," Bette explained later, "trying to pass out and scare me because I had a date with someone else that night. He was in love with me and didn't want me to be with anybody else. So he was always making it difficult for me to have a love life, even though we were no longer personally involved."

Lord, what a night.

OPPOSITE: Clowning as
Nanette in the "Drinking Again"/"Mr.
Rockefeller" barroom segment.

Twelve

As the traveling Bette Midler sideshow made its way east across the country, Bette's third album, *Songs for the New Depression*, was released. It was an odd, delicate mix of material: "Strangers in the Night," Phoebe Snow's yearning 'I Don't Want the Night to End," Bette's "Mr. Rockefeller," the Patti Page hit "Old Cape Cod," "Shiver Me Timbers" along with another Bette composition, the lighthearted nonsense song "Samedi Et Vendredi," the '30s number "Marahuana," a spirited duet with Bob Dylan on his "Buckets of Rain," and what may be the ultimate torch song, Moogy Klingman's heartwrenching "Let Me Just Follow Behind."

The aim of *Songs for the New Depression* was to cheer people up. "I thought 1974 and 1975 *were* a Depression," Bette said, "Desolate. Nixon had quit, all those awful 'snuff' porn murder films came out and the Anvil [a New York S&M bar] was getting a lot of press and I thought, People are going to start killing each other! I have to make some kind of statement. . . at the time, I thought it was the end of the world, so I was making a very whimsical, reactionary album."

The cover photo shows Bette as a white-clad lady with a shoppping bag and a paint brush who has just put a red mustache and beard on a Bette Midler poster. "That little person is supposed to be a harbinger of joy. I love her very much, especially the fact that she never ties her tow shoes. She is the singer on that album. . . it's meant to be very innocent. It's meant to be a harkening back to a kind of innocence that has been bypassed and I feel very strongly a need to return to."

Bette's duet with Bob Dylan was the culmination of a long-time dream for her. When she first came to New York, she has said, she used to "walk the streets hoping to see Bob Dylan." When she finally did meet him, in 1974, he began laughing and told her, "I know what you do but I can't remember your name. I can't remember where I seen you do it."

"I thought the man had lost his marbles," Bette said. "My feelings were really hurt." They met again passingly several times; then, at a party after a Dylan concert in Madison Square Garden, "nobody would talk to him. Here was God again, and the waters literally parting before him. I was just high enough to think it was funny. When he finally made his way over to me, we got into a little conversation. It was a little tit for tat, a little of this and a little of that, and I pinched him on the bottom and the son of a bitch jumped two feet into the air and turned around and let out a laugh. . . then I lost my fear of him."

The duet is very playful; at its end, Bette says, "Bobby, Bobby, hey there, Mr. D., you set me free—I don't believe I really said that. You don't even know. . ." Dylan replies, "I don't wanna know. . . why don't you give Paul Simon a chance?"

Bette was very proud of the album. "It was a great learning experience. On the first two albums, I really wasn't there most of the time. I would come in and do my vocals and go home because I didn't know anything about recording studios. This time, however, I got involved. It forced me to think about what I wanted to do with my music. It also taught me to trust my singing. I was full of self-doubt. I had considered myself a performer, but not necessarily a singer or musician. This record contains some of the best singing I have done, and that made me happy. It filled me with positivism. . ."

Bette and the staggering Harlettes—"the three least depressing aspects of my entire existence"—Sharon Redd, Ula Hedwig and Charlotte Crossley.

Unfortunately, the reviews of the album were filled with negativism; most of the critical reaction to *Songs* was scathing. Steven Gaines wrote in the New York *Sunday News*, "*Songs for the New Depression* doesn't lift mine, financial or psychological. From the art design down to the music on the album, it's a hipper-than-thou package that uses more energy being chic than it does being musical. . . during some of the songs, like the reggae 'Marahuana' or 'Buckets of Rain'. . . you get the feeling you could be listening to a Lily Tomlin comedy album. . . On most of the eleven cuts Midler sounds as if she had nasal congestion or she had regressed to age seven through hypnosis. For a gifted thirty-year-old, that's too infantile. . ."

David Tipmore, in *The Village Voice*, was equally disdainful:". . . each song is like a petite showcase for future movie roles, demonstrating a supposedly versatile actress who, moreover, can carry a tune. . . this extensive posturing makes Midler sound absolutely unavailable: distant, electronic, hoarse, and scared. . . this is not unpredictable. Any 'actress' who also sings is not at home in a recording studio. She needs the dimension of theater to fully incorporate her personality into her product. . . [*Songs*] is the first record I have ever heard which aims for an Academy Award. And as such, the record was a big mistake."

Even Aaron Russo wasn't happy with the album. "Bette loves that album," he said. "I didn't care for it, didn't think it was something the public wanted to hear, and I didn't think they got the essence of Bette Midler on it. The choice of material was not the best, the production wasn't particularly terrific and I thought it was something she was doing for her own satisfaction, as opposed to the public's. I didn't feel anything commercial on that album. . ."

Although there was some favorable reaction, Aaron was right: the record was a major sales disappointment. It failed to enter the Top Forty, and the "Strangers in the Night" single fared equally poorly. It was the first failure Bette had suffered since the beginning of her career, and it depressed her, especially because of the very personal nature of the project. The rest of the tour was somewhat bittersweet: the thrill of the cheering adulation of thousands of people in theaters all across the country was dampened by the knowledge that relatively few people were buying her new album.

The pressures Bette was under—worrying about the record, the rigors of touring, her constant agitation with Aaron—took their toll, and sometimes came out on stage. Charlotte recalls, "Bette could be very schizophrenic on stage. Sometimes we'd see this other personality come out for two or three days at a time. Sometimes she'd be really vicious to the audience, and we'd have to tell her, 'You can't do these things—you're alienating your audience.' And then she'd be remorseful about it—she's not one of those people who can cause harm and not feel the pain of it all."

There was more drama to come on this very *lively* tour. On February 15th, seven members of the troupe—three musicians and four technicians—were arrested by Buffalo police after a raid uncovered a half-ounce of cocaine and one-and-a-half pounds of marijuana in their Holiday Inn room. The police said that while they were on a ramp in an adjacent parking lot investigating a stolen-car complaint, they spotted the drugs by looking in the window.

Aaron Russo was having none of it. He told the press that the arrests constituted part of an anti-vice crusade. "They're against pinball machines here," he said. "The other day they busted three people at a bus stop for reading pornographic magazines. So you can see what's happening. There is no ramp. And they'd have to be pretty tall to peek into a third-floor window...the whole thing seems to be a set-up of some kind, as if the vice squad here was simply waiting for an opportunity to put on their own show for the good citizens of Buffalo...Most towns are liberal in this day and age, and really don't care if they see a musician who seems a little high. But Buffalo is in the midst of this silly anti-vice crusade."

"You know why they got busted," says Charlotte, "because Aaron refused to pay somebody off. And the next night there were plainclothes cops all around the theater, this rickity little theater, and we were just *pissed*. There were these huge headlines. I remember we took the train to New York and my roommate met me at the train station with the newspaper, and it was like right out of some forties movie. She handed me the New York *Post*: 'Bette Midler Troupe Busted in Buffalo.' It was *unbelievable*." The charges against the guys were later reduced, and the matter was settled with a minimum of hassle.

Two days later, a happier occasion: Bette went to Harvard to accept the Hasty Pudding Theatrical Club's award as "Woman of the Year." Driven through the streets of Cambridge in an open car to the cheers of dozens, Bette accepted the award, a gold Boston bean pot. "I showered, shaved and FDS'd myself into a stupor, just to get a crock?" she asked. "This award characterizes what the American male wants in a woman—brains, talent and gorgeous tits." Bette was also awarded a gold lamé brassiere—which she made Club vice-president Chris Ruppenthal put on over his sports jacket—and third-row seats to the Club's traditional drag musical.

Bette proclaimed the whole thing "the most tasteful event with which my name has ever been associated"—and then, as *Time* put it, "showed her class" by twirling on stage to reveal a panty-less derrière. The Hasty Pudding men had met their match. As Boston *Herald American* reporter Harold Banks wrote, "First of all, if I quoted her it wouldn't get into the paper. And if it happened to get into the paper, I'd get fired."

On this tour, it seems, there's a story for practically every city. Bette tells one of them: "In St. Louis, I was on stage for three-and-one-half hours. And I was bombed, just bombed. I was angry and unhappy and I took it out on this poor audience in St. Louis. I was discombobulated. The longer I would ramble on, the worse it got. At one point, I jumped into the audience, ran up the aisle, went to the candy counter in the lobby and bought a candy bar. I

OPPOSITE: Wailing the finale of "Delta Dawn."

112

walked back into the audience, had a dialogue with some shoe salesman and then I started talking to the crowd in a whiny, wasted little voice. *Oh, God!* They had to pull me back on stage. I kept thinking, Isn't this fun, this is the greatest! But no one was laughing because they couldn't believe what they were seeing. It was a scene. . . *so* tacky. After that they sort of clamped down on the booze and they said, 'No more for Miss M.' And anyone who gave me any drugs was going to be fired."

In Cleveland, Bette's show was taped for a Home Box Office television special and a live album. Introducing the Vickie Eydie segment, Bette said, "And now, the Plywood Room, high atop Swingo's Celebrity Motor Lodge in gorgeous downtown Seven Hills, is thrilled to present—"

"We *stayed* there!" Charlotte exclaims. "It's an actual place. Every room had a different theme. Bette stayed in the Elvis Presley room. It had all this *cheese* Italian furniture!"

While they were in Cleveland, the troupe was stranded in their hotel for a day because of a huge snowstorm. Ula remembers that everybody had dinner and then went to the hotel lounge for drinks. "One of our group got up and sang a song, and then everybody sort of expected that we'd all get up. Everybody looked at me and I didn't want to, so Aaron and another guy carried me *bodily* to the dance floor and I did something stupid like 'Summertime.'

"Then we all said, 'C'mon, Bette,' and she said, 'No, I can't'—she had on a wool cap and leg warmers, and she got away with not singing. But toward the end of the evening, we'd all had a few drinks, and there were about five businessmen in the room, and Bette got up and sang for *an hour*. These men had *no idea* who was up there. If they had, they probably would have paid attention. Before long, we were all up there, doing the show, singing 'Leader of the Pack' and everything. The waiters and waitresses were standing around watching—*they* knew who we were.

"Then after everybody left, Bette got up on the stage again and sang for another hour, just her and the piano player. They did a lot of blues. It was *wonderful*."

After a show in Detroit, the members of Bette's company got word that there would be an important meeting with Bette and Aaron. As Ula recalls, "We all got dressed real quick after the show and went to this big meeting room. There was going to be a party after the meeting, and there was food out on the table, and crepe paper hanging across the ceiling.

"We were told to sit down, Bette would be here shortly, this was a very important meeting. And we're wondering, 'What could this be?' The door opens, and there is Bette, in her green bathrobe and a shower cap, carrying a cream pie in her hand, and there's a man behind her with a *tray* full of cream pies. She goes, 'You're wondering why I gathered you all here'—and throws a pie at us. A major pie fight starts, and Sharon and Charlotte and I are screaming and hiding behind these big amps in the room—we had our *good* clothes on. The crew, they had flannel shirts on, and they're *pummeling* each other with these pies.

"I just hid behind the amp and took pictures. Then when the pies were gone, I came out and for some reason there was a water gun that I picked up and squirted at somebody. So that started a *food* fight with the stuff that was on the catering table. What a *mess*. Everybody was soaked, and the crepe paper was falling down on the people and the dye was running all over them. The room was in a *shambles*. I felt sorry for the people who had to *clean* it. I

OPPOSITE: As Miss Liberty, Bette sings "Friends" in the finale of the "Depression" show.

114

don't know what possessed Bette to do that—she just got into a goofy mood, I guess."

Bruce Vilanch adds, "Ever since that first food fight in Detroit, it was a tradition. And Detroit always seems to be the place where *strange* things happen during our tours."

One of the reasons Bette may have staged the food fight was to relieve some of the pressures of touring. Certainly, the tensions between her and Aaron were always present. "Once when we were in Vancouver," Charlotte recalls, "Aaron said something to her that she didn't like and she walked over to him and *punched him in the stomach*. In front of God and everybody. She screamed at him 'You fat SOB' and just went *whomp*. And my heart went out to him, because he stood there and *took it*. He took it, I'm telling you.

"He would go through periods where he would be immaculately dressed every day for weeks, then we'd get on the road and, just to be rebellious, just to get her goat, he didn't bathe for days and days. He'd come in looking like something the dog dragged in, and she'd say, 'Why do you bother to come in and check on me when you look like shit and you smell?' And she would humiliate him in front of the whole company—just saying the most horrible things about him in front of *everybody*. We'd all laugh about it, but privately, we thought it was pretty sad.

"He said to me, 'Why does she treat me this way?' And I said, 'Because you dig it. Because you come back for it more and more. You can handle her in a lot more effective way, one that's a lot gentler.' But then I thought about it and I said, 'But maybe she won't let you.'"

The tensions between Aaron and the rest of Bette's troupe would come to a serious head on the last stop of the Depression Tour—Las Vegas, Vickie Eydie's spiritual home. Things were bad all around because Vegas audiences, as usual, weren't as responsive to Bette's show as most others. "Vegas was a debacle," Bruce Vilanch says. "It was like two weeks in Viet Nam. They weren't ready for her—they're never ready for anybody. The *cognoscenti* who came up from Los Angeles on weekends loved it, but during the week it was *death*. There were dinner shows on Tuesday with 400 Japanese tourists. Las Vegas is like that. Half the people there don't know who you are if they haven't seen you on television every week. They just figure you must be good or you wouldn't be headlining there.

"A lot of people thought there should be more glamour in the show, and the only time there was any was when she was doing Vickie Eydie, which was parodying Vegas—which they *really* didn't get. Bette's timing would really get thrown off.

"Plus, in Vegas she suddenly got the reputation for being a *dirty act*. Across the street, Buddy Hackett is telling fart jokes and all kinds of off-color material, but she was being called bawdy and worse. She and I got into a cab, and of course no one recognizes Bette when she's off stage. The driver said, 'You seen that gal who's working at Caesar's? Geez, what a mouth! *Filthy!*' And Bette is sinking into her seat."

There were, of course, many people who found the show fabulous—including some of the Caesar's Palace staff, who were seen running around during the first act saying, "This is the best show we've ever had!" But onstage, the gig was only partially successful—and backstage, it was a disaster.

"There was a money dispute between Aaron and a lot of people in Bette's troupe," Vilanch relates. "No one was getting any money from the Home Box Office special or the live album, which they felt they deserved, and Aaron

Bette mocks the
attitude of the Harlettes
as she introduces
them to the audience.

wouldn't listen, apparently. Finally it came down to people threatening to stop working because of it. He went to her and said, 'They're all against you,' and she freaked out. She had no idea what was going on. He had kept all this from her. All he told her was that her people were trying to screw her, rip her off. It caused a lot of bad blood. I myself wasn't getting any extra compensation for the Home Box Office special, and I thought what Aaron did was wrong. Bette and I barely spoke for a year because of all that."

According to many of those involved, the Cleveland taping was supposed to have been for Bette's personal use, and when it wound up being sold to cable television for airing, all those involved in the show rightfully felt they should be a part of the additional profits—and they felt the same way about the live album. Charlotte Crossley relates another money dispute with Russo which resulted, as Vilanch puts it, in "a vicious fight, on the floor, screaming and throwing things . . ."

According to Charlotte, the main problem in Vegas was that "we agreed to do Vegas for our usual rate of pay, and we travelled one day to get there. He *docked* us for that travel day—the stagehands and everybody. That wasn't right, and everyone was angry—there was already a lot of animosity among the company. Especially because, here he was wanting to dock our pay and he was going around just being flamboyant and obnoxious, playing the casino tables. He came into Bette's dressing room with a bagful of $100 chips and poured them out on her table. She said, 'You give these girls some chips,' and he *reluctantly* gave us some.

"He created all this antagonism, so that when he wanted to dock our pay we had just had it, and some of the stagehands started rumbling about not working. So he goes back to her between shows and tells her, 'They don't give a fuck about you—they're gonna strike for more money and not do the second show. Charlo doesn't give a damn about you...'

"Well, she doesn't know what is going on and she just got livid, and the first person she came after was me. She stormed into our dressing room and just *attacked* me and Ula. She screamed, 'After all the years of our friendship!' I saw red. We got into a fistfight, and they had to separate us. I went, 'I can't wait to feel my nails digging into your flesh!'—I'm telling you, it was *intense*.

"We finally got it all settled, but man, we had to go out and do a second show, and we were all crying, and finally we went in and told her what Aaron had done and *she* made sure that we were compensated. None of it had been her fault. My boyfriend wanted me to leave after that. But we all stuck it out, because of Bette."

Although Bette continually had to deal with crisis situations like this one, she still felt at this point that Aaron was a vital contributor to her ability to function in the show business pressure cooker. He handled the everyday business affairs of her career—something she did not want to be bothered with—and he was, according to Bette, an important creative ally as well.

"I consider myself lucky," Bette said, "because he pays a lot of attention to me—he doesn't have any other clients, you know. He thinks I'm the greatest thing on God's green earth...It's rough sometimes. I won't say it isn't rough—but it's satisfying in the long haul because of the caliber of work we do. Our shows are consistently good, and they prove that this whole thing wasn't just a flash in the pan...I could go on forever with what he's built for me. I mean, I will always be able to work. The fact that I don't have a hit record one year isn't going to make a lot of difference to a career like mine. That's what Aaron has given me, so I consider myself not only lucky but blessed."

Aaron said in 1978, "We still fight on the average of once a day. The usual reason is that I have to tell her things that nobody else will tell her, and who wants to hear that kinda crap? But there's a very deep love between us, and...I think I would die for the woman. If it came right down to it, I'd give up my life for hers."

Bette took another long period off after the Depression Tour, which must have been sorely needed. Her only public exposure for the rest of the year was on television. ABC had been courting Midler for years to sign for a series of specials, but, fearing that her show would be too risqué for network censors, they refused to allow her the creative freedom she demanded. The obvious solution for Bette was cable television, the new, uncensored subscription service.

On June 19, Home Box Office aired a two-hour-nineteen-minute tape of the Depression show, completely unexpurgated. *The Fabulous Bette Midler Show* came as close as is probably possible to capturing the Midler onstage magic, and it created a furor, winning effusive reviews from critics and dazzling viewers who had never seen Bette as she *really* is. George Maskian wrote in the New York *Daily News*, "Rush on down to the nearest bar, or a friend's house, anyone who has Home Box Office and see the sensation of the

OPPOSITE: Revealing her assets as she accepts the Harvard "Hasty Pudding Award" as Woman of the Year, February 1976.

'70s . . . Miss M really doesn't have to rely on the risqué. Her other talents are too vast and great. She's Martha Raye, Carmen Miranda, Fanny Brice and Judy Garland—all rolled into one. . . To sum up, Bette is a wow!"

The next Midler television appearance wasn't nearly as successful: the Neil Sedaka network special on September 17. It started out well enough, with Bette doing an effective restaging of the "Drinking Again" sequence from *Clams*, complete with mannequins. But her segment with Sedaka bordered on the embarrassing. Like Vickie Eydie, Bette here seemed "trapped in an act not of her own design." She and Sedaka emoted over something that was "bigger than both of us," and Bette announced what it was: lunch. "In fact, you can tell everyone that I'm out to lunch." She then walked off, and after a card appeared on the screen reading "Three weeks later," she returned carrying a picnic basket filled with fried chicken.

"Bette, don't tempt me with your breasts and thighs," Sedaka quipped. Then he and Bette did a duet of his lame hit "Love Will Keep Us Together." Sedaka's soprano warble did little to complement Midler's voice, and though Bette did her best to inject some funkiness into a dance routine, Sedaka's hamminess and painful lack of soul defeated her. She seemed to know it, too: during the routine, she looked at him and asked, "Where's the chicken?"

It was not Bette's finest hour (nor television's), but it did not reflect badly on Midler. During the rest of 1976, Bette made plans for a new album, prepared to make her debut as a singer with George Balanchine's New York City Ballet—and became involved in an important new romance.

OPPOSITE: With Neil Sedaka on his TV special, September 1976.

Thirteen

After Bette had recovered sufficiently from the turbulence of 1976, she began making some interesting career plans. An acceptable network television contract was worked out with NBC, and taping was set to begin on the first Bette Midler special in May.

First, though, Bette announced an unusual project. She would sing and dance—a little—in the New York City Ballet's production of the light opera *The Seven Deadly Sins*, by Kurt Weill and Bertolt Brecht. Bette and the celebrated director of the ballet, George Balanchine, held a press conference to announce her participation. Explaining the unusual choice of Midler, Balanchine said, "Bette could do anything."

"I'm in shock! I'm in awe!" Bette exclaimed. "I expected him to be quite grand, aloof, staid. He's really down-to-earth. And what a wicked sense of humor. And the cold sweat that breaks out on those little ballerinas' faces when he passes by—you know you're not dealing with just another person. The way they feel has rubbed off on me."

Bette and Balanchine posed for an evocative series of dual portraits for famed photographer Richard Avedon, and Bette began rehearsals despite a threatened strike by the ballet musicians' union. It materialized, and when negotiations dragged on, Bette was forced to cancel because of her television commitment. "I was just getting down my moves," she said sadly. "There are movers who sing, singers who dance, and dancers who move while they sing—and trashy people who get away with everything. Honey, all I wanted to do was just open my mouth and *circulate*. . ." It was hoped that Bette's appearance in the ballet could be rescheduled, but nothing was ever worked out.

Bette had been receiving a great deal of press attention in New York, and one item in Liz Smith's gossip column in February raised Bette's ire. Smith had reported Bette's new romance with actor Peter Riegert, whom she had met in October. Midler gave Smith a blistering phone call, according to Liz, "wailing that such publicity 'only serves to ruin the relationship.'"

"Let's be realistic," Bette later said. "I don't think the public is craving to know who I sleep with or what I ate for breakfast. My God, look at Cher. She can't even break a nail without having to give an interview about it. That stuff takes all the mystery away."

Liz Smith reported the phone call in her column, of course, and added: "Naturally, I don't agree with Bette, but I'm glad to present her point of view. As much as I admire Bette's extraordinary work—and have since the first moment of her early fame at the Continental Baths—I think when you are a colorful performer you have to accept some public interest in your colorful life. . .people want to know more about [performers'] inside story and the way they live offstage."

Bette met Riegert, who later went on to fame as the social chairman in *Animal House*, while he was performing off-Broadway in the show *Sexual Perversity in Chicago*. "There was this guy with this beautiful face and this great body and these gorgeous eyes and this wonderful manner," Bette gushed. After the show, she went backstage to meet him and said, "Well, why don't we just go out for a little drinkie, what do you say?"

They got drunk together, and Bette, more forward than usual, asked him for

Bette arrives with Paul Bloch
at the 1977 Grammy Awards, at which
she stole the show by
descending a staircase with a 20-foot
train on her gown.

his number so she could call him up. "Sometimes I think I'm turning into a man," she said.

Before long, Bette and Peter were living together, and it was the most satisfying relationship Bette had ever been in. "I'm having a ball right now," she said. "I wake up and have to pinch myself all the time. I can't believe it."

Peter and Bette discovered quickly that they had a rare rapport. They constantly went to late-night movies together, and when other forms of amusement weren't available, they entertained each other. "We give each other a show every night until we collapse about four in the morning," Bette said. "We get totally caught up in characters that we invent, jokes that we tell each other. Peter is the first man I've really felt this way about—been able to be myself with.

"He and I have a relationship that's utterly painless. We're great companions—we keep each other company, and we lift each other up when we're down, and it's very simple and straightforward. There's none of the game crap between us. . .I love to talk to him and look at him, and I think I even understand him. I can see why people get married now that I have Pete."

123

In May, Bette made a guest appearance on a Bing Crosby television special. It was a wonderful stint, everything that the *Neil Sedaka Show* appearance was not. Dressed as an usherette, Bette begins to sing along in the audience as Crosby is crooning "Attitude of Doing Right."

"Now, there's a child that really got the message," Crosby says. "Oh, I'm sorry, I don't know what came over me," Bette says. It happens again, and Crosby invites her up on the stage, asking if she knows "Accentuate the Positive." "Yes sir," she replies shyly, "I know every word."

"I suppose you're going to tell me your mother sang it to you when you were a baby."

"No sir, my grandmother sang it to my mother when *she* was a baby."

"Would you like to have a go at it with me?"

"You want to sing with *me*? Oh, I couldn't, after all you're *Bing Crosby* and I'm just a little usherette trying to make ends meet. I'll just stand over here and worship you from up close."

Bette did join him for a charming duet, then Bing asked her how she knew all the words. "Music is my life. Music and ushering. Actually, I know songs older than that. I know songs from the turn of the century."

"I know *people* from the turn of the century," Crosby replied.

Bette then did a solo—"Glow Worm," complete with a skin-tight sequinned blue dress with a bow in back which lit up whenever she sang, "Glow little glow worm, glimmer, glimmer." Midway through the song, the Mills Brothers joined her to complete it, to great effect. "I don't believe it," Bette cried. "Me and Bing Crosby and the Mills Brothers on the same stage." Then she grabbed Crosby's arm and said in her best Divine Miss M voice, "I think I am going to *pass out!*"

Bette then asked Crosby to sing "Dinah."

"Do you want to join us?"

"Oh, no, honey," Bette replied. "I'm gettin' tired of carrying you guys." And off she walked. It was a totally captivating turn for all concerned.

Bruce Vilanch recalls Bette hearing from her mother that this was one of the first times in years that her father had watched Bette on television. "I suppose he thought if she's appearing with Bing Crosby, how offensive could she be?," Vilanch says. "And Bette's mother said her dad enjoyed it."

In June, Bette's two-record *Live at Last* album was released, to excellent reviews. Robert Hillburn said, "*Live at Last* finally documents on record the captivating spirit and enormous talent that Midler has long exhibited on stage."

Frank Rose in the *Village Voice* added, "Her singing here has a limpid, liquid quality that never made it onto her previous recordings. She sounds spontaneous—eager and breathless...one-half dewy-eyed ingenue, one-half master of boogie. She is screamingly funny. Her timing is perfect, her ability to play off herself unfailing—no need for a straight man here. The set is sensational."

In addition to the Cleveland show, the album contains a bonus "intermission" of a song written by Bette, Carole Bayer Sager and Bruce Roberts, "You're Moving Out Today." Peter Reilly in *Stereo Review* called the song, released as a single, "the most amusing/touching song since 'Second Hand Rose,' and it is as irresistible as its singer."

"I have never been prouder of anything I did in my whole life than I am of that single," Bette said. "It's scary and exciting, and it's all the nicest things you hope will happen. You ring up the record company and ask, 'Oh, how's my little record doing?' And you look at the charts, and it's really great. I tell ya, it's

OPPOSITE: Singing "Glow Worm" on the Bing Crosby Special, May 1977.

like the pros."

Unfortunately, the single fared very poorly on the charts, but *Live at Last*, while not a blockbuster, did much better than *Songs for the New Depression*, cracking *Billboard's* Top Forty. As Peter Reilly predicted, the album became "the watershed album in Midler's career." It is the one record on which every facet of Bette Milder's incredibly multi-dimensional appeal is captured, and in its broad spectrum it may indeed rank as one of the two or three finest live albums ever recorded.

By now, Bette Midler was an international superstar, and her beginnings as a gay cult figure were merely an interesting footnote to her career. But Midler herself always felt a debt of gratitude to her gay fans, and in September of 1977, she had an opportunity to give something very special back to the community: she and Aaron decided to produce a "Night for Rights" at the Hollywood Bowl. The show would star Bette, Lily Tomlin, Richard Pryor, David Steinberg, Tom Waits and others, and raise money to help fight the Anita Bryant-led fundamentalist Christian forces who were attempting—with some success—to reverse many of the advances made in gay civil rights across the country.

Aaron Russo produced the benefit. "I was so proud of him pulling it together," Bette said. "The logistics were next to impossible, and he worked like a dog for weeks on end."

On September 18, 17,000 people jammed the huge outdoor theater—including Paul Newman, Robert Blake, Paul Lynde, Olivia Newton-John, Rona Barrett and many other liberal Hollywood celebrities—and paid $25 to $50 a seat to help fight prejudice against lesbians and gay men.

The evening started off wonderfully, with Lily Tomlin touching the crowd deeply by saying, "In the '50s, no one was gay—only shy" and telling a moving and funny story of her crush on one of her female grammar school teachers. After the Los Angeles Ballet and the Lockers, Richard Pryor made his entrance. His monologue, delivered with his patented scatology, was nonetheless funny, and surprising—Pryor chided the other performers on the bill for failing to admit to homosexual experiences, and he proceeded to tell about some of his own, much to the delight of the audience.

But then, something went wrong. Pryor's monologue lost its direction, and he began to ramble. Suddenly, he turned ugly. "We got a lot of faggots in the ghetto, but not a single homosexual. Niggers don't want nothing to do with homosexuality." The audience, confused, began to murmur. "All I see are white faces out there. There's only a nigger here and a nigger there." He suggested that the audience was racist because they had given a bigger hand to the white ballet troupe than the black Lockers.

There were catcalls from the audience, and Pryor's vitriol got worse. "Fuck you," he called back. "When the niggers were burning down Watts, you motherfuckers were doing what you wanted on Hollywood Boulevard and didn't give a shit about it."

After vicious remarks about women's rights, Pryor said, "I wanted to come here and tell you to kiss my ass with your bullshit. Ya understand? Kiss my happy, rich black ass." And he walked off the stage.

The audience was shocked into total silence, which hung in the air like a foul odor. Because Pryor had left the stage early, there was a long wait for the next act—Tom Waits—which allowed the audience to stew in its numbed puzzlement. Co-producer Ron Field came onstage to apologize, and so did Aaron Russo—but to say that a damper was put on the evening would be ab-

Bette and the Harlettes
do their "Philadelphia Medley" for the
"*Rolling Stone* Tenth
Anniversary Special," November 1977.

OPPOSITE: Onstage with Lily
Tomlin at the "Night for Rights"
concert.

surd understatement. Bette Midler was scheduled after Waits, and the shock and confusion backstage was no less than that in the audience.

Bruce Vilanch recalls standing in the wings with Lily Tomlin, watching Pryor. "I thought to myself, This is turning, when Pryor called Anita Bryant a 'cunt.' Lily turned on her heels and went back to her dressing room at that point – she'd had enough. Bette came out of her dressing room with curlers in her hair and asked me, 'What is he *doing*?'"

"I was talking to Richard backstage before he went on," Charlotte relates, "and I thought he was being real weird and aggressive and cruisy. I suppose, with his history, it would be safe to say he was on something. I don't think he wanted to be there. There weren't too many black people on the bill, and he was looking for black people to relate to."

Pryor's actions created a great deal of tension and apprehension backstage. "Aaron walked up to me," Charlotte says, "and asked me why he did it. I said, 'Aaron, Richard Pryor isn't a friend of mine. I don't know how he feels. Why

the fuck are you looking at *me?* Do you think because I'm black I have an answer to that question? Well, I don't.'"

All three Harlettes were worried about the audience reaction to their planned opening bit–especially Charlotte. "After this totally derogatory, homophobic, sexist, racist, anti-human diatribe by Richard Pryor, we were supposed to go out there dressed in *Klu Klux Klan* outfits, dragging Bette, who was dressed as the Statue of Liberty, bound and gagged. I was supposed to be the first one out, and I'm thinking, Somebody's gonna *shoot* me. It was a great idea, but after what happened, I didn't know if the audience would misconstrue it at first, or what. I thought there was gonna be a riot after what he'd done, and I was afraid we'd just re-ignite the audience's anger, you know. That didn't happen once we got out there, but the audience didn't react very much to the humor of what we were doing."

It was without doubt the toughest thirty minutes Bette Midler had ever had on stage. "We *hauled ass* through that set," Charlotte says. "We even cut a couple of songs."

"I was in my dressing room running lines with the PA system off," Bette said. "I had no idea that anything unusual was happening until one of the Harlettes came back and told me Richard Pryor had walked off the stage and told the audience to kiss his 'rich black ass.'

"Hmn, I thought...that's interesting. I've said worse than that to a lot of folks, and so, not at all grasping the context of how he'd said it, I went on stage and said, 'Who'd like to kiss my rich white ass?'

"I sensed right away that something else was going on out there besides me...something scary. Still, I really didn't have any idea how deeply Pryor had offended the audience until after the show when somebody described to me what happened, and then I went into shock, too."

Bette's set–she introduced 'Red,' did several of her hits, some Sophie Tucker and Anita Bryant jokes–was not nearly as well received as it would have been under normal circumstances. Knowing something was wrong, Bette said at the end of her truncated appearance–during which she cut both her knees, requiring bandages–"We're all tired; it's been a long evening. Don't you want to go home? I think I really need a few friends." She then called back Lily, David Steinberg, Tom Waits and several others for a reprise of "Friends."

"The evening should have been a 10," Charlotte says. "Richard made it a 1, and Bette brought it back up to a 6. But we didn't save the day. There was just a pervasive sense of loss all around, a feeling that Pryor had ruined what should have been a very special evening."

Keith Lyle, who now works with Charlotte in connection with her new group Full Swing, remembers the party afterwards. "A lot of people didn't go, but Bette and Lily had to. People were coming up to Bette and trying to be real positive and say, 'You were so good,' and she was just going, 'Cut it out–*no.*' Lily was real pissed, and everybody was on her about *why*, because she and Richard are friends. She was in tears the next day, she was so upset about it."

Bette made her opinion of Pryor quite clear a little later. "...as to where all the heavies were during Watts, Pryor's manager was backstage that night and he said, 'I can tell you where Richard Pryor was during the Watts riots. He was at my house watching them on television.'...Mr. Pryor came to his consciousness a little late in life, too, and...he's a bit of a fraud."

Bette's next gig was considerably more successful: an appearance on a television special, "*Rolling Stone*: The Tenth Anniversary." She and the Har-

130

lettes, dressed in the same red Chinese print dresses they wore at the Hollywood Bowl after removing their Klan/Liberty costumes, sang "Red" and the "Uptown"/"Don't Say Nothing Bad About My Baby"/"Da Doo Run Run" medley. Bette also did a rock 'n' roll medley with Jerry Lee Lewis.

During the early fall of 1977, while Bette was preparing another interesting career move—a tour of small clubs across the country—a complication arose. Charlotte Crossley, Ula Hedwig and Sharon Redd had been striking out on their own as Formerly The Harlettes, making club appearances and cutting an album. "The consensus," Ula relates, "was that we should use the name Harlettes in some way at first, just for recognition, and then we would drop it. Sharon went to a lawyer to find out how we could use the name legally, and he suggested that we call ourselves Redd, Hedwig and Crossley—Formerly The Harlettes. I thought that was a real strange name for a group, but that's what we did."

Still, Aaron Russo was not pleased. Formerly The Harlettes were appearing at Hollywood's Studio One, Charlotte says, when Russo "stormed into our dressing room and started screaming at us that we couldn't use the name Harlettes, that we were ripping Bette off and he'd sue us."

Ula picks up the story from here: "We told him that we had been to a lawyer and that it was all legal and we weren't going to change our name. So then he sits down and tells us that if we let him *manage* us, we can keep the name. Charlotte gets up, opens the door, and says, 'Goodbye, Aaron.' He starts yelling again, 'You're thieves, I'm gonna sue you.' We said, 'You *try* to sue us!' and he just split.

"So then we were appearing at Reno Sweeney's and there's an item in the paper that Bette Midler is suing us. Well, this was news to us. They interviewed us on the TV and we said, 'We don't know anything about this. Bette Midler just came to *see* us. *She* doesn't care.'"

Still, Aaron's threats of a lawsuit—and his reasonable contention that the name Formerly The Harlettes might confuse people into thinking Bette no longer had a backup group by that name—resulted in a compromise. The group would be called Redd, Hedwig, Crossley—Formerly *of* the Harlettes.

That was, in fact, the name of their first album—and a terrific one it is—which had just been released as Bette began her club tour. Bette offered to allow the girls to open her show with a thirty-minute set of their own if they would also sing backup in her show. "We talked it over with our management," Ula says, "And we all agreed that it would be a great opportunity—it was a built-in audience. And the record had just come out. I'm sure we sold one or two records from going on the road with Bette."

"Bette was wonderfully supportive of us," Charlotte adds. "She wanted us to open for her—but Aaron didn't. He did everything in his power to sabotage us, because he didn't want us to steal any of Bette's limelight—he just wanted us to augment Bette. But we did that anyway. Our main commitment was to her. She was giving us a chance to be seen and we really needed that at the time. She said to him, 'I'm giving it to these girls. They stood by me. Now I want them to have it.'"

With these matters settled, Bette began her club tour. Both she and Aaron felt that this would not only save her energies, but return her to the intimate relationship with her audience which had started her on the road to stardom. "I had offers for Bette to play the huge halls—the Madison Square Gardens, the Forums," Aaron said, "but it didn't seem to make sense. We also didn't want to go back and play the medium-sized halls right now—so the clubs were a natural. That's really her milieu. She really comes alive on stage. Other things add to the excitement. The fact that she's playing a week in a city rather than just one or two nights means people are talking about the show all week. . . It stirs people up."

And stirred up they indeed were. Bette's club tour began in Vancouver and played San Francisco, Los Angeles, Chicago, Detroit and New York. It was hugely successful, taking in nearly $300,000 for her two California gigs alone—in San Francisco, scalpers were getting $100 for a $15 ticket. The intimacy of clubs added poignancy to her ballads and zing to her humor. In San Francisco, she said, "Everyone told me not to call this burg Frisco, that you natives just *hate* that—Well, *Frisco!Frisco! Frisco!*. . .Oh, I just love a city in a fog. You know that disco down the street called Dance Your Ass Off? I'm gonna open a joint just like that and call it Boogie Till You Puke. . .You hubba-hubba queens have been doing Quualudes again, haven't you? Kids, the sixties are *over*. . .

"Did I sing the ballad yet? Where was I? Oh, God, Oh, God—from the film of the same name. Starring Geoge Burns and John Denver. It's so good to know that George is still working with a dumb blond. . .I want to sing you a song now, so shut your tacky gobs. It's called 'La Vie En Rose,' and it shouldn't be confused with *La Viande Rose*, or *The Red Meat*, which is a very famous French film of the fifties about a young girl who longed to be a prima butcherina. Maestro? Hello? Is the band here yet?"

Bette celebrated her thirty-second birthday while appearing in San Francisco, and Charlotte recalls that the Harlettes gave her "a $200 Teddy bear from FAO Schwartz. It was as big as she was. We gave it to her on stage and she started rolling around the floor with it."

Bette's ten-day stint at the Roxy on Hollywood's Sunset Strip was an even greater success. Coupled with the airing of her first network television special, it put Los Angeles into a Midler frenzy. "Oh, I just love *El Lay*. You can always tell when you're approaching it because of the sound of 100,000 blowdryers wafting across the Hollywood Freeway. I moved here not too long back. I keep going to Tower Records to move all my albums from the Pop bin—where they rest next to Liza Minnelli—and put them in the rock bin, next to Joni Mitchell. I moved here because I wanted to break into the movies. They were going to star me in a movie called *Close Encounters of the Worst Kind*, but I declined. Then Roman Polanski offered me the lead in *Close Encounters with the Third Grade*. . .

"And Universal wanted me for the Pat Nixon story—*The Woman in the Iron Mask*. Quite a challenge—the actress who plays Pat isn't allowed to move her face for 200 years. Did I tell you I slept with Dick? Yeah, it lasted eighteen-and-a-half-minutes and it was quite painful—for *him*."

Robert Hilburn's review summed up the audience reaction well: "I know the critic's handbook says avoid absolutes, but there's no way around it this time. Bette Midler is the *best*. No other female performer has the range, vitality, or ultimately, the emotional impact. The only reason 'female' is used is that I haven't seen all the male contenders. But my suspicion is that it's an unnecessary qualification.

"As with all good performers, Midler responds to her audience. In San Francisco last weekend, the crowd at Bimbo's was—in the Divine Miss M's parlance—the *pits*. Not that it didn't enjoy itself and the show. But most people that night came to celebrate Midler's past. . .she wanted to move on, to explore new areas. Without the audience's concentration, however, it was im-

After the Roxy audience gives her a greaser jacket, a teddy bear and a rubber fried egg, Bette looks at them and asks, "Is this what you *really* think of me?"

OPPOSITE: Bette bursts out of the clamshell to the strains of "Oklahoma" as her first network television special opens.

"We are living proof that the moral standards by which this country lives have died."

possible. She had to repeat lines and underscore meanings in ways that broke her timing and overturned the subtlety. At the Roxy, the audience kept up with her. The difference was enormous. Rather than working to keep the audience alert, she was free to explore and maneuver. From the music to the jokes, the 90-minute set was crisply paced and strikingly executed."

During her December 8th show, Bette asked the audience, "Anyone see *Baretta* last night?" Robert Blake's popular series was scheduled opposite Bette's NBC special. "Did you like my special" she asked to cheers. "I did. . . I was real proud of it. The network was very nice, too. The only thing they asked me not to do was mention drugs. Gee. . . I didn't realize drugs were the enemy in television. I thought they were the *sponsor*."

Bette's special *Ol' Red Hair Is Back*, produced by Gary Smith and directed by Dwight Hemion (who had helmed most of Streisand's television specials) was a gorgeously mounted show which showed Midler off to wonderful advantage while diluting surprisingly little of her bawdiness. She had said, "I really want to do a shabby show, a really sleazy, tacky, shabby show. But the networks are a bit conservative. They want Johnny Mann, they want the Ding-A-Lings. I want sleaze, I want sequins. We'll see how it works out."

At first, it seemed as though it might not work out at all. Bette was terribly frustrated by the network strictures, especially on her humor. She called Bruce Vilanch in desperation: "She told me, 'They don't know what I'm about, Bruce. They don't understand me. I need you to help me.'

"I was torn, because I hadn't worked with Bette since what happened with Aaron in Vegas. But I felt for her, because I know that she needs people who are in tune with her, and she didn't have me, and Ula was the only Harlette she had worked with recently who did that show. So I just decided to bury the hatchet for Bette's sake, and I helped out. And I'll tell you, Aaron treated me wonderfully from then on. I guess he appreciated my coming through when she needed me.

"She was very apprehensive. She'd never done anything on TV as grand as a special, and Aaron had done only the Manhattan Transfer series, and she was worried. The biggest problem was that she felt, like Vickie Eydie, 'trapped in an act not of her own design.' On a TV special, everything has to be big and grand and slick, and that wasn't Bette—she had been unhappy about those aspects of her *Clams* show, and that's why she pared it down for the 'Depression' tour.

"A perfect example were the orchestrations. Bette came in with these ancient charts that Barry had done on *papyrus*, all yellow and crumbling, stuff she'd used in her *nightclub* tours. Of course, they had Peter Matz and they wanted all new orchestrations. Peter did this grand, sweeping, gorgeous arrangement—with tons of strings—for 'Shiver Me Timbers.' It was a lush, beautiful chart—but it wasn't right for 'Shiver Me Timbers.' The beauty of that song when Bette does it is its simplicity. That didn't cause a problem—Peter is a pro and a great guy and he understood Bette's objections, and we went back to the old arrangement—but it was just symptomatic of what Bette was having to deal with.

"Bette had a deal with ABC as far back as 1973, and I remember sitting on the plane with her and Barry and planning the special we were gonna call *Bette Midler—You Gotta Have Friends*. All of Bette's friends would be on it—Barry, Melissa, the Andrews Sisters, the Pointer Sisters, Manhattan Transfer, Peter Allen. And there was going to be a bar sequence—which evolved into 'Drinking Again' in *Clams*, and lots of Hawaiian stuff, which of course got used later.

After filming this segment, Bette decided to wear a corset and leotards rather than this chiffon prom gown, which interfered with her movement.

But needless to say, it never came about—and if it had, at that time, the guests probably would have been Loretta Swit and the Johnny Mann Singers."

Despite Bette's fears, *Ol' Red Hair* turned out beautifully, a seemingly perfect blend of what a TV network wants in a special and the very singular elements that made Bette Midler a phenomenon. Bette not only got her sequins (a gown designed by Bob Mackie) and some stunningly beautiful sets (including a backdrop for "La Vie En Rose" complete with Gustav Klimt paintings) but also just enough sleaziness and questionable taste to put the inimitable Midler stamp on the show. While Bette did have to launder her jokes a bit (instead of FDS'ing themselves into a stupor, the girls *gargled* themselves into a stupor) she got away, by television standards, with murder.

"Try to remain vertical, girls, at least until the first commercial," Bette tells the Harlettes. After "In the Mood," she lies face-up on the floor—"My favorite position"—and says "How does Marie Osmond do it? You mean she doesn't do it? I heard that she *did!*...I promised myself I would never sink this low again—but old habits die hard. Ain't that right, girls?" The Harlettes respond with their patented whine, "Unnh hunnnh."

"Oh, my girls. So verbal, so articulate, so rife with *bons mots*. I told my girls, I said, 'Girls, I want my show to be illuminating, uplifting, I want the show to be a vindication of Tolstoy's innocence.' I want an hour devoted to the twin deities of truth"—she points to one breast—"and beauty"—she points to the other. "Talk about your *big events*."

All the while, Midler has a twinkle in her eye—she knows she's coming *real* close to the TV borderline. At one point she says, "We're gonna shake *everything we own* for you tonight" with just the slightest pause to allow her faithful to fill in "our tits" where it usually goes.

"One of the reasons Bette wanted someone like me around, I think," says Vilanch, "is that she needed someone to tell NBC that yes, we can get away with certain things. The show was going to be on at 10 p.m., and we just pushed and pushed to keep certain things in. And we got away with a lot more than most people. I'll never forget, a while later I was working on another NBC show and I was talking to the NBC censor, who was cutting 'your ass' out of the script. She said, 'That's the anatomical ass, we can't have that.' It seems that if you're referring to a donkey, or even someone making a fool of themselves, it's okay, but the 'anatomical ass' is taboo. So I said to her, 'I've done that before.' 'Not on NBC you haven't.' 'Oh yes, on the Bette Midler special she sang "I don't care if I'm hungry and freezing my ass" during "Friends."'

"And the woman said, 'Oh, she couldn't have—we have a hard-and-fast rule about the anatomical ass,' and it went on and on like that. It was one of those conversations you read about in people's memoirs and you don't believe they actually took place. It did.

"But I think NBC made a conscious decision that if they were going to do a Bette Midler special, they would have to relax some of those strictures. And that's what happened."

The show opened with a scantily-clad Bette popping out of the clamshell, after which guest Emmett Kelly helped Bette introduce "Friends." Later, Bette sang "La Vie En Rose," looking lovely in a red satin gown. Then guest Dustin Hoffman and Bette sang a duet of a song they'd written together, "Shoot the Breeze."

Afterwards, Hoffman insists on playing Rachmaninoff's "Prelude in C-Sharp Minor," despite Bette's protestations that he has to change into their formal attire for their waltz. So, while he plays, Bette strips him to his underwear and redresses him in a tuxedo. Hoffman's appearance ends with a lovely waltz, which they complete by posing to recreate one of the Klimt paintings on the wall, "The Kiss."

"Originally, Laurence Olivier had agreed to be Bette's co-star," Vilanch recalls, "but at the last minute he called her and said, 'I've got an offer to do a movie in Brazil and they're paying me a lot of money. I'm old and I'm sick and I have to think of my family.' Bette said to me, 'What can I do? Tell the man he shouldn't do a major movie for my little TV special?'"

The last segment has Bette singing "Do You Wanna Dance," wearing a fluffy blue housedress instead of the chiffon prom gown she had planned to wear, because she kept getting her heels caught in the material. Singing a rocking version of "Higher and Higher," Bette rips off the housedress to reveal a merry-widow corset and leotards. After "Boogie Woogie Bugle Boy," the Island natives from the opening return and carry Bette down a runway into the audience as confetti falls on everyone.

Ol' Red Hair Is Back was a big ratings winner and got excellent reviews. It won the Emmy Award as the Outstanding Variety Special of the 1977-1978 season. "Bette was in London when the awards took place," Bruce Vilanch says, "but Aaron flew back for the show. When he accepted the Emmy, he forgot to thank Bette. He never heard the end of it."

Bette Midler had conquered yet another entertainment medium. As a star of Broadway, records, the concert stage, clubs and television, the only frontier left to Midler was Hollywood. It wouldn't be long...

OPPOSITE: At the finale of her special, Bette is showered with confetti.

Fourteen

Bette's club tour continued apace as 1978 opened, heading for its culmination in New York. Compared to Bette's other tours, this one was calm and uneventful. It was a relatively short and simple tour, of course, and the pressure on Bette was lessened considerably. She was in an excellent frame of mind, delighted with the response to her special, looking forward to beginning her first movie–and, most of all, she was in love. Her relationship with Peter Riegert was in full flower, and it served to becalm Bette Midler remarkably.

"When he came around, we all breathed a *big* sigh of relief," Charlotte says. "It was important to us that that relationship be okay. When he wasn't around, she could get crazy, but she was very calm and normal when he was around. He was the sweetest man I've ever known who was involved in her life. He was so bright, so smart–he taught English and Drama before he became an actor. And he just loved her and said, 'I'm here for you.'

"We were always concerned about whoever it was in Bette's life, because we knew how it is on the road . . . you haven't seen your old man for a month and *you're a bitch*. And you literally don't have *time* to go out and pick up a piece. It gets real lonely.

"And Peter was always so concerned about Bette. He'd show up wherever we were and he'd take me aside and say, 'What's happening?' And I'd tell him, 'I'm just so glad you're here . . .' because I knew it would calm Bette down and make her happy."

Still, no Bette Midler tour would be complete without *some* drama. "There was an altercation between Aaron and Bill Graham in San Francisco," Charlotte recalls, "and Aaron threatened Bill Graham. You don't threaten Bill Graham. Bill Graham is one of the biggest rock promoters in the country, and a lot of the smaller promoters take their cue from him. Within twenty-four hours, the shit was out–all the promoters in the country had heard what happened.

"By the time we got to Los Angeles, Aaron had *bodyguards* around him because he was afraid of what might happen to him. He had these paid *goons* with him at the Roxy. And I thought, What is this? The Mafia? I tell you, it was very intimidating–and just *nuts*."

Nothing came of that, nor of another somewhat frightening occurrence. Ula remembers, "We were at the Roxy, and in the middle of the show, this big dyke person gets up on top of the table in front of the stage–where people are sitting and drinking–and *walks across it*, on to the stage, and gets Bette in a bear hug. Charlotte–you know Charlotte–comes to the rescue and screams at this woman, 'Okay, that's enough!' The woman just had this impulse to hug Bette and *went with it*. But that can be real scary.

"Another time, someone in the audience started throwing *green bagels* at the stage, and one of them konked Bette on the head. Well, she got pissed–she'd just gotten hit on the head with a *bagel*–and she ran off the stage. So the three of us just stood there going 'Oookay.' Bruce Vilanch threw a newspaper to us and we started reading it, 'cause nothing was happening. She came back out,

OPPOSITE: Famed Hollywood portrait photographer George Hurrell's unusual interpretation of the Midler countenance, 1977.

138

but she was really annoyed. Bagels are not soft."

The club tour ended in January at the Copacabana in New York. It had been almost six years since Bette Midler had played a club in New York, and she was welcomed back with a frenzy of adulation. The demand for tickets was so great that the Copa management felt justified in charging $20, plus a two $3 drink minimum, for admittance. According to Rex Reed, all was chaos: "It wasn't just crowded, it was miserable...long banquet tables with cheap fly-stained pink tableclothes were jammed against walls to accomodate the overflow while mobs pushed, shoved and groped their way along the narrow stairs in a reckless disregard of the fire regulations...my seats were so lousy that I could hardly see the backside of her left earlobe without a mariner's telescope...sweat poured down our faces and the smell was indescribable in a morning newspaper.

"Was it worth it? Well, it all depends on where you place your Bettes. I thought the girl was stupendous. Few contemporary performers could hold and electrify an audience under such intolerable conditions...For any act of less magic and magnitude, I would have walked out. Instead, Bette didn't get off until almost 3 a.m., and I stayed to revel in every delicious moment of her irreverence and showmanship."

Despite the conditions, most of Bette's audiences agreed—even Arthur Bell gave her a generally favorable notice this time—and Bette was once again the toast of Manhattan.

Since December, Bette's fifth album, *Broken Blossom*, had been in release. There were considerable problems during the recording of this album, which took nine months. Bette's rented house was broken into while she and Peter slept; the thief fled after Peter confronted him in the living room. Bette was so shaken by the incident that she moved to a hotel for several weeks until she felt safe enough to return.

Not too much later, the owner of the recording studio drowned in his swimming pool, and just a few hours later Bette got word that her friend Carole Bayer Sager had been in an automobile accident.

David Shaw, describing the scene in *Cosmopolitan*, wrote: "Bette's eyes widen in horror. Her face crumples. Her fingers fly to her cheeks—frantically, like so many tiny birds frightened by a sudden loud noise. To anyone who knows Bette's history, it's obvious what's running through her mind...'Is she dead?' The words are whispered, half in disbelief, half in resignation. [Producer] Brooks Arthur...puts a consoling hand on her shoulder. 'No, Bette,' he says. 'Everything's okay. Carole's going to be just fine.'"

Broken Blossom was arguably the slickest Midler album to date, with little of the rawness and emotion of Bette's first albums, and as such it elicited contradictory critical reactions. Steven Gaines said in *Circus* magazine, "*Broken Blossom* is Bette Midler's clearest, most striking album, with vocals worthy of Streisand backed by the superb production by Brooks Arthur."

Reviewer Robert Stephen Spitz disagreed: "*Broken Blossom* is, as the Divine Miss M would say, the bottomless pits. What she has so shrewdly cultivated in the past—the essential *emotion* of the vocalist—is missing completely. Instead, we are mistreated to naked songs lacking the substance supplied by the interpreter. That's not Bette's style, and the rest of the ingredients are too thin to slide the album by."

Still, many of Bette's fans consider it one of her best albums. Her voice is in

On a London street,
Bette poses with a fireman.

fine form, and it contains some magical moments: a lovely version of "A Dream Is A Wish Your Heart Makes;" a sensuous "Make Yourself Comfortable;" an amusing duet with Tom Waits on "I Never Talk to Strangers;" a hard-rocking version of "Red;" a raunchy "Empty Bed Blues;" a lush "La Vie En Rose," and a touching rendition of "Storybook Children," which was released as a single.

Once again, though, Bette's latest effort landed with a thud in the marketplace. Both the album and single fared poorly on the sales charts, and Bette feared she was becoming a laughingstock. "I wasn't *even* being laughed at," she said later. "I was being *snickered* at. That's much uglier."

Bette's perception was much too self-denigrating; but in any event, in early 1978 she had little time to worry about the charting of her latest album. She was preparing for two highly important events in her career: her first movie and her first world concert tour. The tour, arranged by Aaron Russo, scheduled Bette to perform in eighteen cities in eight foreign countries from England to Australia, and would last three months.

According to Bette, the main reason she agreed to do it was because Aaron's "incessant yapping in my ear about Launching Pads and Smart Career Moves made me so furious I would have gone anywhere to get away from him." Unfortunately, Russo was planning to accompany Bette on the entire three-month trip. "Suddenly I understood why he planned the trek in the first place. After all, the most exotic place the man had ever been to was Las Vegas."

One of the principal reasons for doing the tour, in fact, *was* a smart career move: to increase interest in Bette abroad prior to the release of her first film, *The Rose*. Often, foreign box-office receipts can more than double a film's income, sometimes saving a picture from financial loss.

Bette asked Charlotte, Ula and Sharon to come with her, but their career as Formerly of the Harlettes was doing well and they decided not to sing backup for Bette any longer. So once again, Midler held auditions, this time for all three girls, and for the first time she advertised, in *The Hollywood Reporter*:

"New Harlettes for world tour. Sing great, dance great, have great attitude."

The first audition was open call, and Aaron, Paul Rothchild and choreographer Toni Basil heard 250 girls (two of whom were men in drag), narrowing the field over the next week to sixty, then thirty, then fifteen, then ten.

Linda Hart had been called back each time. A promising solo vocalist, she had always refused to sing backup. But after seeing Bette in concert in 1975, she felt that if she were ever to do it for anybody, it would be Bette because, she says, "it would be like getting a scholarship to Yale for a singer to go on the road with Bette Midler." And so, when she saw the ad, she decided to audition despite the fact that she had an offer to open for Roy Clark in Lake Tahoe.

"Bette had never been at any of the auditions so far," Linda recalls. "Then I got a call and they told me they had narrowed it down to six. At that point, Bette was there, and they told us, 'Obviously, you're all very talented. What we want you to do is something you think makes you absolutely unique.' Well, my father is the minister of a black church in Detroit, and I have a strong gospel background. So I sat at the piano and sang 'Amazing Grace.' I thought they'd think I was crazy—I'm singing religious songs to audition for this rock 'n' roll show—and I didn't even look up until the last couple of lines. I saw that both Aaron and Bette had tears on their cheeks. I almost froze, almost didn't finish—I was mesmerized by their reaction. I thought, Well, even if I don't get the job, at least I touched them."

Linda did get the job, along with Katie Sagal and a black singer. "The first day of rehearsals was a disaster," Linda says. "Katie and the black girl were having a disagreement over who should sing high, and Bette started to get vibes she didn't like. So all three of us were *fired.* I took Paul Rothchild aside and told him, 'You can't fire me. I had seven weeks in Lake Tahoe at $3500 a week and I just cancelled it. That's a lot of money to me. The tension is between Katie and the other girl, it has nothing to do with me. *You're not firing me!'* "

Rothchild agreed that Linda had a point, and she and Katie were rehired and joined by Frannie Eisenberg to make up the new Harlettes. Another grueling round of rehearsals followed. "I had never experienced such overwhelming rehearsals," Linda says. "We'd start at ten o'clock in the morning and do vocals until 5, then we'd break for dinner. From six until midnight, we'd do dance routines. But we never got pissed because she didn't go home either—she stayed after we went home. I learned from Bette the value of listening and learning—and *working hard."*

Bette's show was set to open in Seattle—something of an out-of-country tryout. By 7:30 opening night, Bette and the girls were still on the stage, in street clothes, rehearsing—and the show was set to begin at 8:00. "All the sets hadn't arrived, and a trunkload of our costumes had gotten lost on the plane," Linda relates. "Bette said, 'Fuck it, I'm wearing what I'm wearing'—which was black pedal pushers and a print blouse. We said, 'Bette, you *can't!'*

"By this time it's 8:30, and people are around the block waiting to get in, they're banging on the windows and *screaming* to get in. And I hear this incredible yelling coming from Bette's dressing room—'No! *I'm not wearing that!'* I said to the other girls, 'She's not gonna wear what she did for rehearsals—she *wouldn't!'*

"Well, at 9:00 the show goes on, and Bette's wearing the black pants and the

At a press conference
in London, Bette poses demurely with
a rose. When a photographer
asked her to put the flower in her
mouth, she replied,
"*You* put it in *your* mouth."

print blouse. And I realized that she's the most predictably unpredictable person in the world. She'll always do what you're sure she'd *never* do."

Bette had wondered what she could bring to Europe with her act that was distinctly American. It had to be in the form of a costume, because the travel difficulties of the trip precluded any elaborate sets. Inspired by a Red Sox game on the radio, she decided to wear a hot dog costume. What could be more American than that?

"The hot dog was a big hit in Seattle," Linda says, "but it only lasted two nights. She brought it with her on the tour but she never wore it again—it was just too difficult to get in and out of. It took too long for her to change between numbers."

Peter Riegert visits
with Bette backstage at the London
Palladium, September 1978.

The first stop for Bette's world tour was London and the famed Palladium. "We got off the plane and there were probably a *thousand* people at the airport waiting for us," Linda says. "It was unbelievable, like the Beatles or something. We never expected it. All England had ever known of Bette were her albums. But I guess that was enough.

"She was a little nervous in London, because of all her royalty jokes. She didn't want to offend the audience. The jokes went over great with them, but then we heard rumors that members of the R family were planning to come to the show—maybe even the Queen Mum. They never did—and I doubt that Bette would have changed a word, anyway."

"What a thrill it is to be here playing the Palladium right in the heart of The Old UK—or the YUK, as we sometimes call it," Bette told the Brits. "Well, there'll always be an England, they say. Tonight we put that to the ultimate test. Oh, I tell you, we are so excited. We have done it all. We read our Shakespeare. We boned up on Blake. We read Milton till we went blind. . . . I'm so glad you've heard of me. I've never heard of *you*. But you know what they say, when it's 3 o'clock in New York, its 1938 in Britain.

"I'm just crazy about royalty, especially queens. Your queen, for example . . . she is the whitest woman of them all. She makes us all feel like the third world . . . who do you think makes those hats for her, anyway? She's probably got a little hat fairy chained to the basement saying, 'Queenie's gonna love this one!' . . . and of course I just adore Charles . . . I read somewhere that he can marry a commoner. I guess he wouldn't want someone as common as my own self . . . But you know, my very favorite is Princess Anne. Such an active, outdoorsy lass. She loves nature in spite of what it did to her. Oh my

God – did I say that?"

During the second half of one of her Palladium shows, Bette looked up toward the balcony to see a huge sign painted on a sheet – "We Love Your Tits." "She genuinely cracked up," Linda says. "She fell on the floor with laughter. And I guess she just felt *obligated* because she got up and said, 'Okay, here they are!' and pulled her corset top down. The place went *crazy* with cheers and flashbulbs."

Bette's five-night Palladium gig was extended to ten as "Midlermania" – as one of the local papers put it – swept London. The press greeted her show with double-page spreads dubbing her "The Golden Girl" (a reference to Aaron's demand – which was met – that she be paid in gold for the tour), and rave reviews headlined "Legends are Made of This!"

"Miss Bette ('really a librarian under all this drag') Midler has hit London," the Daily *Telegraph* critic wrote, "and London will never be the same again. In a series of dazzling solo performances she has rediscovered and updated for all the essentials of great music-hall."

John Blake in the *Evening News* wrote, "With this one, dazzling, magic, spellbinding show, Bette Midler conquered Britain." And Sunday *Times* columnist Philip Oakes began his interview with Bette, "If you have spent the past seven days, lightly sedated, in a back room in Bangkok you might have missed the news that Bette Midler's in town."

Derek Jewell's review, also in the Sunday *Times*, indicates how impressed Britain was with Bette Midler's talent: "...her records and her powerful musical persona could scarcely have prepared anyone for the full impact of her Palladium first half. For 75 minutes, between songs, she told bawdy tales, scored off politicians and peasants, royals and renegades, all at a blistering pace that would have destroyed other artists. The pace is part of the Midler illusion. She can be highly offensive and crude – but she moves so fast that no barb or vulgarity festers. She has, too, a glittering vocabulary, like a Broadway moll who has swallowed Roget's 'Thesaurus,' which is superbly deployed with every suggestion of total spontaneity.

"That, however, was only the first half. The second began with high camp music from the 1940s and lewd tales. Then, suddenly, she was sitting on a bench, miming and singing a string of desperately sad-funny songs, throwing in poetry and character sketches in a *tour de force* which suggested a cross between tragic Judy Garland and Charlie Chaplin's universal pathos. The audience was stilled, enraptured. They recognized the vulnerability behind the flashy sophistication. And that remarkable surprise was her final stroke. She received the kind of tumultuously genuine reception which only a star who is many stars in one can evoke."

The next stop on Bette's tour was Britain's "provinces," then four nights in Sweden and Denmark. "They were nuts in Copenhagen," Bette says, *"nuts! They loved me!"* Indeed, her show there may have been the best of all – certainly the audience reaction was unrestrained. People threw bouquets of flowers on the stage during the performance; one young man came onstage during "Do You Wanna Dance?" and, instead of feeling threatened, Bette sang the song to him, then danced with him at its conclusion. It was a memorable night for all concerned.

Bette was next scheduled for a series of one-night stands in three German cities. Her arrival in Germany was not a pleasant experience for her. "I'll tell

Bette tears
into a number on the stage of the
Théàtre Palais. One French
reporter described her as *"Le personnage
le plus extravagant de la chanson."*

you the truth," she later said. "I avoided going to Germany for many, many years. I'm Jewish and I've had that with me ever since I was a kid and I've been unable to lose it. I had a sorrow—a sorrow so deep inside you that you don't even know you have it until you're there in the country. I tell you, I was drunk the whole time. I couldn't face it.

"And when we got off the plane, they were still looking for the Meinhof gang and there were all these soldiers with machine guns along the ramp and all around the airport. I had never seen anything like that and it put me in a terrible frame of mind."

Linda Hart says, "The audiences in Germany weren't sell-outs, and they weren't *that* receptive. They were polite and they seemed to enjoy the show, but there wasn't the kind of screaming and carrying on that we'd had in all the other countries. She really wanted to *get the hell out of there*. On stage, we saw her not taking as many chances, and not going back for encores because she just wanted to get it over with."

She did take one major chance in Germany, however. In the other countries, she had been singing a ditty about Nazis' private parts: "Hitler had only one big ball/Goering had two but they were small/Himmler had something sim'lar/But Goebbels had no balls at all."

"Before the first show in Germany," Linda recalls, "she told us we weren't going to do it. Then she went out and *did* it. It's almost as though she *dares* herself with these things. Not only did she sing it, she had the audience *sing along* with her. I figured, it wasn't Bette out there, it was the Divine Miss M."

According to Linda, they *are* two quite distinct personalities. "Bette is *very* different offstage. A perfect example is when we were in Australia. We were on incredible time change—we kept waking up at five in the morning. One day Bette calls me at 5:30 and says we're all going to the beach. So we go, and I'm wearing this two piece bathing suit. It was something my *grandmother* could see me in and say, 'Oh, it's *darlin'*, hon!'

"Bette looks at me and says, 'Linda! Cover up!' I grabbed a towel because I was sure my top had fallen down. But it hadn't, and I said, 'Cover up what?' Bette said, 'Your *breasts*!' I said, 'I'm wearing a *bathing suit*, what's the matter with you?'

"She was absolutely serious. That was the first time I saw that side of her personality. The other two girls and I just said to each other, 'What is she talking about?' And I thought, This is a whole other girl here . . .'"

Bette has admitted, "In real life I'm terribly prudish. But there's something about getting out on a stage that fills me with this determination to surprise—and shock."

The stopover in France became a mini-vacation for Bette's troupe. "Paris was a honeymoon," Linda says. "We had eight days off and performed on the ninth night. Bette was most generous to us. She got us all suites in the Marisse Hotel for the whole time we were there. My boyfriend flew over and our suite overlooked the Eiffel Tower. It was incredibly romantic. Then we did this one sensational show."

"We are thrilled and delighted to be here in the town where good taste was born. And—judging from the front row—died not moments ago. . . Ladies and Gentlemen, a hearty Parisian welcome to three items I picked up on discount at the Common Market—*Les Harlettes Formidables!* Show them Paris when it sizzles, girls. Aw right, girls. Enough sizzling. Strike a Gallic pose. *Gallic*—not

OPPOSITE: In Copenhagen, Bette's Dolores De Lago routine was taken by the citizens as a tribute to their city's "Little Mermaid," and they loved it.

garlic! Oh, my, *c'est difficile de trouver des domestiques, n'est-ce pas?*"

While Bette was on tour, Peter Riegert flew over twice to join her, once in Paris. "Peter was an inspiration," Linda says. "Not only to Bette but to the whole tour. He was so lovely and so nice and always optimistic. He always had a joke or something fun to relate, always made us laugh. He'd come to the dressing room to buck us up before a show and tell us how great we were the night before. I have terribly fond memories of Peter. When he was around, there was a contentment and a real inner peace about Bette. They seemed to always have great fun together, going out for Chinese food.

"Peter made her laugh. She loves for other people to make her laugh, and he had a real knack for doing that. When Bette was having an awful day and was depressed and difficult to deal with, if Peter was there he could really help to get her through that. If he wasn't there, she'd get lonely and things would be even worse than they had to be.

"It was lonely on the road. Sometimes we four girls would go out and see a good-looking boy and we'd be like sixteen-year-olds–'Ooh, isn't he cute–*look at him*. Who's gonna talk to him first?' Usually, none of us did, because we're all a bit shy in that respect, especially Bette. None of us is the sleep-around type, so we'd figure, 'Eh, why bother'–and go back to our hotel and order room service."

Bette created excitement everywhere she went, but nowhere more so than in Australia. Her original two-week stay in that country was extended to four. Her twelve scheduled shows mushroomed to twenty-three, and all were sell-outs, grossing more than $1 million. In all, Bette performed in front of 70,000 people in Australia.

Bette's reception by the press and her fans in Sydney made all the other countries seem disinterested. Photographs seven-by-eleven inches in size appeared in newspapers, accompanied by headlines like "Divine Bette Plunges In," "Magic from Miss Midler" and "Bawdy Bette Bowls 'em Over."

A press conference held upon her arrival in Sydney created a sensation. Wearing a revealing low-cut electric blue dress and a pink feather boa, Bette fielded questions from the Australian reporters. What did she think of the Women's Electoral Lobby's complaints that her show did not advance the cause of women's liberation? "What, more trouble? I think I'm a great woman. . . great women are those who get out, are not afraid to be themselves and speak their minds."

Did she plan to clean up her act after criticism of its vulgarity? "The police here are going to keep an eye on me? Are they cute? The French police were adorable. They came every night."

Had she gotten caught up in the star syndrome? "Do I look like I'm caught up in the star syndrome? How many people do you know who go around dressed like this in the middle of the day?"

While Bette was in Australia, *Ol' Red Hair Is Back* was aired there for the first time, to rave reviews. The combination of Bette's concerts and the TV special put Australia into a dither over Midler. One newspaper used *three-inch-high* headline type to announce "Bette Midler Drama" on its front page as it reported that band member Ted Irwin had set fire to a fellow band member's hotel room. Irwin was made to pay a $100 fine.

According to *Variety*'s correspondent, "Sydney has never responded better to a visiting artist. In any country her performance would be considered a total triumph, and unless she is a consummate actress, the warmth of her reception

At a press
conference in Sydney, Australia, Bette
looks as much like
Marilyn Monroe as she ever will. Her
comments made headlines.

and its intensity clearly surprised her."

"Oh, Sydney, Sydney! How you have received me! What love you have shown! I'm so glad this turned out to be a deep, meaningful relationship and not just a one-night stand...Of course, we have had a wonderful time flipping and flopping around the world, but on the morrow, my dears, we get to go *home!* I mean I do love you down here—I *do*—but honey, I'd *kill* for a Fatburger!"

On November 27, Midler and Company left Australia and returned home. Bette was tired, and she had reached an important decision about her career. As 1978 turned into 1979, events would evolve—both within and beyond Bette's control—that would fundamentally alter her life, personally and professionally.

PART FOUR

GOING HOLLYWOOD

(1979–1984)

Fifteen

Not long after she returned from Australia, Bette Midler made a decision that was at once surprising and seemingly inevitable: she fired Aaron Russo as her manager. Her action put an end to what perhaps had been the most volatile and tumultuous artist/manager relationship in show business history. It may have been the staggering adulation she had received from seven foreign countries which made her realize after all this time that she didn't need to rely on Aaron Russo in order to be a star.

Or it may have been, in Linda Hart's opinion, the three months of unrelieved Russo Bette had just been through: "There wasn't any *one* incident that I recall. But I think it was the concentrated three months together—every day, every night, every airplane, every restaurant. There was no way for Bette to get away. It was very tense—there were years of problems that had built up. Bette just said, 'That's it!'"

Later, Bette said, "At the moment that our relationship was at its most even, I chose to leave. Because I couldn't take it anymore. I felt that what he was doing for me professionally wasn't worth what he was doing for me personally. I couldn't sleep. I was in a state of anxiety all the time because I never knew what he was going to pull on me next. It was either, 'I'm dying of leukemia' or 'I'm carrying guns because they're out to get me. You're all that's left'. . . always, of course, there was drama, much, much drama. Eventually, I outgrew my need for drama."

She added, "There were certain kinds of withholding-approbation type games that went on between us that were not really healthy." (Reportedly, Bette did not feel a concert was good unless Russo told her it was. And, more often than not, he withheld that approval. "That's a real horrible mindfuck to get into," she said.)

As Bette put an end to this undesirable relationship, one of the most important relationships of her life ended tragically: Ruth Midler died in January of cancer of the liver and leukemia. She had been quite ill for some time, but Bette was not able to get to Hawaii before her death—and that devastated her. It was a terrible time for the entire family; Ruth's illness and her chemotherapy had taken its toll. Bette and Susan felt particularly bitter toward their father. "Toward the end," Bette said, "it got very ugly. There were a lot of accusations flying through the air because he couldn't deal with her illness. He just pretended like she wasn't sick."

A year later, Bette would find it impossible to hide her bitterness toward her father on a nationally televised awards show. But she took some solace in the fact that her stardom had made her mother's last days happier ones. Susan said, "Bette made her very happy with the things she had done, and reading some of the articles about her, and fan mail, and talking to fans on the phone, things like that made her very happy."

For several months after her mom's death, Bette would break into tears without warning, and it was something that would affect her physically as well as emotionally for several years. She did make efforts to cheer herself—and her friends. Linda Hart relates, "Bette said to me, 'Linda, I want to have a party for my mother. I want everybody to feel better.' So I made about six pies and brought them to her place. Everybody tried to be very up. Peter was in an

OPPOSITE PART FOUR: Bette is aglow at the Hollywood premiere of her first film *The Rose*, November 7, 1979.

OPPOSITE: The opening number of *Divine Madness*, "Big Noise from Winnetka."

improvisational group called War Babies and they put on a fabulous improv show with about ten people. Tom Waits was there, and it was very, very nice. But Bette did have a rough time getting over the death of her mother."

This was apparent during Bette's appearance on *Saturday Night Live* in May. She sang "Married Men" in her first segment, then returned to sing Tom Wait's "Martha," a sad song of missed opportunities for love. By the time it was over, Bette was crying and seemed completely oblivious to everything around her. "That song calls up a lot of deep things for me," she said later. "That night on the show, I was thinking about my mom."

Bette made no more public appearances until the late Fall; she was working on a book about her world tour which was set for release in 1980, and a new album, *Thighs and Whispers*. Released in the Fall, this latest Midler recording effort seemed to bring it all together: slick production and fine Midler vocals with some of the passion and emotion many felt her last few albums lacked. Songs like "Cradle Days" and "Millworker" summoned up the affecting Midler pathos, "Big Noise from Winnetka" and "Married Men" her sexy theatricality and "My Knight in Black Leather" the high campiness with which Bette had made her initial mark. In many ways, *Thighs and Whispers* was the most Midleresque Midler album in years, and as such it received highly favorable notices. Peter Reilly wrote in *Stereo Review*, "...her wonderful new Atlantic album...certainly shows that she hasn't forgotten any of her old tricks...not that she doesn't do some very fine straight-out singing here, too, particularly in the disco-slanted 'Hang On In There Baby' and the soul-brushed 'Cradle Days.'

"The Midler voice is like the Midler figure–pint-size–and it is not nearly as vividly colored as she is herself. But it *is* enormously expressive and musical. Moreover, she is a natural, instinctive editor, and any Midler reading of a lyric can be depended on to emphasize just *the* right word or *the* phrase that nails the meaning down absolutely.

"[Bette's] outrageousness is quite real...it has its origin in and is designed to *protect* a vulnerability that is just as real. And it is that vulnerability, I think, that accounts for her unique appeal, because it is never consciously displayed, never capitalized on (as it surely was with, say, Judy Garland), but only suggested. It lends a touching truth to almost everything she sings, no matter how raunchy, how gamey, how impertinent."

Bette was very proud of the album. "People say it's the best thing I've done in a long time and that's gratifying. I really do love the ballads. For someone like me, they keep you alive. I think 'Cradle Days' is one of the best things I ever did. I love old tunes and disco and rock, but ballads really are the key to my soul."

There was some criticism of Midler because of the disco flavor of some of the songs on the album. She didn't take it too seriously; discussing the nascent new wave movement, she said, "The new wave thing is going to be bigger than anything else next year. The groundswell is building everywhere. Not only is it infectious, it's art school, which appeals to intellects. Will I try some? I don't mind if I do. I think I should jump on every musical bandwagon and really drive people mad, just irritate them to shit so they say, 'She's such a cow –she'll jump on any musical bandwagon.' Why not? I'll bleach my hair and rip my clothes. I think it's fun. I'm getting silly in my old age."

Thighs and Whispers did better commercially than *Broken Blossom* –and won the German Record Award as international album of the year–but still sales continued to fall short of the success of her first two albums. A single of "Mar-

Wearing a "Miss Community Chest" banner, Bette sings "Boogie Woogie Bugle Boy."

ried Men" peaked at #40 on the *Billboard* Hot 100 singles chart.

"Radio is very fickle," Bette said. "If you can't get your records played, you can't sell those records. The stations change formats frequently, and the formats are very narrow. You can take six months out to do a movie, and when you come back you find all the formats have changed. So you're working with musicians, browbeating yourself to make a record you're not sure anyone's going to hear."

Within a year, ironically, "taking six months out to make a movie" would result in Bette's first #1 single, "The Rose."

In the early summer, Bette and the Harlettes went back to Europe for a brief promotional tour on which they made several television appearances. "We went to Germany again," Linda Hart says, "and this time Bette seemed much better able to handle it. I guess it was the lack of pressure of having to perform. She always did think it was a beautiful country, and this time all we did was sightsee. We had a great time."

Upon their return, Bette and the girls prepared to take the European show—now called *Bette! Divine Madness*—on a brief U.S. tour and then to New York City's Majestic Theater. Katie Sagal left the Harlettes, and Paulette McWilliams took her place.

The show was altered somewhat from the European version, mostly incorporating more new material (Bette did a great deal of her early material in Europe because they had never seen her do it before), but its essentials stayed the same: a hilarious bit as Dolores De Lago, the toast of Chicago, a beached mermaid who is something of a piscine Vickie Eydie; jokes about the English royalty and some new Sophie Tucker stories; and a lengthy character sketch as the Magic Lady.

This latest tour was typically successful; Bette broke house records in several cities, notably San Francisco. Other cities on the tour were Seattle, Portland, Los Angeles, Phoenix and Detroit. Interest in Bette was unusually high, because of advance word about her first film *The Rose*, which was scheduled for release in November. Talk had already begun that Midler was a sure-fire Oscar nominee for her portrayal of a burnt-out rock star, and fans hoped she'd sing some numbers from the film.

She didn't disappoint. Only four songs into the act, Midler let loose with a gut-wrenching, passionate performance of "Stay With Me Baby" that electrified her audience and won her a standing ovation night after night. Linda Hart remembers the impact the song had on her. "When I heard her do it, I couldn't *wait* to see the movie. It was *mesmerizing*. I'll tell you, 'Stay with Me' and 'I Shall Be Released' were the only two songs that I left the dressing room every night to stand on the sidelines and *watch* her do. It was part of my learning process.

"What was really phenomenal was that sometimes by the third song of the night she had lost her voice, and you'd wonder, 'How is she going to do *seventeen* more songs? What is she gonna do?' Then she'd do 'Stay With Me' and she'd hold those notes and you'd see her veins pop out of her neck and she'd be singing her heart out and I'd think to myself, My God, does she ever *deserve* what her audiences give her. She was relentless. And she never, *ever* cut one number from a show when she didn't feel well. Where she got the strength I'll never know. She has more guts than any person I've ever known."

Critical reaction to her new show was comprised of the usual valentines. Martin Kent in the *Hollywood Reporter* wrote, "A Bette Midler concert is an exquisitely packaged theatrical experience that seems to suggest if not encom-

Backstage on opening night, Bette poses with new Harlettes Franny Eisenberg, Paulette McWilliams and Linda Hart.

The Magic Lady
sings "Do You Wanna Dance?"

pass the history of show business. . . Midler is larger-than-life—a silo of excess. Bursting out of her skintight outfits, she is a science fair project on kinetic energy gone out of control. Armed with a voice that is so powerful, expressive and versatile, her ballads are as devastating as her wildest rockers. . . the diva, a title truly deserved by this great lady, once again stretches her enormous talents and perpetuates the love affair between herself and her fans."

During the *Divine Madness* tour, there was one remarkable incident in Detroit (where else?) that was particularly memorable for Linda Hart. Her family had come up from Texas to see the show, and although they found the language offensive, they weren't upset enough not to fly Linda's 85-year-old grandmother to Detroit for the show.

"My grandmother sits in the second row, and Bette puts on such a wonderful show that after she leaves the stage for good the audience won't quiet down: they want her back. She's already in the shower, and Jerry Blatt comes in her dressing room and tells her that she has to come back out, they're *screaming* for her, they won't leave until she comes out for one more bow."

Bette picks up the story: "I wrapped myself up in a towel, and Jerry said to me, 'Please, whatever you do, don't flash 'em.' Gee, it never *occurred* to me! So what else could I do?"

Linda: "When I saw her in that towel, I knew we were in big trouble. She came out on stage and the drummer started playing this stripper music, and she said, 'Don't give me any ideas.' And I'm going 'Oh, no. . . .'. Bette gets to the mike and thanks and thanks them and says, 'We don't know anymore songs, we don't know anymore jokes. All I can say is goodnight, Detroit, I love you!'

"And with that, she whips the towel off and starts flinging it around her head. Then she skips off. This wasn't flashing, this was definitely, 'Check out

OPPOSITE: At New York's Majestic Theater, Bette sings "My Mother's Eyes" early in her sold-out *Divine Madness* show, December 1979.

BOTH PAGES: The blushing
bride changes her spots after singing
"Chapel of Love."

what's going on here.' I looked down at my grandmother, who has never seen *any* human body naked, let alone on stage with spotlights. She covered her face with her hands and fell on my mother's shoulder. I was sure she'd had a massive coronary and the paramedics would be there any second.

"I saw Bette backstage and I told her I would have given a thousand dollars if she hadn't done that tonight, and explained why. She said, 'Have your grandmother come backstage and I'll talk to her.' I said, 'That's if she's still alive.'

"So my grandmother comes backstage and she's absolutely white, and I said, 'Grandma, did you enjoy the show?' She said, in her deepest Southern accent, 'I *loved* the show, honey, but I just thought that towel number was very unnecessary.' I said, 'Grandma, that wasn't a number, that was spontaneous art.'

"Bette comes in, gets down on her knees in front of my grandmother, who's just this precious mint julep with her silver hair and white gloves, and says, 'Please forgive me–I've never done that before, I'll never do it again. Your granddaughter doesn't work for somebody who does that all the time.'

"Then she said maybe the worst possible thing. She said, 'I don't know what got into me. *God* made me do it.' Now my grandmother is *very* religious, and she looked quite puzzled and said, 'What do you mean?' Bette replied, 'Something came over me, a divine power'–and I'm behind my grandmother, trying to signal to Bette, 'No! No! That's the *worst* thing you could say!'

"Anyway, it turned out to have a happy ending because my grandmother is a big fan. She's been to five or six shows, and she always comes backstage to see her. Back home, she tells everyone that she's a *personal* friend of Bette Midler's."

Bette took a month off before bringing *Divine Madness* to Broadway in December. By the time she did so, in the words of Peter Reilly, "probably the only thing hotter than Better Midler–and surely for quite a while in the foreseeable future–is that English muffin one of the crew was preparing the night the alarm bell rang at Three Mile Island."

The cause of this thermo-nuclear reaction was the explosive combination of her album, the show (described by *Time* as "the hottest ticket in Manhattan") and the rave reviews and huge box-office grosses of Bette's first film, *The Rose*.

Finally, the years of anticipation on the part of Bette and her fans had become a reality: Bette Midler was a movie star.

Sixteen

Ever since Bette Midler burst upon the national entertainment scene in 1973, there was something of a *noblesse oblige* about the fact that she would someday become a film star. After all, hadn't Barbra Streisand, Liza Minnelli and Diana Ross turned cabaret and record careers into Hollywood stardom? And Midler was clearly talented and larger-than-life enough to make the jump herself. Bette and Aaron certainly thought so. "Aaron always understood that it was the movies for us," Bette said. "We never talked about it much, but it was always in the back of our minds."

The only surprising thing about Midler's conquest of tinseltown was that it took so long. Part of the reason was that Aaron Russo continually refused to consider anything but a major star vehicle for Bette. "I wanted her first film to be a role that only Bette Midler could play. I mean, who else could play The Rose? Liza Minnelli? You know what I'm saying?"

In addition to the *Fortune* fiasco, Russo turned down offers for Bette to appear in Talia Shire's role in *Rocky*, Jessica Lange's in *King Kong*, Barbara Harris' in *Nashville*, Goldie Hawn's in *Foul Play*, Madeline Kahn's in *Won Ton Ton, The Dog That Saved Hollywood*, as well as film biographies of Sophie Tucker, Dorothy Parker and Texas Guinan.

"The one we really wanted," Bette said, "was the film version of *Little Me*. Now we lost that one under very unusual circumstances. It all goes back to when Ross Hunter's *Lost Her-Reason* came out. Well my dear, they threw us out of the theater we were laughing so hard...I *never* miss a Liv Ullmann musical...Aaron is not one to mince words and when he met with Ross Hunter about another project, he said something to him about questioning his judgement because he thought *Lost Horizon* was abominable. Well, word got out that we were after *Little Me* and wouldn't ya know it, Hunter went out and bought it for Goldie Hawn."

The difficulty in getting Bette the right film role had also to do with Bette and Aaron's concept that her first film should be a blockbuster offering Bette a chance at *tour de force*. As early as 1972, Bette was quoted as saying, "When Miss M does a movie, it's going to be a blast! A true mind shaker! Something nobody would imagine." Russo's determination was that Bette would be so central to the film that "if she couldn't make the picture, the project would have to be abandoned."

While Aaron's holding out for a Midler blockbuster, in hindsight, was clearly the smart thing to do, one could have been forgiven in 1975 for thinking he was nuts. Particularly since the main reason Bette wasn't getting those kind of offers was that movie executives didn't want to take the risk of starring a newcomer in a picture that would rise or fall entirely on her merits.

Ironically, it was a version of *The Rose* which no one wanted to hire Bette Midler for in 1972. Marvin Worth, a producer at 20th Century-Fox, commissioned Bill Kerby to write a script based on the life of Janis Joplin shortly after she died. Titled *The Pearl*, it was sent to director Mark Rydell. "I said, 'I want Bette Midler,'" says Rydell, "and they said 'Who?' I said there was no other human talent in existence who could play this role. But they were not about to risk their money on an unknown girl, so I walked away from it."

Bette wasn't interested in doing the movie at that point, either. She felt the

OPPOSITE: Bette Midler plays The Rose: "You wanna know how I keep this tired, battered body in shape? Drugs, sex and rock 'n' roll!"

Filming on location
in New York City, Spring 1978.

script, coming so soon after Janis's death, was ghoulish. She had a deep regard for Janis, whom she later revealed had been extremely important to the creation of her performing persona. "I saw her for the first time in 1970. She put me in traction. I left the show and I was stumbling. I couldn't find my way. I was just hit in the face with this terrific *womanness*. And when I saw her I said, 'I can *do* that. I understand what she's doing.'

"What she did was let go of a whole group of emotions that I had never seen expressed on the stage before. I had felt them in my life—I'd had great fits of emotion, great anger, great feelings of rage and loneliness—all heightened and exaggerated. Fighting with a lover and begging him to come back—it was always very big in my life, nothing small or quiet. So when I saw her do that kind of thing on stage, I identified with it and I realized that she was using what was an everyday way of relating to people and putting it to music. And I had been afraid to do that myself before that, because I had never seen it done on stage."

Bette was concerned with the privacy issues that doing a movie based on Janis' life raised. And just as importantly, the last thing she wanted to do was imitate Janis Joplin on screen. Bette said no, and for years she believed that the movie would have been made had she agreed. Recently, however, she said that Aaron never told her that the studio didn't want her in any case. (She must have had a clue later, though, because in 1977 she commented, "It's extremely hard to make the crossover from pop music to movies because the studio honchos want you to prove everything to them. You practically have to mount a production of *Hamlet* all by yourself before they'll get the idea you can act.")

Worth kept the project afloat, and it went through eight drafts, several title changes, three stars and six directors—including Ken Russell, Michael Cimino and Richard Donner—before coming back, in 1976, to Bette, who by then was a major star. "By this time, I was worn out," said Bette, "but I wanted to do films. I felt I had a contribution to make." Aaron asked her to take a look at the script again. "For a performer like me, it had a big emotional range, and I was interested in range. It was the one script we'd been offered in all those years that was a real big part and a real big *good* part." Bette said she would do the movie if it contained no direct elements of Joplin's life and retained only the central character's "sorrow and a certain amount of self-hate, this constant seeking of hers for approbation."

The screenwriters (Bill Kerby and Michael Cimino at the time) were happy to make some revisions, and Bette was signed for it, for a reported salary of $500,000 and a "healthy" percentage of the profits—not bad for a girl they didn't want at first. Marvin Worth and Aaron Russo would co-produce for 20th Century-Fox. (The filming took place before Bette and Aaron parted company.) The script went back to Mark Rydell, who had scored a hit with *Cinderella Liberty*, accompanied by a Midler screentest—"which to my mind made it possible," Rydell says.

The final script—credited to Kerby and Bo Goldman, with no mention of Cimino—centered around the last eight days of "The Rose," an enormously talented, insecure, sometimes infantile, self-destructive rock superstar and her relationship with her suppressive, manipulative manager, Rudge. Alan Bates was hired to play the thankless role of Rudge, and Frederic Forrest was cast as Houston, an AWOL sergeant with whom Rose has a tempestuous affair and who offers her a chance to escape from the maelstrom she is caught in. She is, however, incapable of life without performing, and cannot break her strongest emotional bonds – to Rudge. Just before she is set to do her first hometown concert, Rudge fires her – in what Bette would call "mindfuck games." She is left by a defeated Houston and tries to make contact with her parents, without success. Given heroin by an old "friend," she shoots up and dies onstage after performing "Stay With Me" in front of thousands.

Despite Bette's protestations to the contrary, press reports continued to describe the movie as a thinly-disguised version of Janis Joplin's life. Marvin Worth insisted, "Bette is *not* playing Janis. The character is just not her. It's a rock star, that's all. She's already at the top. I'm not showing the one-two-three step rise to the top." Aaron Russo added, "Rose is a composite: Janis, Jimi Hendrix, Jim Morrison – and Marilyn Monroe and James Dean. Characters who get too caught up in the momentum of their lives to know when to stop."

Filming of *The Rose* began in the Spring of 1978 in New York, Hollywood and Long Beach, California. The entire process was a highly emotional one for Bette, because while the screenwriters were taking the story away from Joplin, they were bringing it closer to Midler. Although she has denied that the writers used her life in putting the story together, there are quite obvious parallels, some minor – a scene in a bath house, another with female impersonators in a gay bar; some major – Rose's estrangement from her parents, her neurotic relationship with Rudge.

The Rudge/Rose connection was unquestionably the strongest link to Bette's own life, and Aaron Russo did little to play it down. During the filming, he said about Bette to an interviewer, "If I say 'Jump,' she jumps."

"Our relationship was so much sicker than anything in that film," Bette said after she and Russo parted ways. "He did things that were much worse...He made my personal life so miserable that I became nonfunctional from 1973 on."

The crushing grind of being "on the road" was certainly something Bette could relate to, as was Rose's voracious sexual appetite. In one scene, Rose begins to make love immediately after leaving the stage. Bette admitted that she had done that. "I've made love *before* going on the stage too. Well, you *do* get hot. The crowd is so exciting, how can you help it?"

Particularly painful for Bette to enact was the relationship between the Rose and her parents. "My relationship with my parents was never in any way as grim as the one in the movie, but the telephone scene where I call home is very close to my heart. I had enough of that kind of rejection to be able to use the memory of it..." Bette says that a line cut from the film struck particularly close to home: "I ask them what they're watching on TV, and then I say, 'Oh, she's good. I like her.' And I had that kind of thing with members of my family – we could admire somebody else, but what I do was never talked about. I wish they had left that in."

Sometimes, Bette made changes herself. Claude Sasha is a female impersonator well know for his Midler impression, which he has done since 1972. For the scene in which The Rose sings along with men dressed as herself, Mae West, Diana Ross and Barbra Streisand, Sasha was hired to play The Rose. "While I was rehearsing one day, Bette and Aaron walked in," he says. "They just sat down, never said a word, stayed a few minutes and left. The next day I was told that I would no longer be doing The Rose, but I'd be doing Barbra Streisand instead. I don't know why the switch was made, but I've always figured it was because my impression of Bette made her uncomfortable. It hit too close to home."

Charlotte Crossley says, "That movie was very much about her. The drugs were overplayed, because that's not part of her reality—and neither is the lesbianism—but everything else, all the emotional intensity, that was her. Those scenes of screaming in the parking lot—Bette had *been* there. The woman was drawing on her *experience* for that movie."

Mark Rydell says: "Many's the time she literally *begged* me not to point her in certain emotional directions. She was afraid of being *too* honest, but that's the only thing she knows. The lady has a built-in lie detector. She doesn't lie as a perfomer—ever. So she reluctantly dove into these deep pits of pain.

"We started out in rehearsals playing the script very cautiously. Then Bette pulled herself up short and said, 'We can't be too cagey, too cautious; let's go all the way.' It was very brave of her. She has more to lose than anyone. But she elected to play the role full force, and it works. . . She can be wild, yet she also has the power and dignity. An amazing talent."

The Rose, in addition to its searing portrayal of hopelessness and disintegration, was, of course, also a film with music. Bette Midler would have to appear in concert as a singer very much unlike herself. It was here in particular that observers felt Bette might fall back on Janis Joplin. "I don't do any Janis," Bette said. "I didn't listen to Janis at all. I did not want to concentrate on Janis. I *avoided* Janis."

Someone else she avoided was Bette Midler. It was important to all concerned that Rose not be merely a rock 'n' roll version of The Divine Miss M. The first thing Bette worked to change was her onstage movement. "I have my own style of moving on stage," Bette said. "I shudder along with little mincing steps. Toni Basil changed all that. She gave me broad steps."

The music, too, would have to be very different from what Bette had been doing up to this point. She felt strongly about certain songs, and was instrumental in bringing two of the most important to the film—"When A Man Loves A Woman" and "Stay With Me Baby." "They're songs I always identified with. I was determined just to be genuine, and *good*. I didn't want anybody calling me names. . ."

Talking about the music in general, Bette said, "It'll surprise a lot of people because it's straight-ahead, no-frills rock 'n' roll with gut lyrics and gut emotions. It's loud and screechy and my favorite kind of music. I just love it. It's a thrill to stand up there and get kicked in the head with a bass. It feels like nothing else in the whole world."

For the concert sequences in the film, Bette performed before live audiences in Los Angeles and Long Beach. The cinematography for the concerts was done by no fewer than nine of the most famous cameramen in the business, including Conrad Hall, Laszlo Kovaks and Haskell Wexler. It was an unprecedented crew. "Everybody knew that Bette Midler's film debut was an *event*," says Mark Rydell. "And those cinematographers wanted to be a part of the excitement."

Paying audiences attended the concerts, and the Midler fans were instructed to "dress 1969" and to scream for The Rose, not Bette. No one knew quite what to expect, although few thought they'd see typical Bette Midler. The screaming from the audiences reflected a genuine excitement about what Bette was doing—authentic, hard-edged rock 'n' roll. She was completely believable as a sixties rock star and her fans were jubilant. "All that applause is earned," Mark Rydell said. "It took a lot of daring for Bette to walk out there and introduce a whole new style. She actually prepared a new style of singing.

One of a series
of portraits from *The Rose*.

Her regular fans are not going to expect what they see...I personally think the change will prove to be one of her more courageous career moves. There's a different kind of dignity about her now. I think she's beginning to sense herself in a different way. She's growing."

One segment in the concert sequences came from Bette after the script was written. As Rose prepares to sing "When A Man Loves A Woman" (one of the highlights of the movie), she goes into a feminist rap. "Sometimes people say to me, 'Rose, when's the first time you ever heard the blues?' And you know what I tell them? 'The day I was born.' And you know why? Because I was born a *woman*...Oh, being a woman is so interesting, don't you find it? What are we ladies? We're waitresses at the banquet of life. *Get in that kitchen and rattle them pots and pans!* And you better look pretty damn good doing it, too, or you're gonna lose your good thing...And why do we do that? We do that to find *love*. I just love to be in love...don't you love to be in love?...ain't it just grand to lay there late at night in your bed waiting for your old man to show up. And when he finally does, long about four o'clock in the morning, with whiskey on his breath and the smell of another woman on his person—what do you do? Do you say, 'Oh, honey, let me open up my loving arms and my loving legs, dive right in, the water's fine?' Is that what you say? Or do you say, *'Pack your bags!* I'm putting on my little waitress cap and my high-heel shoes and I'm gonna find me a real man, a good man, a true man. A man to love me for sure...'."

"I was just sharing an experience I had," Bette says. "I'm a great believer in if you're getting shat on you should throw the discontent out of your house—especially if you're paying the bills. I guess that speech is political. But I didn't think of it as political at the time. Just sharing a life experience."

Arranging and supervising the music for *The Rose* was Paul Rothchild—who had, among other things, produced Janis Joplin's last album *Pearl*. It was a calculated risk to use him, since his association with the project would surely add fuel to the reports that this was really the thinly-veiled "Janis Joplin Story." But in many ways Rothchild's presence assured that the story wouldn't get too close to Janis while at the same time keeping the music authentic for the period and the milieu. "I had fought scoring all along," Rothchild said, "There's not one note of scoring in the film; it's all live music except for the diner scene where there's music coming out of a jukebox. I told them, 'We haven't used one violin in this movie and I want to keep it that way!'"

Ironically, it was Rothchild who saved the song "The Rose" from the scrap heap after Marvin Worth rejected it, feeling that a ballad was inappropriate in a rock 'n' roll movie. Rothchild felt the tender song would have tremendous impact at the end of the raucous movie: "The film shows all the negative aspects of a performer's life, and then closes with a song that's a totally positive statement. And Bette's vocal is very melancholy and beaten, which I like as a counterpoint to the optimism of the lyric."

After a while, it became clear that the song had hit single potential—and Rothchild agreed to add the violins to a new, less downbeat Midler vocal. "When it came time for the single, I didn't dare release it to AM radio with just piano and voice. So for the single I added strings, French horns and some woodwinds."

The single of "The Rose" became Bette Midler's biggest hit, hitting #1 on *Record World*'s Top 100 Singles chart. It won the Golden Globe as Best Movie Song, and Bette's performance was awarded a Grammy for Best Pop Vocal, Female. The song was not nominated for an Oscar since it had not been written by Amanda McBroom specifically for the movie.

The soundtrack album for *The Rose* also became one of Bette's biggest-selling albums, rising into the Top Ten.

While *The Rose* neared release, advance word began to filter out that it contained an astonishingly potent performance by Bette Midler. Mark Rydell started beating the drums early. "I think she'll paralyze everyone with her performance. She'll just take your breath away." Bette was pleased too, although, according to Rydell, "She'd still like to make improvements. She keeps following me around like a dog, wanting to change things. 'Can't I re-do that line...?' 'Wouldn't it be better if....'."

Bette was so sensitive about her appearance that she refused to watch the dailies. "I'm a little nutty about my looks," she explained at the time, "although it's not quite so bad now that I've lost weight. I was afraid I would get very self-conscious and start turning my good side to the camera. I don't want to stiffen up. I don't want to freak out, because I've got so many other things on my mind. I'm so crazed that I probably would have stopped it if I had seen anything I didn't like. I decided I will not see any of it and just trust in providence."

Bette did see the film when it opened. "I was nauseated. I had this mental picture of myself, a thin white duchess in a beautiful body, and there was this ratty, broken-down blond creature on the screen. I wanted to find a bridge to drive off."

Of course, ratty and broken down was exactly what she was supposed to be. In fact, the filming was such a grueling experience for Bette that that in itself contributed to the gut-wrenching authenticity of her performance. "We shot the film in sequence," Bette said, "and I was so agitated the whole time we were doing it, that I wasn't eating at all. I had stopped eating—I'd have a carrot—and as we filmed I kept getting thinner and thinner. As a character trait, it was terrific, it worked to show her dissolution."

When *The Rose* opened, the critical raves for Midler's performance were exceptional. Although Arthur Bell, after seeing a preview, wrote, "To put it

OPPOSITE: During rehearsals in Long Beach, Bette reacts to photographer Bob Scott.

charitably, *The Rose* stinks," few others agreed. While the film itself received mixed notices, Bette's were almost unanimously ecstatic.

"Remember this day," Rex Reed wrote. "It's the one that will go down in history as the day Bette Midler made her movie debut. Now *The Rose*, the movie she makes it in, is not all that much to shout about, but Bette's blazing performance saves it from mediocrity, gives it pulse and glamour and heart. Barbra Streisand, by comparison, seems like a has-been...Bette is so great you don't even care how illogical it is...the dynamic Bette sends it soaring into the stratosphere with her throbbing vitality. You can't call this acting debut 'auspicious.' Hell, she tears the theater apart!"

David Denby wrote in *New York* magazine, "What a storm of acting! Midler loads her own brassy, elbow-swinging, big-mama sluttishness on top of Janis's childlike egocentricity, and the results are emotionally kaleidoscopic, draining, yet clear as a series of trumpet blasts...A lot of the time Midler looks awful, partly because she doesn't have the training to protect herself against the camera and partly because she doesn't *want* to protect herself. Instead, she wants to make you feel her pain—at the risk of leaving you appalled.

"There's a startling sequence in which she revs herself up in front of a mirror before a concert: Beating her fists rhythmically against her body, she gasps with every blow, until, at the climax, her eyes, which have been tightly shut, suddenly pop open in terror, like the eyes in a demonic-possession movie. But of course this *is* a demonic-possession movie. Midler's Rose may be too drunk to walk, but when she comes out onstage and the crowd roars, she goes into a full-bodied vamp, shoulders twitching, breasts swatting the air—the transformation is exciting even after you've seen it three or four times."

Gene Shalit said, "With torrential force, Bette Midler sweeps *The Rose* into a film experience...an extravagant performance and an explosive debut." Jack Kroll in *Newsweek* added, "Bette Midler's performance is an event to be experienced—a fevered, fearless portrait of a tormented, gifted, sexy child-woman who sang her heart out until it exploded."

The Rose immediately became an event picture, with long lines waiting for shows four hours later. "New York's on fire with the picture!" Rydell enthused. "Everybody's going crazy over it. I just came from Chicago and the response was sensational. It's so exciting. You don't get this very often in you life. Something spectacular is happening. The feeling is electrifying. It has to do with the fact that we are delivering a new talent. The kind you see once in ten or twenty years. When was the last one? I guess Streisand. But Bette's a spectacular virtuoso, a great artist who should be protected by an Act of Congress, like a natural resource."

The "natural resource" herself refused to read the reviews, as wonderful as they were. "It's just not worth it," she said. "You never know when that one turn of phrase is going to leap out and lacerate your eyeballs and enrage you. I've been through all that and I don't need it anymore. Anyway, there are always people who will call and tell you what is said. They're usually circumspect. They know you don't want to hear the bad bits."

The film's enormous box-office success—it grossed $55 million—the strong sales of the album and single, and Bette's sold-out *Divine Madness* show on Broadway made Bette Midler more of a phenomenon than she had ever been before. Millions of young people who had never even seen her were flocking to their local theaters to see *The Rose*, and Midler suddenly had a whole new audience. Another *People* cover quoted Bette from her show: "Give me some

OPPOSITE: After a fight, Rose pursues Houston into a turkish bath. Running past a shocked man in a shower, Rose says, "If you keep watering it, it might grow."

respect. I'm a screen goddess now!" And *Time* headlined its article detailing the Midler mania, "Make Me A Legend!"—quoting Bette's directive to Aaron Russo with the implication that she had achieved her desire.

Bette's extraordinary new success put her under a microscope of public scrutiny the likes of which she had never encountered before. Dozens of newspapers and magazines featured major articles about her; she appeared for an hour on *The Phil Donahue Show* and submitted to two highly emotional interviews by Barbara Walters and Rona Barrett.

Walters referred to Midler's enormous success, and contrasted it to her personal life—losing her mother, firing Aaron, suffering ill health. She asked Bette how she was holding up. "Well, I'll tell you," Bette answered, "It's been very rough. This is not fun. It's hard work and it's terribly exhausting. To be quite frank, I don't like to think about it. It's been very, very hard for me, this last year. There were a couple of times I really thought I was going to go under. I was ready to call in the men in the white suits. I had no idea until I decided to do it myself what Aaron really did."

"How did you keep from falling apart?" Walters asked.

"I don't really know that I have," Bette replied. "I think I'm very close to falling apart. But I don't care, you know. You can always pick up the pieces. It's not like I'm going to die or anything—that much I've learned."

On the Barrett interview, Bette did fall apart, if only momentarily. Rona showed a clip of the telephone scene, when Rose tries to talk to her parents and realizes once again that they have nothing to talk about. A few minutes after the clip, Rona asks Bette, "Why are your eyes tearing?" Bette explains that seeing the clip choked her up and Rona asks her, "What does it remind you of?"

"It reminds me of a lot of things. . ." She wipes her eyes. "You always do this to me, Rona. I'm never coming on this show again. . .Give me something to wipe my eyes. . .This is so mean. . .It was very moving, the whole evening that we shot it was very moving. . .and then there was the memory that I used when I was doing it. . .whenever I see that clip it brings it all back."

"It seemed very real," Rona says.

"To be honest, it was real. . ." At this point, Bette begins to sob openly. "It always comes back. . ." She catches herself and says, "Can we go on to something a little more cheerful?"

Bette was asked by many interviewers how much like The Rose she is. She admitted the similarities were strong, and intimated that seeing herself in the movie had prompted her to cut back drastically on her drinking. "I'm the worst kind of drunk. I'm mean and vicious and I bite people and jump out of cars. I cry a lot, and get on the telephone with old lovers and my family. 'Why did you bring me into this world?' I cry. They don't have an answer for that, of course. I guess it's because I'm half Russian; we tend to be sentimental slobs."

There was some interest in whether Bette's father had seen the film. Writer Dave Hirshey called him for a piece on Bette in the New York *Daily News* Sunday Magazine. Hirshey asked Fred why he hadn't seen Bette onstage: "I'm just not interested in that kind of entertainment. Now I hear she's in the movies, though. Something about Janet Joplin? I think she was some sort of rock singer. I don't like to spend money and I think charging four or five dollars to see a movie is outrageous. But to see my own daughter. . .well, I guess I'll splurge."

By all accounts, Fred never did see *The Rose.*

The Rose starts to
fall apart after her manager fires her
and Houston leaves.

OPPOSITE: Singing "Midnight in Memphis" during filming at the Wiltern Theater in Los Angeles.

Bette Midler was now exactly where she had fantasized about being for the last twenty-five years of her life. But she found that reality didn't come close to what she had *thought* stardom would be like. ("I saw the superficial things, the limousines and the furs, but I never imagined the underpinnings.") Barbara Walters asked her an interesting question: "What do you fantasize about the future? Is the best yet to come?"

With great resignation, Bette replied, "I think this is it. I do. What else is there? You catch me at a very peculiar period of my life, because everything has been leading up to this moment—and here I am. At the crossroads. And she's standing right in the middle. She's not giving an *inch*."

Peter Riegert escorts his
lady to the New York premiere of *The
Rose*, November 6, 1979.

OPPOSITE: Moments after somehow
summoning up the strength to give a
devastating performance
of "Stay With Me Baby," Rose succumbs
to the effects of
alcohol, pills and heroin.

Seventeen

Riding the crest of an incredible wave of popularity and success, Bette Midler should have been on top of the world. Instead, she was an emotional wreck. She never had been able to handle the pressure of stardom; more success seemed only to make her more insecure, more unsure that she can live up to the ballyhoo—and her paychecks. As *Divine Madness* wound down its six-week run on Broadway—and Bette prepared to transfer the show to film as her second movie for a salary of $850,000—she broke under the strain. Once again, Aaron Russo was at the center of Bette's emotional storm.

Bette was already quite sensitive about her show, because although it was doing tremendous business, the New York reviews were lukewarm. This was the first time Midler had been in New York without Russo, and Rex Reed's uncharacteristic reservations hit home more than any rave: "Unfortunately, there's a lot of trash cluttering the stage at the Majestic between solos that convinces me she needs outside help. This is a show that has been poorly organized and badly put together."

So incensed was Midler about this and other mixed reviews that she took an atypical and ill-advised action, one which unfortunately made Liz Smith's column. According to Smith, ". . . SRO audiences who adore her crazy campiness and torchy singing aren't enough for Bette. She wants the critics to stand up and cheer, too. . . the result is a star who makes wild frenzied telephone calls to her press agent between acts, blaming and threatening and ranting and raving. Now Bette is saying that from now on, *she* will be the only one to say who reviews her work. She is even on the record as frothing that she knows reviews can be 'bought' or 'arranged' and she intends to see that justice is done to her in the future.

"Journalists who have supported Bette for years and been her most fervent admirers," Smith continued, "find that they can't get near the star these days. There is enormous unreality concerning the rise of this truly great talent. Lots of us hoped that the unrealistic, high-toned arrogance surrounding Bette Midler would disappear with the tempestuous end of her management by Aaron Russo. But it hasn't happened. Things are worse."

Things for Bette were certainly *made* worse by Aaron Russo's return to the scene. He attended the show on its last night, then went backstage to talk to Bette. "He told me it was a terrible show. He said I was ruining all he had done for me and I looked like an albino onstage. When he told me this, I was sick with bronchitis. I had my head in the toilet, barfing. Aaron always *did* know my weakest moments, and then he would strike."

It was a *very* weak moment for Bette, and Linda Hart remembers the result vividly. "It seemed to be very distressing for her. They stayed in her dressing room for hours behind closed doors. I don't know what they talked about, but it upset her a great deal. It was the last night of the show, and we were all set to go back to California to make the movie of the show. Well, the next day, *we were all fired*—the three Harlettes and fifteen musicians. And the same week, she and Peter broke up. It would be safe to say that she was under a lot of pressure."

When Linda got back to California, she was greeted by a telegram informing her that her services would no longer be required—as was everyone else.

Liberace presents Bette
with the Entertainer of the Year
award from the Conference
of Personal Managers West, 1980.

"We were all pretty much flipped out. We couldn't understand it. We had already signed contracts to do the movie. And I felt very personal about it, because Bette and I had been close. Franny and I decided we'd just go over to her house and confront her. This was a pretty courageous thing to do, because we'd heard she was really furious with us. But the way I looked at it, she hadn't hired me by telegram and she wasn't going to fire me by telegram, either. She was gonna look me in the eye and tell me.

"We went to her house, and as luck would have it, she was home alone. She let us in and we saw right away that she was under a terrible strain, that she was about to really fall apart. We talked for two hours and it got *loud*. But it was very confusing, and we still to this day don't know exactly what she was pissed about. And she said, 'I'm gonna use different girls and that's that.'

"As we were leaving she said, 'You girls kissed my ass.' I looked at her and said, 'Bette, I loved you. But I never kissed your ass.' And Franny—thank God for her sense of humor—said, 'I kissed your ass but I never loved you.' And you know what? Bette cracked up and said, 'You know, I gotta hand it to you girls, you had a lot of guts to come up here and I respect you for it.' But she was under a lot of pressure from *somewhere* and she just felt she had to make changes."

The Harlettes' attorney was less understanding. His clients had signed a contract, and from his point of view, Bette's action was a clear-cut breach of it.

Bette is triumphant after winning two Golden Globes ("Best Actress in a Musical or Comedy" and "New Female Star of the Year") at the 1980 Awards.

OPPOSITE: Chaz Sandford escorts a radiant Bette to the 1980 Academy Awards, where she has been nominated as Best Actress.

In February, he filed a $3 million suit against Bette and the Ladd Co., which was producing the *Divine Madness* movie, charging a breach of contract and claiming that Bette had persuaded Ladd to break the contract by "falsely claiming they were not competent artists." The suit sought $1 million in punitive damages.

The *Divine Madness* contract would have brought the Harlettes $14,500 each per week. "I didn't want to sue anyone," Linda says, "but I was confronted with the fact that I had planned on that money and we had a contract with the Ladd Co. Anyway, we won the suit and we were paid in full what we would have made on the picture if we hadn't been let go."

As puzzled as Bette's friends were by her actions, they were positively shocked by her breakup with Peter Riegert. Bette and Peter had seemed to all the perfect couple, but although they saw each other intermittently for a while afterwards, this was the point at which they went their separate ways. Some observers theorized that Peter's success with *Animal House* threw the relationship off-balance, but Charlotte Crossley feels that Bette was in no way threatened by Peter's burgeoning fame. Rather, she feels the strain of dealing with Aaron Russo took its toll. "Peter was another one who had his battles with Aaron. Aaron was very jealous of him, very intimidated by him, because he was another person in her life who was an artist and had an affinity with her that Aaron didn't. He wanted to get Peter out of the picture. It was a battle,

180

Bette wears an airplane
hat of her own design as she shows off
her first book, *A View From
A Broad*, at a Los Angeles book-signing.

OPPOSITE: In New York, Bette
wore a typewriter on her head: "All lady
authors should wear hats."

and it was very painful. And it affected the quality of that relationship—long after Aaron was out of the picture.

"Bette puts a time limit on her relationships. There comes a point where there's angst and anxiety, and you have to decide how much of the relationship works and how much doesn't. And when Bette comes to the point where she has that anxiety, she runs away. It's more important to her to keep the men in her life as friends than to keep a relationship going after it should end."

"Relationships are so *hard*," Bette has said. "It's difficult enough to come to grips with your own self, but to have to deal with another self, with that little spirit that's living in somebody else's body—you have to *worry* about them and put them *above* you. You have to *nurse* them when they're sick. My father always wanted me to be something steady, like a nurse, and sometimes I think: Daddy, I wound up a nurse after all."

She doesn't expect that kind of devotion from another person. "I don't like to ask for that support from people I don't pay...It's so draining on someone you love to have to keep lifting you up all the time. I should be on top of the world, pleased and happy with myself. People don't understand if I say, 'I *hate* myself; I can't *bear* it.' The thing is that I go overboard. When I am unhappy or depressed, I am a tidal wave of misery."

Despite the hell Bette was going through during this time, she looked positively radiant at the Golden Globe Awards in February, where she won twice—as Best Female Newcomer and as Best Actress in a Musical or Comedy. Accepting the first award, she looked out at the audience and said, "I'm reminded of something...no, I can't do it...I'm reminded of what Joan Crawford said when she got one of these: 'I'll show you a pair of Golden Globes!'"

The audience roared, and when Bette got up to receive her second statuette, there was laughter even before she said, "I wish I'd had both of these before." After thanking the co-workers she forgot the first time, Bette said, "I'd like to thank my Mom—" She stopped, looking as though she were debating with herself whether to say it, then, quietly and begrudgingly, added "and my Pa." It was a bittersweet moment, and one remarkably revealing of Bette's ambivalent feelings toward her father.

A short while later, Bette was nominated for the highest honor the film industry can bestow—an Academy Award. She wanted the award badly, but there was significant competition from Sally Field in *Norma Rae*. Most insiders agreed that one of the two would win the award.

Bette said later, "I walked into the auditorium and I knew I wasn't going to win, because all the winners were lined up in a row—Meryl, Dustin, Bob Benton, Sally Field. It was like they made space for them so they wouldn't have too much trouble getting up to get the statuette. I'm over here next to the john and I said, '*This is not the hot seat*—I guess I lost.'"

She added, "I was very disappointed not to win, but I thought Sally Field deserved it. She's worked a long time and she was terrific in the film..."

Even without an Oscar for its star, *The Rose* was still a memorable film and an enormous hit, and Bette's performance will remain one of the most impressive debuts in screen history. Midler was soon to make another debut—as an author.

In April, Simon and Schuster published Bette's memoir of her European tour, *A View From A Broad*. It is not a strictly accurate account; she admits "Most of it I made up, because I didn't get out of my hotel very often." She never wore the hotdog suit anywhere in Europe, for example, and some of the

In the film version
of *Divine Madness*, Bette is carried
onstage atop an ear of corn.

OPPOSITE:
Bette sings "Shiver Me Timbers."

other events are out of sequence, but it is a funny, beautifully illustrated book reflecting perfectly the humor and the spirit of Bette Midler. It was well-reviewed, and by the end of May was on the New York *Times* non-fiction bestseller list. Midler had conquered still another medium, and her book-signing parties in New York and Los Angeles became almost as raucous as one of her concerts. In New York on May 1, she signed 750 books for fans who had begun lining up at 8 a.m. Bedecked in a typewriter hat of her own design ("all lady authors should wear hats," she explained), Bette was protected by two burly bodyguards—whose presence turned out to be needed.

"The crush was unbelievable," the New York *Daily News* reported, "with fans turning over bookshelves in an attempt to touch the star. . . 'Bette, we love you!' came the shouts from the throng. . . 'I love you, too,' Midler shouted back. . . the crush got so heavy that a nearby stack of books suddenly tumbled to the floor. 'Now, now, children,' scolded Bette. 'Kiss, kiss, kiss!'"

It was just as hectic three weeks later in Los Angeles; this time, Bette made the *Guinness Book of World Records* by signing *fifteen hundred* books between 7:30 and 1:30 a.m.—three-and-a-half hours after she was scheduled to stop. This time, Bette wore a hat complete with globe and whirling airplane. One little girl asked her, "Why do you have an airplane on your head?" Bette laughed. "It's to make you laugh—and so people will ask me, 'What's that airplane doing on your head?'"

The film of *Divine Madness*—or, as Bette called it, "the time-capsule version of my act"—opened in New York in late September. It had been filmed over three days the prior March before a live audience at the Pasadena Civic Auditorium, with Michael Ritchie (*Smile*, *Semi-Tough*) directing ten cameras to capture the essence of Midler for the big screen.

Two brand-new Harlettes (Jocelyn Brown and Diva Gray) and the newly-anointed "Oldest Living Harlette" Ula Hedwig shared the stage with Bette. (Formerly of the Harlettes had disbanded.) Ula remembers that filming was an

Dolores De Lago, the
Toast of Chicago—and a piscine
Vickie Eydie.

OPPOSITE: The
"E Street Blues" segment.

ordeal. "It was when California was getting this incredible amount of rain, and the basement of the theater was under two feet of water. There were all kinds of delays. It seemed like all we did was wait and wait to go on. The poor audience had to sit there from seven until midnight after coming out in the rain—and they had to pay $10 on top of everything!"

The filming was an ordeal for Bette, too. Her fragile emotional state had resulted in a bout with pneumonia, which she was not over when the time came to begin filming. In many of her numbers, she sounded as though she had a head cold, and on the second day of filming, things caught up with her. "It was toward the beginning of the show," Ula remembers. "Bette came out and then she turned real pale and just stood there. She ran off the stage and collapsed. They had to revive her, and an announcement was made that there wouldn't be anymore show that evening."

Since Bette was ill, why wasn't the filming postponed? Bruce Vilanch, who co-wrote the film with Bette and Jerry Blatt, says, "They would have had to make an insurance claim, because lots of money was at stake, and she was loathe to do that because it's a bad thing to have on your record. It was only a four-day shoot to begin with, and to have all that scrubbed would not have been a good thing, so she just decided to go forward with it. She had a 103-degree fever the second night."

Bette did not sound good on many of her numbers, and she re-recorded some of them in the studio. Her vocals were thus improved on some songs, but this gave the film an uneven quality and a sense of unreality when Bette's lip-syncing was evident. It also pointed up the poor quality of her voice on several numbers, most notably "Paradise," the second song in the film.

Bette's humor, though, was top notch; she included her royalty jokes and Sophie Tucker stories and added caustic comments about her trip to Europe, especially Germany. The show began with a stream of highly literate humor at the beginning of the concert: she introduced the Harlettes as "my three favorite *chotchkes* on the breakfront of life. I'll never forget the first time I found these girls, selling their papayas on 42nd Street. So flush, so filthy—the astonishing verbal abuse they heaped upon me made me certain we were destined to share the stage some day. Not only are my girls fine singers and dancers, not only are they gorgeous and talented, but they also *think I'm God!* Ain't that right girls?"

"Unnh hunnh!"

"Oh, my girls! They function as a Greek chorus. These girls don't know shit about Euripides, but they know plenty about Trojans!...Oh God, once again behaving in a manner I had sworn to eschew"—someone in the audience yells "Gesundheit!"—"Thank you. Once again falling into the vat of vulgarity. Oh, tut, tut. We did so want to leave our sordid past behind and emerge from this project bathed in a new and ennobling light...I wanted to show you the good beneath the gaudy, the saint beneath all this paint, the sweet, pure, winsome soul that lurks beneath this lurid exterior.

"But fortunately, just as I was about to rush down the path of righteousness and respectability, a wee small voice called out to me in the night—and reminded me of the motto by which I have always tried to live my life: *Fuck 'em if they can't take a joke!*"

Divine Madness received excellent critical response. Kevin Thomas in the Los Angeles *Times* wrote, "...for those of us who think Miss M really is divine, *Divine Madness* is pure, exhilirating joy, a definitive concert film culled from more than 90 hours of footage shot during three shows...Dynamic,

BETTE MIDLER
is *Divine Madness*

Written by JERRY BLATT, BETTE MIDLER, BRUCE VILANCH

Produced and Directed by MICHAEL RITCHIE

A Ladd Company Release · DOLBY STEREO · R

Through Warner Bros. A Warner Communications Company

The witty advertising campaign for *Divine Madness* featured this ad and another with Dolores sitting in the Lincoln Memorial.

uninhibited, electrifying–all such familiar adjectives seem threadbare to describe the Hawaiian-born superstar...Midler's immense talent is matched by her energy, but she's clearly having such fun she charges rather than drains an audience...*Divine Madness* is definitely, most definitely, not for prudes. But, oh, is it a winner!"

Janet Maslin in the New York *Times* commented, "*Divine Madness* presents Miss Midler's act in all its gaudy, irrepressible glory...Even more impressive than her way with an off-color punchline–which is certainly impressive–is the control in her delivery. Miss Midler knows full well what her audience expects of her, and what the traffic will bear. Only a thin line seperates her from vulgarity, from maudlin excess, from material that shows her off to poor advantage or gives her self-deprecating humor a nasty edge. And her ability to steer clear of such things is remarkable."

"*Divine Madness*," wrote the New York *Daily News* reviewer Ernest Leogrande, "captures the essential Midler...the audience in the movie blends into the audience in the movie theater, unifying their applause...on its own terms, *Divine Madness* is a Grade A achievement...the seemingly inexhaustible Midler ends her screen performance standing on her head, a fitting symbol of the lengths she goes to in order to deliver the show she feels is expected of her."

Despite these raves, *Divine Madness* was a major box office disappointment, especially compared to *The Rose*. Aaron Russo felt the entire project was ill-advised: "You don't follow a picture that got four Academy Award nominations with one that has no dramatic impact, a concert that in parts had been seen before in various theaters and on television. She's a special person and has to be treated a certain way. With me, everything Bette did was eventlike; it all had a certain air that the concert film didn't accomplish. The thing about Bette is her heart; the film missed that essence. From a creative standpoint, it was wrong. It didn't have any importance. It was terrible."

Many of those whom Bette calls "the hard-core fans" agreed. They felt the movie failed to capture Bette nearly as well as the Home Box Office special had, and Bruce Vilanch feels there was a reason for that. "They played around with the sequence of the show," he says. "The wedding cake, 'Chapel of Love' and 'Boogie Woogie Bugle Boy' was the *finale* on stage. Bette would never, *ever* end a show with 'I Shall Be Released' by itself–she'd come back and sing 'Friends,' because she always wants to leave her audience with a smile. But the producers felt that because *The Rose* ended with a dramatic song and it had been so successful, so should this movie. They told Bette it would show her off as a dramatic actress, and she thought that was a good idea. I fought for her standing on her head at the end. I just thought we had to leave 'em with *something* funny, something up.

"This was a 94-minute version of a 2¾-hour show. My big fight with Michael Ritchie was to maintain the balance in her act. Jerry Blatt and I were the only two people there who had been with her for a long time, except for Ula. There was no one else to say, 'Hey, you're losing sight of what Bette Midler is.' That was a constant struggle. They wanted the brassiness and this and that–but the only way you can get away with Sophie Tucker jokes is if you follow them up immediately with a heart-wrenching ballad. Because that shows you that this isn't really a dirty broad, this is a vulnerable little girl. Her whole show is carefully constructed to show you all those sides, and when you start truncating it, and fooling around with it, you lose that.

"Bette didn't have creative control. She surrendered that. At one point she was going to be the producer, but then she decided just to be an ac-

"Uncle Bette wants you!"
The Harlettes—Jocelyn Brown, Ula
Hedwig and Diva Gray—join Bette
for a rousing rendition of "Boogie
Woogie Bugle Boy."

tress for hire."

Charlotte Crossley had problems with the movie, too. "I didn't feel any of Bette's optimism there. I thought, This woman is weary. It was like it was *The Rose Two*. There were wonderful moments, but she was very drained. She had been running a race for years, and I think it really showed there."

At first, Bette was pleased with the film. Referring to the Home Box Office special, she said, "There will always be a place in my heart for that special. But first off, I'm twenty pounds lighter. Second, my hair is blond. Third, the movie looks beautiful, and compared to TV, the sound is 400 per cent better."

Bette felt the movie would serve to introduce her act to her new fans. "Actually, *Divine Madness* is like the background for *The Rose*. I have a whole new audience that had no idea how I was eking out a living all those years."

Asked if *Divine Madness* doesn't exhaust her stage material, she replied, "It sure does, and I'm relieved and gloriously happy. Some of that material I've done for a long time, and I'm pleased as punch to kick that act off."

Later, Bette was less positive about the film. "Michael Ritchie hates music," she said, "Who knew? I didn't find out until the movie was edited that he not only dislikes music, he can't count a bar. I didn't choose him to direct. The Ladd Company came to me with Michael Ritchie under their arms...Immediately, the project became nervewracking. I had a band that would tear their clothes off because they didn't like their costumes. I had a choreographer who screamed at the designer. The man who did my lighting and Michael Ritchie despised each other. In the middle of all this, I came down with pneumonia...Finally, all I could do was put my best face on and drag the little bastard out to the public."

Talking about the film's financial failure, she said, "It was an enormous thing to do alone [without Aaron] and I made some mistakes. It was all my fault. I made all the mistakes. The concert picture is a scary form. I felt it should have been peddled as a spectacle rather than as a concert, because there I was, making a spectacle of myself. In France, it was sold that way and did very, very well."

To this point, as a movie star, Bette Midler was batting .500. Her next motion picture, however, would be the worst experience of her life and leave her at the lowest emotional ebb she had ever reached.

Eighteen

While Bette was making her third film *Jinxed*—which turned out to be prophetically named—Aaron Russo went public with his feelings about their breakup. "When I met Bette," he said, "she needed somebody, a manager who would dominate her life, give her everything she had...Eventually she started resenting it. I did dominate her, never allowing enough room for the person inside to come out. But if I hadn't, her career wouldn't have gone anywhere.

"I don't think she ever understood what I did or what it took to do it. She was incapable of making decisions. She'd get angry when the press or somebody else would give me credit for something. She wanted nobody else to get the credit.

"She doesn't come to me for advice anymore. We don't have a relationship. I wish we did...I miss her. I know the pain, the insecurity she lives with all the time. That's who the girl is. I want to put my arm around her and give to her. I want her to understand that.

"I do have a broken heart and although I've moved on, there's still that piece of my heart she can have whenever she wants."

For her part, Bette has said that she misses Aaron, too. "He did things that made enemies for me throughout the time that we were together. But he also did a lot of good things...he had a plan. With all the brutality, he did have a plan...I may call him up, have him come back—only this time there would be some ground rules."

At this writing, Bette hasn't called Aaron up, and it seems unlikely that she will. But it's safe to say that Bette wished Aaron had been around during the filming of *Jinxed*. "I had a terrible nervous breakdown," Bette said. "I was sick for a good three months. I was very, very ill." She began to see a psychiatrist "because it was too much for me to deal with by myself."

The project began promisingly enough. Bette had script, director and co-star approval on the film, a black comedy about Willie, a Lake Tahoe dealer jinxed by Harold, an arrogant Twenty-One player who follows him from casino to casino, winning so much he costs Willie his jobs. To break the bad luck, gambler's lore says, Willie has to take something away from Harold; this turns out to be his live-in girlfriend, country-singer Bonita Friml. Willie and Bonita fall in love and conspire to kill Harold, so that Bonita will be free of his physical brutality and psychological dominance, and Willie will be free of his jinx.

Just before they are to go through with the plan, however, Willie finally beats Harold. As far as Willie is concerned, there is no reason now to kill him—but Harold kills himself, and in order to collect on the insurance money, Bonita convinces Willie to go through with their plan to make it look like an accident.

When Bonita discovers that Harold had not paid the insurance premiums, Willie accuses her of lying to him, and they split. But Bonita has a letter from Harold which sends her on a wild chase to track down clues which will bring her money. Finally she realizes that Harold has transferred his power over Willie to her, and she returns to the casino in triumph and wipes him out.

As Willie is leaving town in despair, Bonita pops up in the back seat of his car

OPPOSITE: Bette as Bonita in her prophetically-titled third film, *Jinxed*.

190

and tells him that they have a good thing going, that they can travel from casino to casino and share the money she wins.

To direct, Bette chose Don Siegel, best known for his direction of Clint Eastwood's *Dirty Harry* and the 1956 version of *Invasion of the Body Snatchers*. He was an odd choice to direct a Bette Midler film, but because it had elements of murderous drama, Bette explained, "I thought with Siegel being good at that and me being good with comedy, we'd have a nice marriage."

Her choice to play Willie was Ken Wahl. Although he was a virtual unknown, he was enormously good-looking and had an arresting screen presence. "I felt Ken Wahl had what we used to call animal magnetism," Bette said.

Filming on *Jinxed* began in the Spring of 1981. By August, reports of trouble on the set began to circulate. Gossip column items appeared intimating that Midler's "shenanigans" on the set were causing cost overruns and that Bette was "driving people crazy" by being "over zealous" in using her power. Producer Herb Jaffe seemed to confirm the reports when he was asked if they were true. "When did she change? You talk as if suddenly the moon comes out at night." He said that they had successfully figured the overruns into the budget. "That is what is known as the *mishegas* column in the budget."

Both Don Siegel and Ken Wahl made disparaging comments about Bette to the press. "I've worked with several tough characters, but she's the toughest. It's been the most unpleasant working experience of my life," Siegel said.

Wahl told a reporter that in order to act love scenes with Midler, he had to think of his dog. "She was hard, and in control, and the vibes were bad from the start. If I'd known what it would be like, I never would have accepted the assignment to begin with. Who needs this aggravation?"

On September 15, Army Archerd wrote in his *Daily Variety* column, "As for 'Jinxed,' starring Bette Midler, Siegel adds, 'It was miserable, a very unpleasant experience.' He says Midler was able to demand '20-25 takes and print four or five.'"

On September 27, the story broke wide open with a major article in the Los Angeles *Times* entitled, "Trouble on the set of 'Jinxed'? You can Bette on it." The article detailed the gripes against Midler and carried new quotes from Siegel and Wahl.

"It's just obvious she's insecure," Siegel said. "It's equally obvious she has a great talent. But from out of that enormous insecurity she trusted no one. Consequently, it was very difficult working with her. She comes on as an expert in every facet of the business. . . In her mind she thinks she's a much better director than I am."

Wahl: "It's been miserable with her and took all my concentration to get up and go to work in the morning. . . She doesn't talk, she yells. I think the main problem is that she's so insecure about everything. I enjoy being happy; Bette's the kind of person who thrives on being miserable."

Don Siegel and Herb Jaffe complained that the studio (United Artists) always sided with Midler because they were "in awe" of her. Indeed, Anthea Sylbert, vice president of production, came to Midler's defense throughout the *Times* article—not, apparently, out of awe but simply because she felt "everyone got into a habit of blaming everything on her. Bette Midler is an extremely hard worker and conscientious."

The *Times* reprinted a memo to Sylbert from Dennis Brown, vice president of production management, detailing the fact that the average number of takes with Bette was 3.9, without Bette 2.7. "Over a third of the scenes with Bette were done in only one or two takes and over half were done in three or less takes."

With Ken Wahl in a
tense moment from the film. There
were tenser moments
off screen. Wahl bad-mouthed
Midler to the press
so badly that her lawyer warned
him to stop.

Thus, Sylbert said, Siegel's contention that Bette demanded retake after retake was not true. "The dailies were consistently wonderful," she said, "and one of the people responsible for them being wonderful was Bette Midler. She is obsessed with perfection. Some people are troubled by that, but I've always admired it . . . we're talking about a director who spent most of his career dealing with men . . . There may have been resentment for a woman having some kind of power."

An unnamed stage hand also came to Bette's defense: "Bette can be difficult but it's only because she wants certain things from the project. At any moment her creative input is enormous. If you have someone this strong on the set, you'll have problems. But she's not a malicious or evil person. She just wants to rehearse things that one more time. That's Bette, a compulsive worker. It's her talent, remember, around which the picture is made."

The *Times* piece ended with a story about the complicated filming of the scene in which Willie sends the mobile home containing the body of Harold over a cliff. Action director Sam Peckinpah, a friend of Siegel's, was brought in to help with the shot. The trailer was set on fire, a stuntman jumped out of the truck pulling it and the two vehicles exploded as they fell down the 70-foot drop. Everyone was pleased; a dangerous stunt had been completed without a hitch, and filming was over. The assistant director was heard to say, "If Bette was here, she'd want one more."

In the ensuing months before the film's release, Siegel continued to badmouth Bette. "[The studio] gave her anything and everything she wanted, which made it totally difficult for me...I wasn't totally without rebuttal, however, and didn't always give in to her...I realized we were in trouble [from the beginning]. She hated the script, all the scripts we rewrote. Both of us tried to get off the picture before it started but we had signed contracts. I was afraid they'd sue me.

"I know Midler wasn't pleased with the way she looked. I think [cinematographer Vilmos] Zsigmond did a very good job with her....If I could have my name taken off [the movie] I would. I wish to God I hadn't made it. There were many things I expressly wanted to do but they were all blocked by those two women who work there [at UA; Sylbert and studio president Paula Weinstein].

"It shouldn't have [cost] anywhere near $15 million. It's not up there on the screen, but Midler was constantly rewriting, rewriting, rewriting. All this from a girl who made two pictures, one a bomb."

Bette refused to be drawn into the fray, and would not consent to an interview, but her attorney, Jerry Edelstein, sent Siegel and Wahl letters demanding that they stop making "defamatory" statements that "are not true and will not be able to be proven true." Edelstein commented, "My client has been more cooperative than anyone has a right to be. She waived her overtime. Why anyone would say anything derogatory about her we can't understand ...quite frankly, we don't want to deal on this level, badmouth anyone or make statements on any of it. I don't understand why Siegel is on this vendetta."

The *Times* article prompted a rash of letters to the editor in the following weeks, all of them in Midler's defense. One writer commented, "If a man is bold and forthright, knows what he wants and how to get it, we call him a real go-getter, success-oriented and clever. But if a woman lives by these same principles she is labeled pushy, overbearing and unfeminine...also, along with being in bad taste, it seems like bad business when the producer, director and leading man knock their leading lady publicly, telling nasty tales out of school before the release of a multimillion-dollar film. So who are the real culprits here? Personally, I smell some badly decaying male egos in this bunch." The controversy and recriminations spread; Howard Jaffe, in a later L.A. *Times* piece, called the behavior of Sylbert and other studio executives "execrable. Their total interference made it very difficult to function as producer...what Sylbert did was to pass me by, go over my head, and it was all done with the support of the studio."

Sylbert replied, "I wish we could have relied on him. Nothing would have made my life happier but...he seemed to care more how his percentages were affected by overages than the creativity of the whole thing."

The entire affair was an unprecedented airing of cinematic dirty laundry, and although Bette remained silent for almost a year, when she did talk about what happened on *Jinxed*, an entirely different picture emerged—and the full extent of the toll it took on Bette became clear.

"I couldn't walk, I couldn't get out of bed. I just cried for weeks on end. And anything would set me off. I couldn't control myself. I had just been so *attacked*, so *humiliated*. It was as though they wanted to destroy me, and I couldn't understand what I had done.

Bonita tries to figure
out how to dispose of the body of
her husband (Rip Torn).

"I was trying to make the best movie I could, and I was resented for it...when somebody gives you that much money to make a picture, you can't shortchange them. But these people...there wasn't a single one of them who wasn't out to stiff the studio...they're lazy and they're uncommitted, and they resent you for being so square...They didn't want to work that hard. They didn't want to make it the best *Jinxed* they could make it. So it was like pulling a caravan up Mount Everest all by myself."

Later, Bette revealed that Don Siegel had "*slugged*" me. We were filming a scene he didn't want to do—the one in which Bonita sings in front of the class reunion—and we started to fight over it. It got pretty ugly. He started calling me names and he jumped out of his trailer and I followed him. His wife—she's very large, about six feet tall—grabbed me because I was getting ready to haul off and hit him. She held me from behind, and instead of me hitting him, he hauled off and hit me. I was livid. It was terrible, just traumatic."

According to Bette, the rest of the crew didn't like Siegel, either. "Part of the set was a dungeon with an entrance from above and very little room underneath. One day the crew pushed him into it, locked it and went to lunch."

In *Rolling Stone* several months later, Bette went into more detail about the disastrous personality clash between her and Ken Wahl. "Ken was unbelievably hateful to me...the first time I met him, the first thing he said was, 'I want you to know I hate niggers and faggots.'. . .I had no idea why he said that because we had neither of those in our picture. . .By that time, of course, I knew what particular terrain I had stumbled on to."

After reading with Wahl, Bette said, she felt he wouldn't work out, and neither did Don Siegel. "But Steven Bach [then head of UA] wanted him, so we were gracious about it. However, Mr. Siegel immediately told Ken that he had not been our choice, which right away set the guy's teeth on edge."

Obviously, *Jinxed* was a jinxed movie; rarely has the chemistry on a set been worse. Don Siegel's insensitivity to Midler and Ken Wahl's "*mal* vibes" sent Bette into a paroxysm of insecurity, which caused her to make demands that were met with further hostility. "On the set, it was as though a wall had come between them and me," she said. "I kept thinking, If I can just get through one more day; one more day of having to face them and their awful hatred. . .every day I walked between those walls feeling completely alienated and alone and worthless."

Bette felt that a big part of the problem was male chauvinism. "I had always been 'one of the boys.' I never thought about being 'a woman in the business.' For me it was always, 'This is how it is, and if you don't like it, goodbye.' And because I was inventive and people wanted to work with me, they listened. A lot of times during the woman's movement, I would think, What's all the fuss about? If you're smart, you go in and say what you want and that's that. Well, that's *not* that. This picture opened my eyes to the world. I said to myself, 'I'm not the only woman who has gone through this.'

"I made the biggest mistake anybody can make: I did it for the money. I would rather work for free than do something I don't believe in for money."

All of this took an enormous emotional and physical toll on Bette. "Every day, every morning toward the end, I felt I was holding on for dear life. I would wake up with heart palpitations. And sometimes, in the middle of the night, I would wake up, not screaming but not being able to breathe. . ."

The psychiatrist helped Bette "bounce back" from the trauma of *Jinxed*, and she was hopeful that the film would be such a hit that all the problems would be worth it. Anthea Sylbert noted optimistically that the last time such director/actress problems had been reported was on *Funny Girl*. It would be more than a year before *Jinxed* was released and observers were able to judge the results for themselves.

Midler stayed largely out of the public eye during the interim, but she did make one memorable appearance on the 1982 Oscar show in March. Wearing a tinselly gold gown with red and blue lace hankies on one shoulder – which, in the words of fashion observer Mr. Blackwell, "fluttered like disaster signals on a ship's bow" – Bette twirled around as she walked on stage and said to the audience when she reached the podium, "I guess you didn't think it was possible to overdress for this affair."

She then began a series of improvised gags which livened up the proceedings considerably. "So this is what it feels like to be up here. This is fantastic. I've been waiting for two years for the Academy to call me up and say they made a mistake. . .Don't you hate it when presenters come out and use this moment for their own personal aggrandizement?

"This is the Oscars. We have to be as dignified as possible. That is why I have decided to *rise* to the occasion"–she puts both hands under her bosom and lifts–"and give the nominations for the Best Original Song all the respect I think they deserve. All right. . .the Best Original Song is a song written expressly for a picture and not just some piece of junk the producer found in the

Bette arrives for the 1982 Oscar show. "I guess you didn't think it was possible to overdress for this affair," she told the audience.

piano bench, you dig. . ." She then made disparaging comments about most films: "That endless movie, *Endless Love*; *For Your Eyes Only*—it was. . . I couldn't watch it."

Bette's appearance created a sensation. Commentators suggested Midler should get an award for the presentation, and video bars ran a tape of it for months afterward. "That sure was fun," she said. "And the feedback on it was extraordinary! I couldn't have had more people call or wire or send flowers if I had actually won the damn thing."

Asked if it had been spontaneous or planned, Bette suggested it was spur-of-the-moment. "You had to be at rehearsal to understand. It was stiff. Lots of tension, like lava flowing toward Pompeii. 'You have to lighten this up a bit,' I said to myself. Is it really that important? The Oscars are about movies, c'mon. I was clowning around a little at the rehearsal, and I decided to do the same on the show. There's a certain kind of pomposity that I cannot bear. . . ."

As the release of *Jinxed* became imminent in the Fall, Don Siegel continued to spout off against Midler, and there were strong signs of potential box-office trouble. Anthea Sylbert ordered an entirely new score written, one that would point up the comic elements of the movie. Lalo Schifrin, who wrote the original score and was not asked to supply the new one, blamed Bette. "She's a musician. I'm a musician. We could have communicated. . . I knew there was tension, but not of this proportion. There was a real war going on. . . I could have done something. I didn't have the opportunity. I never even met Midler, who assumed I was on Don's side. . . I wrote music for a thriller, and the studio thought they had a comedy. If we could have put our brains together, I could have done it."

Siegel said a few weeks before the picture opened, "I'd let my wife, children and animals starve before I'd subject them to something like that again." But, perhaps because "I have a piece of the gross," Siegel saw fit to praise Midler, too. "To my great surprise, I like the picture. I like Bette Midler's work in it. She was absolutely awful in *Divine Madness*, but there are moments in this when she's brilliant."

Whether it was the tension on the set or the fact that Siegel was making a drama and Midler was making a comedy, *Jinxed* turned out to be an oddly unsatisfying, highly schizophrenic movie. There were moments of moving pathos and moments of rousing comedy, but audiences were never quite sure which was which, and the parts were decidedly better than the whole. Bette's performance, too, vacillated wildly, never quite finding a center and confusing audiences about just how to take Bonita Friml.

The reviews of *Jinxed* were, on the whole, quite bad. David Anson's comments in *Newsweek* were typical: "What Bette Midler did for last spring's Academy Awards show she does for *Jinxed*. That's saying quite a bit, but it's not saying that *Jinxed* is much of a movie—only that when she's on hand, done up in platinum-blond hair and doing her dynamo waddle across Nevada, it's hard not to be entertained. . . Midler is not overly concerned with building a plausible characterization. Her performance is more on the order of creative sabotage; injecting sassy Midlerian one-liners to pep up a discombobulated story line. There's no way of knowing what this bizarrely patchy movie started out to be—a love story? A comic *Double Indemnity?*. . . Director Don Siegel (*Dirty Harry*, *Escape from Alcatraz*) is hardly known for comedy. On *Jinxed* he may not have known he was making one until he saw the rushes."

Rex Reed wrote of *Jinxed*, "Sorry to say it is never very funny, only occasionally wry, and often just downright embarrassing. It is a comic idea in

Bonita embarks
on her mysterious chase.

Looking for all the world like the librarian she says she is at heart, Bette makes an appearance at a 1982 anti-nuke rally.

search of a script, a series of character sketches in search of characters, a cast in search of a director and just about everything else a movie is not supposed to be. . . With a little age and a few lines in her peachy brow, Midler is going to grow into a great broad like Italy's Giulietta Masina, or even Judy Holliday. . . bad movies like *Jinxed* are going to drive her—and the rest of her fans, too—right around the bend. There is nothing more annoying than to watch a genuine talent fall into the hands of fools. Dear Bette, come home. All is forgiven. But first, burn the negative to *Jinxed*.

"P.S. There is one funny line in this otherwise hopeless misfortune. Bette stares at Rip Torn's wet corpse, bloated, turning blue, toupee askew, eyes at half-mast, and squeals: 'God, Harold, you look like Frank Sinatra!' You had to be there."

Unfortunately, not too many people were. By the third week of release, the audience for *Jinxed* had dropped 56% from the week before, and after a month the box-office receipts were so small, the industry stopped tabulating them. *Jinxed* became one of those genuine Hollywood horrors, a total box-office bomb, losing more than $20 million for the studio.

Columnist Marilyn Beck neatly summarized the result: "That has to be a crushing defeat for Bette, because, flawed as the movie might be, it is not bad enough to deserve the whipping that it is receiving."

"I liked the picture," Bette said later. "It was peculiar, but at least it wasn't the same old junk. I felt it didn't get a fair shake because of the publicity about the infighting and the bad feelings among the people who made it."

As if her experience with *Jinxed* weren't bad enough, Bette found that the devastating publicity and box-office tallies had effectively blackballed her from films. She was not sent good scripts. "I keep hoping. I keep thinking, Surely something must turn up. But it doesn't. Where do all the scripts go, do you suppose? Is there someone in the middle there, stopping them getting to me? I'd like to do another film, but they aren't exactly beating down my door." It would be two years after the release of *Jinxed* before Bette would begin to make another picture.

Nineteen

Linda Hart was sitting at home in November of 1982 when the telephone rang. It was Jerry Blatt, one of Bette's comedy writers. "Linda," he said, "you're never going to guess why I'm calling you."

"You're right, Jerry," Linda replied. "I'm not."

"I'm sitting in West L.A. in a Chinese restaurant with Bette—now don't answer me until you hear everything I'm going to say. Bette has been in rehearsal for a new tour with Katie and Ula and a new girl, and she can't stand the new girl. She's firing her at nine o'clock tomorrow morning—and she wants you to be there at ten."

"BETTE WHO?" Linda screamed into the phone. "What are you *talking* about?! We don't speak for two years and suddenly I'm going to *be there* at ten o'clock *tomorrow morning?*"

"She really wants you," Blatt pleaded. "She's very sorry about everything and she's willing to let bygones be bygones. She never wanted to fire you, she adores you and she'll pay you a *lot* of money this time."

"*How much?*" Linda asked.

And thus was the hatchet buried—Linda rejoined the Harlettes. "I was really, really reluctant," Linda says, "but it *was* good money and I felt very bad about what happened between me and Bette. I was afraid there would be tension, you know, or weirdness, but there wasn't after a few days. And I'll never forget our first night on stage. She introduced me as 'Linda ("I sued and won") Hart,' and I knew then that for her to make a joke about it, everything was okay. It took a lot for her to swallow her pride and call me up when *I* had sued *her.* I really respected her for that."

"De Tour," as it was called, presented a vastly different Bette Midler show. Influenced by New Wave and Bette's new-found passion for art, the show was a highly stylish one, with colorful costumes and gorgeous sets complete with Continental, Art Deco and German Expressionist influences, Bicycle Playing Cards come to life, ballerinas, giant balloons simulating bazooms, and the entire De Lago family—four mermaids who put on a hilariously-choreographed wheelchair ballet while singing "We Are Family."

"There are *tons* of props," Bette said. "It's prop city. And I've culled ideas from performers long gone, old ideas that are like standards nobody does anymore—just fun things, silly things that are in such terrible taste everybody will groan and say, 'I can't believe she's foisting this on us.'"

Actually, the show was much more visually impressive than it was tasteless, and it contained a great deal of new musical material as well: "Pink Cadillac Walk," "It Should've Been Me," "Pretty Legs and Great Big Knockers," (with balloons), a mermaid-family medley of "Rolling on the River" and "We are Family," "My Mother's Eyes," "Broken Bicycles" and "Everyone's Gone to the Moon," as well as songs from an upcoming album, including "That May Be All I Need To Know," "Beast of Burden," "Got My Eye On You" and "Favorite Waste of Time."

In her concert souvenir program, Bette explained the genesis of her "De Tour" show. "Art! That amorphous, elusive, flighty little bird of the spirit that will betimes flutter to my shoulder, hopefully for more than just a preen. Of late I have dwelt with the muses...What you are about to experience—on

Much more glamorous, Bette raps with the audience at the Universal Amphitheater early in "De Tour," December 1982

page and stage—is the result of the greatest intellectual struggle of my life, Hegelian in intensity, Homeric in scope. Forgive me, I must sit down."

"This was her show from the word go," says Bruce Vilanch. "It was the product of really wanting to do something different. *Divine Madness* was basically the act she'd been doing for ten years, and she wanted to do something quite different this time. She wanted a different look and feel. Of course, we did wind up using the mermaids, but that was for the sight gag of having all of them in wheelchairs. We were going to have Dolores at an anti-nuke rally, coming out on a bomb and all, but we thought it would get tired real fast.

"She'd been sitting in the house after *Jinxed*—suffering—and read a lot of art books and got influenced by bauhaus and Walter Gropius and all those people and she wanted the show to reflect that. She'd been dabbling in new music; she'd gotten all excited about Jack Mack and the Heart Attack and a lot of L.A. bands she was hearing and thought were quite wonderful. So she wanted the show to reflect her new enthusiasms and what was going on in the L.A. arts scene. Of course, being Bette, she made fun of the whole thing: 'This show is so new, so artsy-fartsy, even I can't keep up with it. But do I give a shit? *Noooooo.*'"

Bette's humor in this show wasn't all that different—just typically top-notch. "Have you noticed that whenever anyone has a problem these days, they blame it on cocaine? Your marriage is collapsing—it's the blow. Can't keep a job—it's the blow. Liberace is accused of being a homosexual—now that *was* the blow! The nerve of that worm, trying to tell us that Liberace is a homosexual! Does he really expect us to *believe* that?!

"And then there's herpes. Oh, God...'You always herpe the one you love...'

"I love Olivia's new song, don't you? 'Let me hear your body talk'...Mine said, 'Fuck you!' Have you heard Richard Simmons's new record?—'Let's get pitiful.'"

She also had some choice new Sophie jokes, including this one: "I fell in love with my boyfriend Ernie not long after I buried my husband Jake. I'll never forget the first time we were in the sack. It was right in the middle of the action. Ernie broke down in great, wracking sobs. I said, 'Ernie, get hold of yourself. What's the matter?' He said to me, 'Soph, I can't stand it. I can't stand the thought that I'm in Jake's place.'

"I said to him, Ernie—don't worry about it. Jake's place was about five inches further down."

One of the funniest bits in the new show was a spoof of *Jinxed*, a film which, Bette said, "suffered from projectus interruptus—it went before it even came." A screen was lowered, and a clip from the film—dubbed in Italian—was run, along with subtitles explaining what was *really* going on. The scene was the one in which Bonita goes to the old prospector who tries to rape her. As she enters the ghost town, the subtitles read, "Oh, the MGM lot! I can't believe it. Louis B. Mayer must be turning over—in Joan Crawford's grave."

As she is hit with a tumbleweed, she says, "Ah, flowers from the director." The grizzled, crazed prospector—a director named Mr. Sea-gull who is having readings for his new film—shows Bette down a shaft and says, "Let me show you to your dressing room."

"Dressing room?" says Bette. "You call this a dressing room? I played a Turkish bath that was cleaner than this!"

When Bonita sees the package Harold has left with the prospector for her, Mr. Sea-gull says, "That's the script. But your skin is the wrong color."

OPPOSITE: Awe-inspiring production values accompany the "Pretty Legs and Great Big Knockers" number.

"Wrong color? What are you talking about?"

"Aren't you the girl who played that rock singer who did drugs and died?"

"Yes."

"Well, isn't Diana Rose black?"

A few moments later, the director starts to shoot his gun and Bonita screams in terror. "You wouldn't treat me this way if I were Meryl Streep!"

"I'll read you for the part but let's have a drink first."

Bonita puts a mickey in his drink. Then he says, "You may be a good actress. Show me your tits." She strips down to her bra and as he begins to pass out he blurts out, "I think I'm gonna shoot!" and collapses as his gun fires away.

As Bonita leaves the mine shaft, she says in English, "Dirty Old Fart"—which appears in Italian in the subtitles.

"De Tour" took Bette to nineteen cities between December 6, 1982 and March 21, 1983. On New Year's Eve in Los Angeles, Bette came onstage once again in a baby diaper with a 1983 sash—accompanied by old man time representing 1982. To the surprise and delight of the audience, the old man turned out to be Barry Manilow, who joined Bette and the audience in singing "Auld Lang Syne."

"De Tour" was Bette's most successful ever. Since *The Rose*, her audience had greatly increased in size and diversity, and this was her first tour since that film's release. She broke records in city after city, and her appearance in New York—at the enormous Radio City Music Hall—broke that theater's box-office record with a take of $1,327,000. Fans had lined up in frigid temperatures to wait all night to buy tickets. It was clear that no matter what her fortunes in Hollywood, Bette Midler would always be a concert superstar. This tour grossed an incredible $8 million.

The reviews were extraordinary as well. John Karr said of her San Francisco show, "Bette Midler peaked with this concert. I've always loved her, laughed and cried with her. But I was caught unprepared for this sort of unity of conception, assimilation of styles and increased singing prowess. Here is the Bette we've always predicted. It's as if the struggles of Hollywood were a cocoon, from which Bette has emerged transfigured."

Stephen Holden wrote in the New York *Times*, "Bette Midler has always tried for the nearly impossible on stage: the creation of a show-business personality who could embrace the worlds of vaudeville, legitimate theater and rock all in a single evening...the only uncertain element in Miss Midler's arsenal has been her singing voice...it was a happy surprise, therefore, when [she] unveiled a newly-fortified rock singing voice...not only did Miss Midler stay consistently on pitch, she interpreted demanding rock ballads like 'Stay With Me' with an impressive dynamic control and sustained long phrases that never gave way to amusical histrionics.

"The strength of Miss Midler's singing threw her comedy routines into brilliant relief...her delivery didn't evince the same desperate desire to amuse that sometimes characterized her work in the past. Even her riskiest material was delivered with a new air of dignity. This firm sense of emotional control gave the evening a shape and purpose that her earlier revues have lacked. For the first time on a New York stage, Miss Midler's vaudeville and rock aspirations coincided happily and with total confidence."

According to Ula Hedwig, Bette was much calmer on this tour—and so were things in general. "I think she's more self-assured now. There's less pressure on her. Maybe she just realizes how much people love her. Before, there was a

New Wave and Bette's
recent immersion into art
inspired the "De Tour"
motif. "This show is so artsy-
fartsy even I can't
keep up with it," she said.

constant need to try to please everybody, and not thinking that she was pleas-
ing people, and getting nervous about it."

There were still moments of tension, Ula admits. "I know she has a reputation for being the Queen Bitch, and I can see how a person who's in the firing
line of attack could think that, but if you know her, there's a reason for all that.
It's the pressure she's under. Anyone would snap at people under that kind of
pressure.

"But she's really a very likable person. I love her to death. I've been over to
her house for dinner, and she has on this little apron and she's cooking ribs.
She can be a very sweet person, and if I see that other side coming, I just walk
away. I don't deal with it, you know. If she has to react that way, there's a
reason. It's not that she's a bitch on wheels—that's not it at all. A lot of people
assume that, because that's what they walk in the door and see. But they don't
know what's behind it. She always says, 'I'm hardest on myself'—and she is.
She wants things to be right."

At the Greek Theater in
Los Angeles, Bette sings "Married Men"
during a somewhat altered
"De Tour" concert, Summer 1983.

OPPOSITE: Ten years
after her Philharmonic Hall New Year's
Eve show, Bette puts on
another diaper and is joined by Barry
Manilow at the Universal
Amphitheater, December 31, 1982.

After "De Tour" ended in March, Bette went out again in the summer with a similar show, hitting some cities she'd missed the first time, and revisiting others. This time, the pace got to her, and she had to be hospitalized after collapsing during a performance in Detroit. "I was beat to a pulp," she says. "I was working too hard, and I couldn't stop thinking about my mother. I was racked with guilt—and really terrified. When you're in a weakened condition, all the guilt of your life floods back to you."

During "Pretty Legs and Great Big Knockers," Bette ran offstage to get the giant balloons, and blacked out. Paramedics took her to the hospital. "I was sure I wouldn't get better. I felt panic-stricken and couldn't stop crying. Then I started to take stock. I thought of all the people I hadn't seen. And I really wanted to see my mother, but I couldn't." Bette recovered after a few days in the hospital and resumed the tour, which ended in the early Fall.

Since early 1981, Bette had been living with Benoit Gautier, the Frenchman she had met while in Paris in 1974. Linda Hart says, "When we went back to Europe for the promotional tour in 1979, Bette saw him a couple of times. Then he came over here about a year later."

Gautier, a personal manager who handles Jon Anderson, former lead singer of Yes, "insists on a good time," Bette said. "I'm a workaholic, so it balances out."

Bette doesn't like to talk about her boyfriends. "It freaks them out," she says. "It takes something away from what you've got together." And besides, she says, "I hate to talk about my 'currents' because the old ones always get upset. I hate to hurt the 'exes' because the 'exes' are too divine. And they don't like to think they have been supplanted in my affections."

But Bette has spoken a bit about Benoit. Their relationship is quiet, she says. "We see each other evenings, we have dinner together. It's very traditional; nothing *kinque*. Calm, always calm, because there's so much of people screaming during the day, you really do need a chance to catch your breath." At the same time, though, "he has a lot of oomph, and that's very good for me. I'm a kind of homebody, a stick-in-the-mud. He makes me get out of the house, he makes me travel. He says, 'Get going!' So we do a lot of going. He's also very European, in that he loves to feed me and buy me presents. He's the best wife a girl ever had."

Asked if she would get married, Bette replied, "Oh, *nevair*, NEV-AIR! There's community property in this state! I'm not giving away a nickel, honey! I think marriage is great—if two people are equals. But not if it's a master/slave thing. Not unless that's what they're into, hey! But I'm not that kind of girl."

She has talked quite a lot recently about having a baby, and while she doesn't think it necessary to be married first, she does think a child should be raised with two parents. "That's very important. Children need two parents. Of course, if one of them is a monster, then they're better off with just one."

She worries about her age. "Everybody my age is having babies," she said. "The problem is, we're already close to 40, so we're probably going to raise a generation of 'only' children. And you know what turkeys they are!"

She is non-commital about whether Benoit might be the father of her baby, should she have one. "I've been with him three years, you know, and three years has been my limit with men. His time is nearly up." Although there have been some rocky stretches, at this writing Bette and Benoit are still together. "Benoit always talks about having [a child] and naming it Clovis—that's the boy—and Edmée if it's a girl. Now you know why I'm nervous about having children."

In the late Summer, Bette's ninth album, *No Frills*, was released. As she had threatened to do, Bette "jumped on the New Wave bandwagon" with this one, but not to a ridiculous degree. The record has a new music sound to it, but the material and delivery are well within the traditional Midler boundaries—perhaps too much so. There is a formulaic quality to the album, as though Bette were trying simply to update the kinds of songs she has always done best, rather than truly stretching to encompass new music. There's a Latin-flavored "Only in Miami," a vulnerable torch song, "All I Need To Know," a double *entendre* number, "Let Me Drive," a rock cover, "Beast of Burden," and a bittersweet Midler composition, "Come Back Jimmy Dean." While most of the songs are excellent on their own terms, the packaging of the album may have worked against it: by seeming to promise a radical departure and failing to deliver it, Bette may have disappointed some buyers, who then gave the album bad word-of-mouth.

Talking about *No Frills* while she was making it, Bette said, "With this new record, I'm probably going to put the Divine Miss M on the back burner. I want this record to have passion, but I also want it to have the underpinnings of seriousness...it's music with no strings and no horns. It's bare-bones music, as unpretentious as it can be. Just stark."

Bette was unable to appeal to record buyers beyond her hard-core fans with the album, which didn't get very high on the sales charts. On a *Tonight Show* appearance in the Fall, Bette said, "I like this album, even if it is a stiff. But it's a good album. It's just so hard to get radio play."

It's not easy to keep Bette Midler down, of course, and it wasn't long before she was back on top of the sales charts: not with a record, but with another best-selling book.

The Saga of Baby Divine was a charming poetic fable, illustrated colorfully by Todd Schorr, about a little girl with bright red hair—born wearing high heels—whose first word is "More!" Her parents don't know how to deal with her, and she begins an odyssey of discovery. She meets three fabulous ladies, Lilly, Tillie and Joyce, who are, in the words of *People* magazine, "a combination of the Three Wise Men, the Andrews Sisters and the William Morris Agency." They make a showbiz star out of Baby. The book's message is that one must be proud to be oneself, and should live life to the fullest: "Make sure that your Life is a Rare Entertainment/It doesn't take anything drastic/You needn't be gorgeous or wealthy or smart/Just Very Enthusiastic!"

Bette admitted that *The Saga of Baby Divine* was at least partially autobiographical. "Talking about me is just like talking about her. This book is the history of The Divine Miss M. It's her 'backstory' as we like to say."

Why did Bette write a book like this? "I've always loved children's books," she said. "This isn't a *baby* children's book, it has something for everyone. I was in love with this kind of illustration when I was a kid, very Disney-esque and colorful, real rich. My mother taught me how to read before I was in Kindergarten, and whenever she couldn't mind me she would sit me down in front of a bunch of books, so I had quite an education and I always wanted to be one of those people who write these books."

Bette was extremely proud of *The Saga of Baby Divine*. She felt the message it contained was an important one. "It's a book about being different. I always felt very different when I was a kid. We all want to be king of the playground when we're kids, and we spend our adult lives still wanting to be king of the playground. This book says you don't have to be that—you can be happy just being yourself."

OPPOSITE: At a Los Angeles book-signing party for *Baby Divine*, Bette wears Baby on her head. She signed 6,000 copies of the book on this promotional tour.

Toni Basil, Midler's
former choreographer and now a rock
star in her own right, accompanies
Bette to a screening of her new "Beast
of Burden" video, February 1984.

OPPOSITE: Barry escorts
Bette to the Los Angeles premiere of
Barbra Streisand's *Yentl.*
"I brought tissues in case it gets
weepy," Bette said.

The book's sumptuous look thrilled Bette, too. "The illustrator is brilliant. He's an air brush artist, and air brushing is something that isn't used much in children's books, because it's so expensive. You have to be a fine craftsman to do it. Todd is more than a craftsman, he's an artist. I was lucky to find him."

The reviews of *Baby Divine* were generally good. *People* magazine said, "The book has to be appreciated for its flash and glitz, the way the rest of Midler's act is. As such it is a campy exercise that should, if nothing else, delight devoted Midlerians."

There must be a lot of "devoted Midlerians," because *Baby Divine* was one of the biggest successes of the Christmas 1983 book-selling season. It gained Bette two national magazine covers (*Ms* and *Saturday Review*) and rose to #3 on the New York *Times* Fiction Bestseller list, on which it remained for more than three months. Once again, Bette "flogged myself into a stupor" with an 11-city book-signing tour, on which she autographed 6,000 copies and met her fans face-to-face once again. "How does it feel to be an institution?" one of them asked her. "Don't *say* that!" she replied. "I'm too *young* to be an institution. Besides, I'd rather be a bank!"

According to Bette, her publisher (Crown) asked her to write another book, *Terrible Tasteless Tales,* but she declined. "I'll leave that to the terrible, tasteless people." She has also reportedly been asked to write a beauty book ("I have to laugh!") and her autobiography, but nothing definite is in the works.

On December 1st, Benoit threw a 38th birthday party for Bette, which became something of a reunion. Charlotte Crossley attended, and she remembers that all of Bette's old friends showed up. "Johnny Carson was there, and Barry Manilow, Rosemary Clooney, Martha Raye, Neil Diamond, Burt and Carol Bacharach, Toni Basil, Ula, Katie, Linda—it was just old home day for us. We sang with her and had a wonderful time. We hadn't seen her for a while, it was so nice to see her and share our good wishes with her."

In January 1984, a marvelous video of Bette's "Beast of Burden" was released, along with a single of the song. Filmed at New York's Peppermint Lounge, it begins with newspaper front pages headlined, "Bette Leaves Sheik for Mick" and "Mick Drops Everyone for Bette." Then Mick Jagger comes into Bette's dressing room as she's about to perform the song, to tell her that they're through. She begs him to stay "long enough to hear me sing your song. I sing it better than anybody."

"Well, almost anybody," Mick replies—and Bette makes a "get him" face.

Bette sings the song, looking like a piece of cotton candy with a wildly teased blond hairdo and a pink satin jacket, then Mick comes on stage from the audience to sing and dance with her. At the conclusion of the video, the Sheik approaches them from the audience and throws custard pies in their faces.

For Bette, it was something of a dream come true to work with Mick Jagger. "He was unbelievable," she says. "Infinitely amusing, a complete pro, a gentleman, uncomplaining—and *sexy.*"

As this book goes to press, Bette is preparing to make a new movie—her first in three years. Entitled *My Girdle Is Killing Me,* the film is based on a screenplay by Bette's former lighting man, Peter Dallas. It concerns, according to Dallas, a "lovable and naive movie star who hits the skids and is penniless when the telegram arrives that she has been nominated for an Oscar. Then it's a scramble for the bucks so she can get herself to Hollywood and present herself like a star. It winds up in underworld crime. It's kind of a latter-day *I Love Lucy*—with a black Ethel."

Bette and her man,
Benoit Gautier, attend a Hollywood
screening of *Footloose*,
February 1984. They met in France
during Bette's 1974 vacation.

OPPOSITE: Mick Jagger
and Bette in their funny, sexy
"Beast of Burden" video.

Dallas brought the script to Bette in 1980. "I've always thought of her as a zany Martha Raye type character, and there isn't anyone today like that, a funny lady—Fanny Brice, Martha Raye, Lucille Ball—and I think Bette could fill that position wonderfully.

"When Bette read the script, she thought it was wonderful, but she sort of stayed away from me and it, because of course when you become a big star you don't want to settle for what people *you* know can come up with. You suddenly have access to all the big names and the big talents. So she first had to scour both coasts, and then after four years she came back and said she wanted to do it. Which was gratifying, because I'd written it with her in mind."

The movie, which begins filming in the late Fall of 1984, will be produced by Marvin Worth (a good omen—he co-produced *The Rose*) and released by Paramount Pictures.

As Bette Midler begins her third decade in show business, many of her associates have noticed that she is a changed woman. "She has definitely mellowed out," Charlotte says. Peter Dallas adds, "Bette has grown into a very together lady. She has cultivated herself into a fine person to deal with. Even fighting with her now is not counter-productive because viciousness doesn't enter into it, even in her anger. She's fighting now with more dignity—which is a testament to her personal growth."

Indeed, Bette has grown in many ways. She has proven to herself that she can handle her sometimes dizzying business affairs without Aaron Russo; that she can survive an experience as debilitating and publicly humiliating as *Jinxed*; and that when she is left to her own devices, the public adores the result.

She has even learned to accept the divisions between her and her father; she dedicated *Baby Divine* to him. "I've come to terms with it," she says. "I think it's more his problem than mine, and once you accept that, you breathe easier. He was never interested in entertainment. He thought it was frivolous, and he's never changed his mind. But that's all right. It takes all kinds. I don't like what he does, either, which is to putter around the house, mostly. But I like *him*. He's a big tease, and a cynic like me."

Again, the fascinating dichotomies become evident. Bette Midler is a cynic who's sentimental, a queen of camp who's quietly introspective, a desperately insecure young woman who is maturing into someone who likes herself. When writer Armistead Maupin told Bette that he thought she was getting better with age, she replied, "Thanks. I think I am, too, and I'll tell you why. I don't think I'm anywhere near as crazy as I used to be. I used to be capable of quite serious rages. I'm not anymore. I'm really much more thoughtful. I like what I'm turning into. And I like the fact that I'm growing up; that I didn't, you know, arrest myself at age thirteen. . . One of my big things is to learn, and to keep growing. It's hard sometimes, because things pull away. But that's basically my direction, and I think it's positive."

Calmer,
happier, more self-confident,
Bette relaxes in her
Greenwich Village loft during
the early part of 1984.

ABOUT THE AUTHOR

James Spada's previous books include *Hepburn: Her Life in Pictures; Judy and Liza; Monroe: Her Life in Pictures; Streisand: The Woman and the Legend;* and *The Films of Robert Redford.*

James Spada Associates have also produced the books *Elizabeth Taylor: A Biography in Photographs; The Telephone Book; Bette Davis: A Biography in Photographs;* (to be released in 1985) and the *1984 Marilyn Monroe Pin-Up Calender.*

Spada's interview subjects from the literary, art and show business worlds include James Michener, Norton Simon, Robert Redford, Julie Harris, Stephen King, Barry Gibb, Gore Vidal, Studs Terkel, Peter Bogdanovich and many others.

Mr. Spada has been Editor of *In the Know* magazine and Managing Editor of *Movie Mirror* magazine. He has also been the publisher of *Barbra Quarterly* and *EMK: The Edward M. Kennedy Quarterly.* Born and raised in New York, he now lives in West Hollywood, California.

PHOTO CREDITS